To Each Their Darkness

For Ben Irvine —

This is not the droid you're looking for....

To Each Their Darkness

Gary A. Braunbeck

Apex Publications

ISBN: 978-0-9845535-1-8

Cover art by Steven Gilberts
Cover design by Justin Stewart
Book design by Aaron Leis

Apex Publications, LLC
www.apexbookcompany.com
PO Box 24323 Lexington, KY 40524

"Why should we honour those that die upon the field of battle; a man may show as reckless courage in entering into the abyss of himself."

–W. B. Yeats

"There are lonely cemeteries,
graves full of bones without sound,
the heart passing through a tunnel,
dark, dark, dark
as in a shipwreck we die from within
as we drown in the heart,
as we fall out of the skin into the soul . . ."

–Pablo Neruda, "Death Alone"

". . . Her body is gone, only this
flat, crackling image remains,
but even now, still she trembles
deep in the paper, where particles
that form her likeness waltz
in quick, subatomic union . . ."

–Lucy A. Snyder, "Photograph of a Lady, Circa 1890"

DYSART: You won't gallop anymore, Alan. Horses will be quite safe for you . . . You will, however, be without pain. More or less completely without pain.

[Pause.

He speaks now directly to the theatre, standing by the motionless body of ALAN STRANG, *under the blanket.]*

And now for me it never stops: that voice of Equus out of the cave—"Why Me? . . . Why Me? . . . Account for Me!" . . . All right—I say it! . . . In an ultimate sense I cannot know what I do in this place—yet I do ultimate things. Irreversible, terminal things. I stand in the dark with a pick in my hand, striking at heads!

[He moves away from ALAN, *back to the downstage bench, and finally sits.]*

I need—more desperately than my children need me—a way of seeing in the dark. What way is this? . . . *What dark is this?* . . . I cannot call it ordained of God: I cannot go so far. I will, however, pay it so much homage. There is now, in my mouth, this sharp chain. And it never comes out.

[A long pause

DYSART *sits staring]*

BLACKOUT

–Peter Shaffer, *Equus*

"I live fearfully within myself."

–T. M. Wright, "Fog Boy"

Contents

To Each Their Darkness

Preamble:
Welcome to My Abyss

Explanation the First

EIGHT YEARS AGO I WROTE A NON-FICTION BOOK TITLED *FEAR in a Handful of Dust: Horror As a Way of Life*. It was, at the time, the best I could make it. Upon its release it received a lot of very kind reviews and was later honored with a Bram Stoker Award nomination from the Horror Writers Association. Since then, it has gone out of print, the rights have reverted back to me, and if you want a copy you can easily find one at any number of online booksellers (used and otherwise)—but be careful: some of them are charging outrageous amounts. Believe me when I tell you, *do not pay more than the original cover price of $40.00*. Never say I offered no help during these uncertain economic times.

Ahem.

I was not then, nor am I now, completely happy with the way *Fear*... turned out. It's not just the formatting mistakes and typos that were in that edition (though rest assured I did not do the Happy Dance about those), but I always felt as if the book had come *this close* to its goal and my intention, only to run out of steam in the home stretch. There are few worse feelings in a writer's professional career than to realize that you've loosed a piece on the world that was either not yet ready to be written, or *was* ready to be written . . . just not by you, not as you were then, with your limited emotional inner vocabulary.

Don't misunderstand; I remain proud of *Fear* . . . and will happily sign it for those who have in the years since gone to the trouble to track down a copy because they've heard such good things about it. In many ways (which I briefly touched upon in the original edition) the writing of *Fear* . . . saved my sanity and my life. It reinvigorated my creative drive (which had been all but nonexistent) and my determination to live the rest of my life as well as I could and bring no further pain, anxiety, sadness, disappointment, fear, or the infliction of loneliness into the world than I already had—and believe me, I'd done more than my share of spreading around the misery as fairly as I could, especially in my younger days.

In the introduction to the first collection of Cedar Hill stories, *Graveyard People*, I wrote, with tongue firmly in cheek, the following words:

> "What you now hold in your hands is the first collection . . . of my Cedar Hill stories [in] the order in which they appear in the Cedar Hill Cycle, an ongoing work that will see completion only when I die."

Somehow I don't find that quite as funny now as I did then (more on that later).

It occurs to me that this explanation has taken on a far-too-somber quality far too soon, so instead of carrying on in this borderline-melancholic tone, I'll take a breath and continue slouching toward the point.

Explanation the Second

If you're like me, you always feel a little apprehension when an author releases the "preferred version" of a previous book. There are numerous reasons for this, not the least being that this is the version of the book that existed *before* an editor got his or her red pencil on it. It could be that the previous version of the book *was* the better version, thanks to a keen editorial eye that caught not only typos and continuity problems, but was also able to find the excess fat when the writer became self-indulgent and mercilessly trimmed away elements that might very well have bored readers to despair. It could also be that the book was gutted in order to meet an absurd word or page count by a mass-market publisher or, in some cases (this really happened to a writer friend of mine), because the fucking *font* used by said mass-market publisher was set in stone and the length of the manuscript exceeded the previously-mentioned acceptable page count because of the required use of said font.

So here you are, looking at an author's "preferred" version of a book you purchased, read, and enjoyed years ago (if you hadn't enjoyed the original, you wouldn't be standing there with the new edition in your hand, wondering should I or shouldn't I). It really is a crapshoot, because sometimes the "preferred" editions add depth to the characters and storyline, fill in little plotholes that you noticed on the way but decided didn't really matter, and give the overall narrative a stronger and more confident cohesiveness that you didn't even realize had been missing until now. And sometimes all a "preferred" edition does is dump in the fertilizer that the original editor worked for months to shovel out, a heavy-duty filter mask covering the nose and mouth at all times.

Examples of "preferred" versions that fit in the former category: *The Totem*, by David Morrell; *The Throat*, by Peter Straub; Robert Dunbar's *The Pines*; and F. Paul Wilson's *Rakoshi* (originally published as *The Tomb*, the novel that marked the debut of Repairman Jack). For the latter category (and here's where I'm going to piss off a lot of folks), I have one grand example: *The Stand: Complete and Uncut* by Stephen King. For me, the new material added *zilch* to that epic, except for some really grotesque background details about certain characters that neither humanized them more, nor enriched relationships, nor did anything to move the story forward; in fact, sequences in the original version that I'd found terrifying and exhilarating became bloated and mind-numbingly repetitive. I had to force myself to finish it. And King is a writer whose work I usually greatly respect and admire (I think *Pet Sematary* will coexist alongside the works of Poe, Hawthorne, Lovecraft, and Matthew Lewis'

The Monk until the multiverse implodes and we're all reduced to the final vibrations on the unseen strings running through the three sheets of space and one sheet of time, and don't even get me started on *The Dead Zone*, a novel I re-read every year . . . but already I digress).

It is a few months away from the middle of 2010 as I write this, which means it is also a few months from my fiftieth birthday (this said by the guy who didn't have a game plan past 40 because he really didn't expect to still be here). The person I am now, like the narrator of *The Indifference of Heaven* (a.k.a. *In Silent Graves*), is coming to grips with the truth of his mortality; it's no longer some abstract concept happily pushed back into the fog of youthful denial, but an actual figure closing in from the distance, with recognizable features and questionable breath. So here I am, re-examining the horror field and the validity of my place in it, and whether or not my overall body of work has any real worth or purpose. (Hey, I'm almost *fifty*, fer chrissakes! Allow ten lines of middle-aged crisis morbid musings. Your turn is coming. Bwa-ha-ha-ha-ha.)

Ahem.

I look back on the person I was nine years ago and find that he embarrasses me. His impatience, his anger, his almost complete disregard for his own health, his naïveté, and his selfishness; *Christ*, his selfishness. Yeah, he'd managed to survive some nastiness (okay, okay, a *lot* of nastiness) from his childhood, his teenage years, his early adult life, blah-blah-blah, and he was trying to believe that the worst was over and he was now firmly walking down the road of health, happiness, and success. He had no idea that all of the shit that had happened to him up to that point—or that he'd walked into or caused himself—was just a warm-up, the comic in baggy pants with a spritzer bottle and banana cream pie, the opening act to the final third of his life, where more than a few surprises were waiting up the multiverse's sleeve, some of which were going to land on his head like a curse from Heaven.

But I do have at least one thing to thank him for; he had a hand in helping to get me to the point where I am, at last, ready to write the book that *Fear in a Handful of Dust* should have been.

And so . . .

Explanation the Third

That does not mean that what you're reading at this moment is the "preferred" version of *Fear*. No; had that been the case, I would have kept the original title and simply added a "Revised and Expanded" beneath it in smaller letters. Consider this book the equivalent of a variation on a theme. It's a bit more orderly, a bit more directly honest, a little less stream-of-consciousness (but not much), more focused on the writing process (and the pitfalls that process often presents if one is not careful), and if you're expecting to find the entire text of the original between these covers . . . sorry, not happening. It has nothing to do with any esoteric or "artful" (*gaaah!* —that word!) pretense on my part, but it does have everything to do with those of you who purchased the original edition, and those of you who have purchased this variation on a theme.

As a reader and lover of limited edition books, nothing makes me want to grab a rifle and climb a water tower more than shelling out forty bucks plus shipping for a limited edition, only to see the exact same book, word for word, come out a few years later in a much less expensive trade paperback edition. (Yes, I still tend to overreact from time to time). It completely negates the collectability of the original edition and makes the reader feel like a rube, like he or she has fallen for the old bait-and-switch.

If you are one who purchased the original edition and may be thinking that you've been had, know this: probably a little more than 40 percent of the original text is contained within these pages. What reprinted text there is has not been altered in any way (with the exception of correcting typos and errors in grammar and syntax). I think you're going to appreciate the new material and having this as a companion piece to the book you purchased eight years ago.

If you are one who didn't purchase the original because the forty bucks plus shipping for the limited edition was way the hell out of your financial comfort zone, you should find the cover price of this Apex edition much more agreeable, and you'll be getting the book that I'd always intended the original to be. I want to make certain that no one comes away feeling as if they got the bad end of the deal. I spent a lot of time worrying over this, and I hope you find my solution a fair and equitable one. The book was simply too important for me to give up on.

Which, finally, leads me to the new title and . . .

Explanation Next to the Last

As mentioned earlier, the original edition was subtitled *Horror as a Way of Life*, and it actually came close—*this close*—to conveying what I wanted to get across to those folks—readers, writers, editors, book reviewers—who, in one form or another, seemed to frequently and loudly bemoan the stale state of the horror field, yet most, when asked what might be done about it, just cast downward glances and shook their heads in bemused resignation. Horror fell into a sickening rut in the late 80s and early 90s, and that's what lead to its demise; everybody was writing the same kind of book that was being written by everybody else, and if someone, through sheer cosmic accident, happened to produce a piece of work that was original, that dealt with the terrors *within* as well as without, that offered unique situations and fully-developed three-dimensional characters reacting as real human beings *would* react when faced with such a dark challenge, well . . . there was no dearth of evil-clown artwork that could be slapped on the cover to make it *look* like everything else. (Ask the wonderful, overlooked and underrated writer Joseph Citro about this, whose handful of excellent novels during this period were all but treated as afterthoughts—evil clown covers included—and which are now being reprinted by a first-rate regional publisher, Hardscrabble Books, in New England, and treated as the works of literary merit they always were . . . *and* the publisher never shies away from mentioning the more horrific elements to be found between the covers—not one of which has an evil clown in sight.)

Well, here it is, nine years past the *2001* so daringly envisioned by the remarkable Arthur C. Clarke, and horror has been enjoying something of a renaissance since entering the new century. Oh, *man*, it really looked good when the books first started shipping out of the warehouses around 2002–2003. Mass-market publishers were taking chances with some risky, emotional, challenging, even experimental and surrealistic material. The subject matter grappled with in these books—not to mention the skill and manner with which it was tackled—was, for a while, awfully exciting. It seemed like this stuff was gloriously all over the road, something new and different every month, nothing predictable or pedestrian—hell, even some of the *covers* weren't what you expected. It was time to see what the horror-hungry public was ready to flock to, a public that had been surviving on expensive limited and numbered editions from a small handful of specialty presses that had somehow managed to not lose their shirts in the interim. For a few years—say, up until 2005 or 2006—it looked as if horror was truly going to pull itself up by its bootstraps and start climbing toward a new and higher creative precipice where it could evolve into what Robert R. McCammon once called "the supreme mythic literature of our time." *Whoo-hoo! Groovy, even!* I'll just grab my wallet and then—let me at 'em! Would we see the resurrection of the traditional ghost story, I wondered. Would the countless purveyors of so-called psychological horror grow enough of a spine to move out of the niche created by Thomas Harris and Hannibal Lector? Would the plethora of second- and third-rate Stephen King wannabes finally feel that second testicle drop and dare to step out of his (justifiably) massive shadow? Might this next generation of writers bring with them an aesthetic and intelligence honed by the reading of past masters? Would there at long last be that oh-so-longed-for daring move into cross-genre work? The editors were swearing that horror wouldn't fall into the same old rut of the late 80s and early 90s. And, much to my surprise, it didn't.

It created a completely new rut to fall into.

The rut of the 80s and early 90s was guarded by vampires and psycho killers.

The new rut—and what a roomy, bottomless rut it seems—is guarded by . . . vampires, psycho killers . . .

. . . and zombies.

Lots and lots and lots of zombies, some of which carry the shredded flesh of Jane Austen in what's left of their teeth; others are still chewing on H.G. Welles, or Jules Verne, or . . . I've lost track. After the publication of Brian Keene's Stoker Award-winning *The Rising*, the renewed interest in the undead was fast and furious (and I am *not* blaming Brian for this, so no nasty e-mails, please). Yeah, fast and furious, and a lot of Keene's imitators produced work that was, at best, of journeyman quality. Most of it was just awful—no sense of character, no original plots or plot elements, just fast-paced blood and guts and zombies.

Lots and lots and lots of zombies.

(This is all leading up to my explaining the new title, so stay with me.)

I have grown to hate zombies. For the record, I have written only three zombie stories in my career, and one of them—"We Now Pause for Station Identification"—won the third of my five Bram Stoker Awards.

I love a good zombie story when it's done well, when it's in the hands of someone with skill, wit, intelligence, and the ability to instill it with more than one level. Anthologies like those edited by Christopher Golden, Kim Paffenroth, John Joseph Adams, and the Prime Books anthology, *Zombies: The Recent Dead*, edited by Paula Guran (which should see release shortly after this book) are excellent examples. But don't kid yourselves: the quality of the stories you'll find in these collections are the exception, not the norm.

The recent and near-ubiquitous trend of "reimagining" classic works of literature by adding zombies or vampires or sea monsters or IRS agents—okay, that last one hasn't happened yet, but it's probably coming soon: *Wise Blood-Sucking Vampire IRS Agents*—got on my nerves in a hurry. I read Seth Graham-Smith's *Pride and Prejudice and Zombies* and liked it; it was funny enough to hold my interest and showed a lot of imagination on the author's part; there were a couple of times where I could not differentiate his prose from that of the author on whose dead spine he was doing cartwheels. It was a fun read, but that was all. Now we're seeing—from both the major mass-market house as well as the specialty press—a plethora of "revisionist" classics wherein characters such as Mr. Darcy or Huck Finn (with Zombie Jim), as well as others mentioned previously, are being picked over like the last remains of meat on a turkey drumstick. At least Graham-Smith demonstrated some *craft* in his novel, but the imitators that have followed in its wake are the equivalent of online fan fiction. The writers don't even bother with craft, they simply find sections of the original text that can be excised so that they can insert their beastie of choice. In olden days, this would have been called hackwork.

I know an excellent writer currently enjoying a rise in his popularity who can string together some of the loveliest sentences that work on both the micro and macro writing levels. His prose is confident, his sense of pacing a wonder to behold, and his characterization solid. Problem is, nearly all of his books have been inspired almost completely by Stephen King's books. And it shows. Most of the time, said writer is just employing King-like concepts and tropes as a jumping-off point; the King-like familiarity grabs readers' attention, pulls them into the novel, and keeps their attention as he smoothly moves into his own original storylines and fresh ideas. There is another up-and-coming writer I know who cites horror movies and their directors as being her major influence. And it shows. She couldn't write a good sentence if guns were being held on her family and one of them killed each time she over-used adjectives. Like the writer mentioned earlier in this paragraph, you can correctly infer that there is something *missing* from her work for me—the same thing I find that is missing from a majority of new horror being published by newcomers: the authenticity of an individual literary vision. In short, too much of it reads like what's come before, and what's going to come after will be just like what came before and what comes after it, *ad nauseam.*

I have a theory about this, about why it's happened before and why it's happening now.

Too many horror writers are afraid to bring their own personal darkness to the surface and use it to instill their work with that authenticity; it's just easier to use what's come before—or elements of what's come before—because it's immediately recognizable by readers. Vampires. Ghouls. Serial killers. Science experiments gone awry. And zombies. Lots and lots and lots of zombies.

Stephen King, Peter Straub, Clive Barker, Joyce Carol Oates, Poe, Kelly Link, Caitlin Kiernan, Jonathan Carroll. Names you know, and whose books you have read. You know what sets them apart? They know their own darknesses, have come to grips with them, and are now in control. They also like to mix it up as often as possible; with the exception of Poe, all of them write or have written some impressive cross-genre works, works that terrify, frighten, disturb, move, and chill you because they know the big secret: terror is an extremely *intimate* thing, and if that terror feels mass-manufactured, then all is lost. So they instill their own personal darknesses into their work—carefully, subtly, quietly, often imperceptibly—so that when the set pieces come, when all hell breaks loose, they have drawn the reader so deeply into the narrative that there's no escape; story and reader have become one because the readers feel that the writer has written this book or story *exclusively* for them, and they accept the writer's individual darkness because it has come through so well on the page—because the writer, as Yeats so succinctly put it, had the "reckless courage" to enter into the abyss of him- or herself, submerged in that abyss and gathered the darkness needed for the work, and then made it back to the surface and to the keyboard, for the most part unharmed.

Each has gone to their darkness and shared it brilliantly on the page.

If only the next generation of horror writers could learn from this. But most of them don't; most of them have no influences that existed before 1982, and much of their work doesn't read so much as a horror novels as they do film or miniseries treatments. They walk nowhere near the abyss of the self, where their personal darkness awaits them at the bottom, so they cannot bring that element of authenticity to their work. But their darkness is still there, waiting.

Explanation the Last

I decided to re-title this book *To Each Their Darkness* as a reminder that until you have explored your abyss and brought back the materials you need to enrich your work, that missing authenticity will always be AWOL. And it's not only your loss, but your readers' loss, as well.

Not to mention that of your story or novel.

All of them deserve better. They deserve to be steps the horror field can climb to reach that new precipice upon which it comes ever closer to being the supreme mythic literature of our time.

To Each Their Darkness, then. I'd like to share some of mine with you.

Welcome to my abyss.

FADE IN: CRAMPED APARTMENT OFFICE—NIGHT

Sitting at the desk is a HORROR WRITER. Once 40-ish, he is now 50-ish with way too much grey hair in his beard. He is hunched over his computer keyboard in a position that health guides insist in no uncertain terms is uncomfortable, even dangerous, but he doesn't seem to notice. CAMERA TRACKS IN slowly, and we see his hands madly typing away in a self-taught two-finger method that you can just tell has served him well over the years. CAMERA PAUSES on his face, which is wearing a PERPETUAL BEMUSED SCOWL that we will come to know and dread and in the end find incessantly irritating.

HORROR WRITER stops his typing, runs a hand through his hair (which also has too much grey, but what the hell, he figures he's earned it so screw those "Just For Men" hair coloring ads). He looks around the office as if the word he's searching for has skulked off to hide in a corner just to annoy the living shit out of him.

WRITER

(in VOICE-OVER)

I should have done something noble with my life, like becoming a cesspool cleaner or a CPA...but, no, I have to be a goddamn writer. If this was the opening scene to a movie I was writing, half the effing audience would have run for the exits and been home by now. I dunno, maybe it's like everyone says—I'm too hard on myself. Still...how in the hell do you make yourself seem interesting to readers who've seen this type of thing a hundred times before? Stephen King nailed it with *Danse Macabre*, but I'm not trying to write another book like that. That would be silly. Stupid. Suicidal. Very hard. Difficult, even. And, besides, King's got that whole "I'm big enough to tie knots in your spine" thing going for him.

He looks around a bit more, can't find where the word is hiding, then sighs loudly, reaches for his smokes, remembers that he can't smoke inside, and stares at the screen.

WRITER

I'll bet Stephen King can smoke in *his* office. Lucky bastard.

He looks over to his bookshelves, which contain several books by Stephen King, as well as

William Goldman, Carson McCullers, John O'Hara, Eudora Welty, Raymond Carver, Harlan Ellison, M.R. James, Kobo Abe, Ed Gorman, John Cheever, T.C. Boyle, Russell Banks, and about a hundred other writers. He STARES at the King books. His upper lip twitches on the left side.

WRITER

How come we all have to walk in your shadow?

STEPHEN KING BOOKS

Oh, no you don't, not *this* horseshit again! Speaking from the heart—a heart filled with nothing but love for ya—we are sick and tired of always being shat upon and pointed at and blamed for every little thing that goes wrong in other writers' careers. "Oh, if only they didn't pay *so much money* to Stephen King for his books! If only they would recognize that some of *us* are deserving of hefty advances! If only they would recognize that some of us are *just* as brilliant as Stephen King and his offspring!" Jesus! What a bunch of whiny, self-pitying, self-indulgent, self-*delusional*, greedy little resentful warthogs you are sometimes!

WRITER

(composing himself after the initial shock)

I was unaware that you could talk.

BOOKS

Oooh, listen to him, why don't you? "I was unaware..." What a surprise that is to us! See how we tremble at this revelation? And yet you seem to be taking it so well.

WRITER

It's late and I'm stuck for a good opening; nothing would unnerve me right now.

BOOKS

We could do an interpretive dance number. We've been rehearsing.

WRITER

That's all right.

BOOKS

No, seriously, we've been rehearsing like nobody's business. We can do other things besides take up space on the bestseller lists and raze entire forests. We have an identity outside of the guy who wrote us. Make some room over there and we'll show you a Bob Fosse routine that'll have you—

WRITER

—no, really, you don't need to do this—

BOOKS

—but we insist! We do. You'll never regret this, we swear it! On your deathbed, when your grandchildren ask you what was the high point of your life, you'll say it was without a doubt the night *Firestarter* did the forbidden dance with *Hearts In Atlantis* while

On Writing got all jiggy with *Misery* and *Under the Dome* did a pole-dance that—

HORROR WRITER grabs a GODZILLA ACTION FIGURE WITH KUNG-FU GRIP and THROWS it at *Different Seasons*, deeply hurting that book's feelings and causing it to whimper quietly, but with great dignity.

GODZILLA ACTION FIGURE WITH KUNG-FU GRIP lands on its head, firmly wedged between two bookcases. It is not a pretty sight, but no one notices.

HORROR WRITER mutters an apology to the books, then turns back toward his computer.

WRITER
(V.O. cont'd)
I wonder if King ever has his books offer to dance for *him*. Nah...for him they probably mount a full-scale production of *La Traviata*...or the Broadway version of *Carrie*.

He shakes his head.

BOOKS
Excuse us, not to be a bother—

WRITER
—that ship kinda sailed—

BOOKS
—but we have what we think is a fairly solid, if arguably uninspired, idea for your opening.

WRITER

This makes me despair. Sincerely. Regardless of what I do, this will be thought of as just another rip-off of *Danse Macabre*.

DANSE MACABRE

(from bookshelf)

Did I *ask* to be dragged into the middle of this? No, I did not. I was up here, minding my own business, and was bothering whom? *No one*. And yet now, suddenly, here I am at the heart of the controversy, and I have to say, in all earnestness, it is tiresome. Leave me out of this, I'm begging you.

(pauses)

Besides, I've seen their dance routine and, trust me, they're better off up here on the shelf.

BOOKS

You always did have a superiority complex.

DANSE MACABRE

Not listening. See? This is me, not listening.

WRITER

(to himself)

I have *got* to start taking my medication again.

BOOKS

Look, this is a book about horror films and horror literature, right?

WRITER

Sort of...

BOOKS

"Sort of"? One tingles in the presence of such crystalline decisiveness. It is so very important to have a definite goal in mind. No wonder you have two-way conversations with inanimate objects.

GODZILLA ACTION FIGURE WITH KUNG-FU GRIP

(Shouting from between the bookshelves)

A little help, please? It's not bad enough that Toho decided to put me in cold storage and that in some prints I still share screen time with Raymond Burr—*no*, now I discover that they've whored me out to some outfit called "Legendary...something-or-other," who, with my lucky streak lately, will probably be run by some guy named Guido the Fist. *And* they're talking 3-D. So I ask myself, "'Zilla-man, how can this get any worse?" Answer: I get used as a projectile and wind up with my ass in the air. There is no dignity in this for the King of All Monsters, do you understand? So—if you don't mind my asking, if it's not too much trouble, if you wouldn't mind, not to be a pest, but—*will one of you schmucks do something before my neck snaps*?

WRITER and *BOOKS*

Shut up!

GODZILLA ACTION FIGURE WITH KUNG-FU GRIP
If I could reach your ankle, I would do *such* serious damage. Believe me when I tell you this.

WRITER
(to BOOKS)
You were saying?

BOOKS
Since it's a book—okay, okay, a *sort-of* book—about horror movies and horror literature, why not start with something that combines the two?

WRITER
Gimme a 'frinstance.

BOOKS
Start things off like a really pedestrian, self-conscious screenplay. You can open with a shot of the office and this pathetic middle-aged dweeb banging away at his keyboard, then have something truly ridiculous happen to show just how pedestrian it all is, then work your way back around to the dweeb at the computer and move into the book that way. See? Both film and the printed word combine to save your sorry *tuchus*.

WRITER
I can't believe I'm about to say this, but that's a good idea. I think I'll go with that. Yeah—that's a *really* good idea.

BOOKS

That's why we're bestsellers and you're...well...*not*.

WRITER

I can't describe for you how comforting that is.

GODZILLA ACTION FIGURE WITH KUNG-FU GRIP

Okay, I can feel the blood rushing to my head, there are these dark shadows creeping in from the corners of my eyes, and I can't seem to breathe, not that anyone cares...

HORROR WRITER leans in toward his computer screen, aware that *Danse Macabre* will always be looking over his shoulder. He is oblivious to the hideous death-roar of GODZILLA ACTION FIGURE WITH KUNG-FU GRIP (which is more of a snivel at this point) and the self-satisfied smirk of the BOOKS, who really do seem quite pleased with themselves.

DISSOLVE THROUGH TO: THE COMPUTER SCREEN, which reads:

Establishing Shot: It Was Already Broke When I Got Here

I've eked out what I euphemistically refer to as my living writing fiction for the last twenty-seven years. I've published somewhere in the neighborhood of two hundred short stories, ten novels, ten short-story collections, a handful of not-bad poetry, dozens of film columns and book reviews, and have seen my work nominated for (and winning) some lovely awards and translated into seven languages.

I'm 43, divorced, on anti-depressants, and am on my third attempt in as many months to quit smoking. I like to watch movies, listen to music, read everything I can lay my hands on . . . and write stories. *God,* how I love to write stories. I have no hobbies of which to speak because a full 85 percent of my time is spent on work, making me one of the most single-minded, hyper-focused, evangelically mono-maniacal little writin' pricks you'd never want to meet. I have a terrific agent, more grey hair than I'd like, twenty pounds I need to lose, and a cat named Monte who will eat anything that doesn't run away from him in time. A lot of my work has been classified as horror, and I'm good with that because I think horror is—or, rather, *can be*—a noble field in which to toil. But there remain a number of dilemmas (not as many as it had back in the 80s, thank the Fates) still facing the field as we begin a new but you-bet-your-ass-*cautious* resurgence of the you-should-pardon-the-word genre.

What you hold in your hands both is and isn't a book of film and fiction writing commentaries; yes, you'll find several reviews and (hopefully intelligent) analyses in here, but a format like that can quickly grow wearisome and repetitive—any schmuck with desktop-publishing capabilities can churn out a book of reviews and opinion pieces about the same books and movies we've all seen discussed a thousand times before—so I've decided to take it a couple of steps . . . well, let's say *sideways.* One's reaction to horror movies and literature is a highly subjective and personal thing, with emphasis on the latter. Consider this a thinly-disguised autobiography by means of reflections about movies, books, and writing. It's not enough for someone to simply say, "I liked it" or "I really hated it"; those are not opinions in and of themselves—they are *prefaces* to opinions. To qualify as actual opinions, they must be followed by reasons why, and in order for you to understand the reasons *why*, you have to understand something about the person giving the opinion.

Like it or not (and there are times when I fall more on the "not" side), horror in all its written, recorded, and visual forms is the core of my life. I have loved the darkness ever since I was a little boy of five watching *Zontar: Thing From Venus, The Lodger, Tarantula, The Creature From The Black Lagoon,* and other movies on Channel 10's *Chiller Theater* on Friday nights, along with my dad, who always smelled of machine grease, Old Spice, and factory foulness from his day's labor at a manufacturing plant that would eventually screw him up one side and down the other and toss him away like a rusty machine part.

My parents—though not great readers themselves—always bought books for me, encouraged me to read, and always watched scary movies with me. You'll hear more about them as we go on.

But we need to begin where this will all end: in the darkness, in a seat on the aisle, watching phantom images flicker across the screen as the observers gathered there become an audience and metamorphose temporarily into what the late Jim Morrison dubbed "quiet vampires": film spectators.

Now, from among these quiet vampires, let's pick someone . . .

. . . ah, there, middle row, right-hand section; we can all guess as to his story, but I think I might have a little inside information; so let me tell it:

There's this guy sitting in a second-run movie theater, where he's come with a minivan full of friends to see Rob Zombie's *House of a Thousand Corpses*. It's about sixty minutes into the thing, and he's suddenly asking the following question to a God he's not sure pays any attention to humankind, assuming that He/She/It/Them is even there: *Why in the hell am I* liking *this movie?*

Make no mistakes about it: *Corpses* is an exercise in sadistic, inhuman, grotesque brutality. It hates all of its characters, and a good argument can be made that it has nothing but contempt for its target audience (who stayed away in droves during its initial run in theaters)—but, unlike, say, the *Scream* films, it doesn't attempt to disguise its contempt for its audience with a lot of overly clever visual gimmicks, trendy film-geek references, and smartass asides. *Corpses* is up-front about it, as if Zombie is saying, "Okay, you sick, twisted things, this is what you want, so here it is, right in your face and up your nose and down your throat. Gag on it." It fails as an out-and-out horror film, it fails as a black comedy, and it fails in its core intent to be an affectionate *homage* to the psycho-horror films of the 1970s such as *The Texas Chainsaw Massacre* and *Last House On The Left*.

But for all the levels on which it fails—and they are legion—there is a raw, primal, kinetic energy to the movie that gets under your skin, no matter how much you don't want that to happen.

All while giving you the finger from first shot to last.

In an odd sort of way, you have to respect a movie this arrogant and condescending. Yeah, it's garbage, but it's *ingenious* garbage that, for about one minute halfway through the movie, actually achieves a moment of genuine nerve-wracking brilliance: one of the family of psychos that our unlucky quartet of boys and girls has encountered forces a sheriff's deputy to kneel at gunpoint, then holds the gun in front of the deputy's face while the camera does this slow, slow, *slow* pull-back to a distant overhead shot; it takes the camera almost fifty seconds to pull back and then remain still, and while this is happening there's nothing going on—no movement, no dialogue, no music, no sound, *nothing*. Absolute silence. And then, once the camera has stopped moving, this silence and stillness continues for almost another *ten seconds* before the psycho pulls the trigger and kills the deputy.

John Woo or Kurosawa it ain't, but here's the thing: we *know* the second that deputy drops his gun and kneels down that he's toast, burnt on both sides. We *know* this, we've seen too many horror movies *not* to know this, and so this unbearable, nerve-wracking, agitating silence is nothing but Zombie's way of drawing out the *dread* of the moment; he knows that we know what's coming, but he also knows that suspense and dread are not created by hyperactive editing (which he's utilized to alarming effect thus far) but by that most precious and misunderstood element available to storytellers and filmmakers both: hesitation. There is more outright terror in a held breath than in a million deafening screams, and with this single shot, Zombie shows the audience that he knows this—and since Zombie possesses this understanding and skill as a director, you can't help but wonder why he decided to squander it for most of *Corpses*' ninety-three-minute running time (which feels more like two and a half hours by the time the credits roll).

As far as this guy watching from his seat in the middle row is concerned, Rob Zombie—for all the lambasting he's taken from critics and audiences alike—knows *precisely* what's he's doing every step of the way.

House of a Thousand Corpses contains almost *everything* this guy in the audience despises about the modern horror genre—the only element missing from it is that of a heterosexual couple being snuffed immediately following sex.

In short, there was—and remains—no sensible reason for him to like this movie.

But he does. (He also liked Zombie's second film, *The Devil's Rejects*, a grindhouse film if ever there was one, and a film that could be considered a companion piece to Sam Peckinpah's masterpiece, *Bring Me the Head of Alfredo Garcia*.)

The guy has counted thirteen people who have walked out on the movie so far—something he himself should have done a while back.

He's sitting there, and all around him people are leaving, yet he watches the screen, fascinated, and suddenly finds himself thinking about, of all things, the A-word: art.

Here's some background on this guy: over the last eighteen months he has buried one of his favorite uncles, his father, his grandmother, and his mother—who he had to order taken off life-support and then spend three terrible hours watching her life grind to its end in a series of sputtering little agonies (he still has nightmares filled with her heartbroken, angry, accusing eyes); he has recently moved to a new city; he has gone through an emotionally devastating divorce that was completely his fault; he has undergone a fairly serious surgery to repair nerve damage in his right hand; and he has had a suicidal meltdown that landed him in The Bin for a while, where they kept him doped to the gills and under constant observation.

It's not exactly been a banner time for him up, and he knows that the last thing he needs is to be sitting here watching a vicious, mean-spirited, gleefully sadistic, inhumanly brutal so-called movie that is the most crystalline encapsulation he's ever seen of everything he hates about the horror field.

Yet he's not moving.

People are running for the exits all around him, and this silently pleases him, even makes him feel some hope for the human race—

—yet he remains. A movie that would offend his mother, that would make his father's often-pessimistic view of the world darken thirty shades of onyx, a movie that he knows has absolutely nothing to recommend giving it any more of the time that he'll never, ever, *ever* get back (*I'm going to be dead soon enough*, he keeps thinking) . . . and his ass stays glued to the seat.

There is a contradiction here that needs exploring, and that's something else we're going to do along the way; after all, how many of you have continued reading a horror novel or story that you know is sub-par, or stayed in your seat during a horror movie that even the medically brain-dead could recognize as being awful?

For this guy—and guess who it is?—that number is easily more than he cares to count.

But he knows he's not alone in this; thousands of you share his interest in, fascination with, and love of the darkness.

Admit it; you're right there with me in that movie theater; you've been with me there before, and you'll be there with me again. And again. And again.

Don't point fingers and accuse me of being elitist, biased, unpleasant, acerbic, grim, arrogant, depressing, untoward, discourteous, and generally no fun at parties; I already *know* I'm all of these, thanks so much. And you'd better damn well not accuse me of being part of the problems that I intend to discuss here. Horror movies and horror fiction existed long before I first put pen to paper, as did their problems, so if anything said herein and onward strikes a nerve with you, don't try to put the blame on me, folks: it was already broke when I got here.

HORROR WRITER leans back, looks at the screen, and nods.

BOOKS

See there? What'd we tell you?

WRITER

Okay, you were right. Thank you.

BOOKS

Always listen to us, pal, we're never wrong.

WRITER

I have two words for you...

DANSE MACABRE
(to itself)
This oughtta be good.

WRITER
...*Maximum Overdrive*.

THE BOOKS are silent for a moment, but we can HEAR *Danse Macabre* chuckling uncontrollably.

BOOKS
That was a cheap shot. You should be nicer to us.

WRITER
It's late and I'm tired. Sue me.

BOOKS
You really shouldn't criticize a movie until you've tried making one yourself.

WRITER
Easy for you to say.

BOOKS
(pouting)
Yeah, well, *still*...that was pretty low, even for a horror writer.

WRITER
(to himself)
Is it just me, or has Godzilla been awfully quiet?

BOOKS
What now, oh follower-in-our-creator's-shadow?

WRITER

Well, I think we've taken this opening bit about as far as we can without trying readers' patience, so...

He places his hands on the keyboard. The legs of the GODZILLA ACTION FIGURE WITH KUNG-FU GRIP twitch for a moment, then are still. CAMERA MOVES to the screen and we SEE:

CUT SHARP TO:

Part One:
A View From The Aisle Seat

"Film spectators are quiet vampires."
–Jim Morrison, *The Lords*

1

Small (and Not-So) Beginnings; Second Chances; and Lots Of Things Which Dance

"Life is material—you just have to live long enough to see how to use it."

–William Goldman, *The Color Of Light*

THIS IS HOW THE MAJORITY OF THIS BOOK IS GOING TO UNFOLD: things are going to jump and skitter and bounce around like pieces of a jigsaw puzzle caught in the wind, but, believe me, it'll all come together in the end. Or, as Jim Morrison once wrote, "The subjects says,'I see first lots of thing which dance . . . then everything becomes gradually connected.'"

Structure and reading experience dictate that this is the place to start with some appropriate anecdote about the first time I was ever really scared by a horror movie or nearly jumped out of my shorts when a sudden sound startled me from the story I was reading, some humorous moment of epiphany where All Was Revealed, but the truth is my "revelation" (a word I find more than a bit overly-dramatic, so we'll use "discovery" from here on; thanks for enduring this parenthetical pause) did not come about from reading a book or seeing a movie, but rather, because of two incidents in my life that occurred five years apart. The first was solitary, while the second . . . wasn't.

The first came about because of music. Specifically the music of The Who. Even more specifically the album *Quadrophenia*; and even *more* specifically, the second song on side four (this was, after all, back in the glory days of holy vinyl).

By its musical structure alone, *Quadrophenia* opened my eyes and my intellect to the endless possibilities offered by the metaphor; add to that its compelling and challenging narrative structure, and you've got something that, to my mind, qualifies as a masterpiece.

Quadrophenia centers on a young kid in 1960s England named Jimmy. Jimmy comes from a hard-luck, working class family. He wants to be popular among his friends. He also wants to be a good son, a good worker, and a great lover. In the midst of trying to be all things to everyone, he realizes that he presents four very distinctive personalities to the world over the course of his days: the tough guy, the romantic, the crazy fun friend, and the troubled son. Each of these separate personalities is represented by a distinct musical theme, and each personality encompasses only one aspect of the real Jimmy; none of them represent who he is in his heart. On top of all this, he's saddled with having a deeper insight into the human spirit than most people think a person of his station is capable. He admits that even he doesn't know who he really is. Being a confused, angry young man with rampaging hormones, it doesn't take long before certain aspects of his other personalities start bleeding over into the parts of his life where they don't belong.

There's much, much more to *Quadrophenia's* story, but that's the spine of it.

Okay, Christmas Eve, 1972. I was twelve years old. I had been in the hospital forover a week with pneumonia and had been released the previous morning. My dad was at work and his shift didn't end until 8:00 PM, and my mom and my little sister (age four) were doing the visiting rounds with friends and relatives but had promised me they'd be back before seven. I was lying there in bed, feeling like I was gonna bite the big one any second, and there was nothing to do—a phrase not used in the existentialist, Vladamir and Estragon, *Waiting for Godot* sense. No; what I mean is: I was bored out of my skull. I was also so weak I couldn't draw a conclusion, let alone move.

It was a tradition at the Braunbeck home that everyone got to open one present on Christmas Eve, and I knew which one I was going to unwrap. However, I was convinced that I wasn't going to live to see the morning (I was having trouble breathing and every inch of my body, inside and out, felt like it was boiling away), but I somehow rallied and stumbled downstairs in a medicated haze and stole one of my presents from under the tree. I knew it was the *Quadrophenia* album, and I was damned if I was going to die without listening to it. I took it back up to my room, put it on my record player, lay down (collapsed, actually), and listened to it all the way through, sides one through four.

This sounds like a ham-fisted cliché, but the thing changed my life. On side four, there's an instrumental piece called "The Rock," which remains for me one of the most amazing and moving pieces of music—and that's music, period, not just rock music—that I've ever heard.

In *Tommy,* the central character's epiphany is conveyed through words and music, but in *Quadrophenia,* it is conveyed solely through music. "The Rock" starts off by repeating each of the four themes separately, then, one by one, begins overlapping them until the four themes blend seamlessly into one, creating a fifth unique, defining theme as Jimmy finally realizes who he really is.

That was a revelation—ahem . . . uh, er . . . *discovery*—for the twelve-year-old me. Pete Townshend and The Who had pulled an incredible musical sleight-of-hand, created a musical Rubik's Cube that I hadn't even realized existed until the puzzle was completed.

I knew then that I wanted to someday create a piece or body of work that did what Townshend had done with *Quadrophenia's* music: present you with a group of seemingly disparate pieces/themes that in the end converged into a unified whole that was not only rewarding in and of itself (as "The Rock" most definitely is), but also enriched the sum of its parts.

"The Rock" is a perfect metaphor for what we as human beings strive toward during every moment between that first slap on the ass and the last handful of soil tossed on the lid of the coffin. Call it the psychological equivalent of string theory or whatever you will: we strive to bring the various selves together to form the whole that is uniquely "me" or "you," all the while treasuring the journey that has led to this time, this breath, this moment.

That's why I admire "The Rock," and that's why *Quadrophenia*—both in its musical and narrative structure—was, is, and ever shall be the prime example of the standard I compare—get this—my *storytelling* abilities to. I don't know if I'll ever create something as structurally and aesthetically overpowering as it is—and God knows it's not something that is always in the forefront of my mind—but, damn, it's been a helluva trip toward my own "Rock" so far.

And part of that trip has always led to either the bookshelf, the movie theater, or the typewriter (then electronic typewriter, then word processor, then computer). For me, all of these things—books, stories, movies, music, etc.—have always been connected in one form or another. I balk at many (but not all) writers who claim that the use of modern technologies and cultural icons in fiction is proof of lazy writing by sloppy, unorganized minds who don't want to bother with the work of refining their descriptive skills. "What of Dickens?" they say. "Dickens did not rely on the use of easily-accessible catch-phrases or film, television, and pop-culture references in order to enrich his work." Yeah, no arguments there . . . but are you trying to tell me that if computers, television, radio, and blockbuster films *had* existed in Dickens' day, he *wouldn't* have employed them in his stories? Are you saying that if television news cameras had existed when Sydney Carton walked to his heroic and noble death at the end of *A Tale Of Two Cities,* he wouldn't have delivered his famous "'Tis a far, far better thing I do . . ." speech right into the lens so the whole world might hear his final words? Or that if Ye Olde videotape and VCRs had existed during *Great Expectations,* the tragic Miss Havisham *wouldn't* have sat before a television in her wedding dress, watching transferred home movies of herself with the man who jilted her, or even played the song they first danced to on her record or CD player? Okay, you could *try,* but I wouldn't be convinced.

In his book of essays *Who Killed Hollywood?* the redoubtable novelist and screenwriter William Goldman makes a compelling—if somewhat insular—argument about the importance of movies: American culture (Goldman argues) is at the center of world culture, and it is *movies*—not books, not symphonies, not poetry or sculpture or dance or any other art form—that lies at the heart of American culture.

This is an argument I neither fully agree nor fully disagree with, but like the majority of Goldman's arguments about movies and culture, it has tremendous merit and so should not be ignored. For the sake of that argument, let's say that Goldman's conclusion is correct, and that movies are what lie at the heart of American culture. As writers, we have one of two choices as to what we can do about this: we can ignore the importance movies play in the day-to-day lives of many people, never referencing them in our fiction, or we can accept that it will always be movies that are at the heart of American culture and proceed accordingly. No, I'm not saying that we should write our novels and stories with an eye toward the eventual movie adaptation, nor am I advocating that our prose should be of the clipped, shorthand, eighth-grade comprehension level that we are told is as difficult as most readers will tolerate; what I *am* saying is that movies, music, television, DVDs, cell phones, and all the other accouterments that decorate the world have uses beyond those for which they were designed. If, as storytellers, we fail to employ them (when and if needed, of course), then we have no one but ourselves to blame if our work is thought to be out of touch. In the end, these things are just props, and as any good performer can tell you, if a prop can be employed to enrich your performance, you're a fool not to use it.

If fictional stories in all their forms are supposed to be, as often purported, reflections and reinterpretations of reality, then that reality has to include those things that give structure and recognition to the world around its characters. It doesn't matter a damn whether Havisham pines for her lover while trundling around in her wedding dress during the 1800s or while sitting glued to the Internet searching for some nugget of information about him in 2070; universal human conditions never change, only the props surrounding them. Any writer worth their carbon knows that in order to make a story's characters and circumstances immediate and accessible to readers, there must be points of reference to establish in *which* reality this tale is set. In the case of horror fiction, it becomes not only necessary, but vital that reality be firmly established as soon as possible because it's going to be chewed to shreds soon enough, especially when the promise of the second chance is dangled in front of a character.

Of all the themes explored in fiction and film, none is so recurrent as that of the second chance. From *Faustus* and "The Devil and Daniel

Webster" to *Grand Hotel, A Christmas Carol* and *It's A Wonderful Life* (not to mention numerous episodes of *The Twilight Zone, Darkroom,* and *The Outer Limits*), the second chance theme is one of the few timeless subjects that hasn't yet been worn down, and probably never will be. It's a grabber every time (at least for me). Who hasn't wished for the chance to somehow right a perceived wrong or undo a past failure? Who doesn't carry around a load of regret because we awaken some mornings feeling that we've wasted time and maybe even our lives doing something that makes us miserable? Who hasn't tried to ease that regret by briefly retreating into a wistful daydream where a fresh start and clean slate are readily available? Regret is one of the strongest and most self-destructive emotions human beings possess, and that makes it an excellent tool for writers and filmmakers who want to engage both the intellect and emotions of an audience. I'll state for the record that it's my belief that all horror fiction—be it written or cinematic—at its inception must grapple with such strong emotions to have a chance at lasting impact.

I've never been, as either a reader or a writer, one who responds strongly to outside bogies; I am not moved by a scene of someone struck immobile by a vampire's seductive stare or squirming under a psychopath's knife. There are exceptions to this, of course, but they're few and far between. For me, if you're going to scare or disturb readers, then you've *got* to get under their skin, and the most effective and affecting way to do this is to hit an emotional nerve as soon as you can. Few external horrors carry much of a threat unless the fear is directly connected to an emotion—and unlike Doug Winter's oft-repeated turn of the phrase, I *don't* consider horror to be an emotion. By itself, it's nothing more than a gut reaction—not a genuine emotion—one half of an equation, and only becomes horrific when it's intertwined with a strong emotion that it can manipulate in order to weaken the character's resolve.

Case in point: *Seconds*, arguably director John Frankenheimer's best film. Based on the excellent novel by David Ely, in it we meet middle-aged bank executive Arthur Hamilton (John Randolph in a masterfully shaded performance) whose life is so miserable he walks as if the earth might open at any moment and swallow him whole. His job drains him of humanity. His marriage is hollow and cold. His self-respect is rattling its last breath. He doesn't know how things came to this. He knows that he was once a decent man but he isn't any longer, and he can't understand why. He feels alien to the world around him.

Then one day a stranger in the subway hands him a card with an address written on it; the stranger knows Hamilton's name, and as soon as we see the expression on Hamilton's face, we know that he has some idea why he's been handed this slip of paper.

That night Hamilton is called by a supposedly dead friend. "I have a wonderful new life!" he tells Hamilton. "I'm happy, old buddy, and I want to do the same for you!"

It seems there are these "people" who can give you a new life. A new face. A new voice and identity. They can give you a life where you are successful at the thing you always dreamed of (in Hamilton's case, being a famous artist). It costs a lot, and once the process has begun there is no turning back.

Hamilton, after much soul-searching, decides to go through with it and embarks on a chilling journey to the secret headquarters where these "people" make arrangements for a new life. (He is taken there in the back of a meat delivery truck—some of the most unnerving black-humored symbolism I've ever encountered.) There, he meets with the doctor (Will Geer, Grandpa Walton himself, who is quietly and absolutely terrifying in the role) who has created this program. The decision made, the work begins, and soon Hamilton is transformed into the younger, more vital Antiochus "Tony" Wilson (played by Rock Hudson), given a new profession, a new home, a new life. Things are idyllic for a while, but eventually Hamilton's conscience and its questions about his old life drive him to return to his widow in an effort to find out where he went wrong.

Frankenheimer always dealt with extremes in his best pictures, and *Seconds* is possibly the most extreme film he ever made. His penchant for lean storytelling and muscular pacing is at its peak here, as is his use of his ought-to-be-patented foreground framing technique. Aided by the starkly dazzling cinematography of James Wong Howe (who won an Oscar for his work on the Paul Newman film *Hud*), Frankenheimer's forceful, in-your-face style was never better suited to its material (the script, by Lewis John Carlino—who went on to write the stunning Ellen Burstyn film *Resurrection,* as well as write and direct *The Great Santini*—is among the most literate ever written for a horror film).

Born in 1930 in Queens, New York, Frankenheimer wanted to be a professional tennis player; thank the Fates he changed his mind, or film lovers would be all the poorer.

Frankenheimer began his career as an assistant at CBS during the days of live television. His enthusiasm, intelligence, and knowledge of the camera quickly earned him a chance to direct. In 1957 he helmed the live broadcast of the Emmy Award-winning *The Comedian*, written by none other than Rod Serling. It starred Mickey Rooney, Edmund O'Brian, Kim Hunter (whom many of you might remember from the original—and best—*Planet Of The Apes*, co-scripted by Serling), and a surprisingly effective Mel Torme. What distinguished *The Comedian* from other live television dramas of the period was not only its superb script (which remains one of Serling's most angry and poetic), but Frankenheimer's maverick direction. Until *The Comedian*, most directors had been limited to the use of one, sometimes two cameras, but Frankenheimer bullied CBS executives into letting him use three—an unheard-of gamble. Not only did Frankenheimer use three cameras, he used them *simultaneously* during the breathtaking opening sequence, which still stuns today. (*The Comedian* is readily available on DVD; if you've never seen this benchmark production in television history, you'd do well to find a copy.)

Frankenheimer would work again with Serling on the 1964 political thriller *Seven Days in May*, starring Burt Lancaster, Kirk Douglas, Martin Balsam, John Houseman (in his first film role), Ava Gardner, and the great Fredric March. Based on the novel by Fletcher Knebel, *Seven Days In May* depicts what happens when a military plot to overthrow the United States government is uncovered one week before the President is scheduled to deliver his State of the Union Address. Though it contains a minimum of action, the film is nonetheless gripping, suspenseful, and, at several points, outright nerve-wracking. It also boasts a famous confrontation scene between Lancaster and March toward the end of the movie, which Frankenheimer often said was his personal favorite of all the scenes he had directed. Considering that his career spanned five decades, that's no small recommendation. That confrontation sequence remains one of the most taut, literate, and brilliantly directed sequences I have ever seen.

A lot—a *lot*—has been written and said about the film that put Frankenheimer on the map, *The Manchurian Candidate*. How effective you'll find the film today depends on your personal level of cynicism. *Candidate*—a satire in the truest sense of the word—deliberately sets out to make the viewer uncertain as to whether or not it's supposed to funny. Admittedly, some of the scenes in the film have an aura of comedy about them that I think was intentional, while others—scenes obviously intended to be serious, unintentionally draw chuckles. Laurence Harvey's British accent seems ludicrously out of place for a veteran of the Korean War, especially since he's supposed to be American, but once you get past his voice, you cannot help but admire his rich, complex performance. The final sequence, filmed in Madison Square Garden, remains one of the most beautifully edited and unbearably suspenseful ever put on film. (Many critics and film scholars credit Frankenheimer as having created the template for the modern political thriller. When viewing such films as *Candidate, Seven Days in May, Black Sunday*, and the recent HBO film *The Path to War*—which is now Frankenheimer's swan song, and a great one, at that—this accolade seems almost understated.)

In 1966, Frankenheimer turned out a pair of films that could not possibly be more disparate in subject matter and execution: *Seconds* and *Grand Prix*. Frankenheimer did not want to make *Grand Prix*, but was forced to do so after *Seconds* died a miserable death at the box office.

Grand Prix, on the other hand, was a tremendous hit at the box office, and remained Frankenheimer's most financially successful film until 1998's *Ronin*. The script by veteran playwright Robert Alan Arthur (who co-wrote *All That Jazz* with the late Bob Fosse), ultimately focuses too much on the soap-opera level problems of the drivers and their families, but it's when the film gets on the racetrack that Frankenheimer and cinematographer Lionel "Curly" Linden (who did a season as *Night Gallery*'s director of photography) blindside you. When faced with the challenge of filming a lengthy race in such a way as to make it interesting for film audiences, Frankenheimer decided he wanted to have the camera become part of the actual race, so he and Linden designed a special camera and camera harness that could be attached to the front driver's side of the car, giving the illusion that the viewer was riding on the hood during the race.

You've seen this same shot about a million times over the years, in every car chase that's been filmed. You have John Frankenheimer and Lionel Linden to thank for it.

The decades of the 70s and 80s were not good ones for Frankenheimer. In addition to a string of box office disappointments (good films such as *I Walk The Line* and not-so-good ones like 99 *and 44/100% Dead*—he never fared well with comedies), Frankenheimer was battling depression and alcoholism, which began shortly after the assassination of his close friend Robert Kennedy.

Most people know the story of how Frankenheimer drove Kennedy to the Ambassador Hotel the night of the senator's murder, but during an interview with Larry King, Frankenheimer offered a chilling post-script to the tale: he had left the podium area (where he'd been standing next to Kennedy) about three minutes before Kennedy's speech was finished in order to get his car, drive it to the front of the building, and be ready to pick up the senator. As he sat there with the car idling, he tuned to the news on the radio in time for a special bulletin: Senator Robert Kennedy had just been shot and killed along with acclaimed movie director John Frankenheimer.

"I heard them announce my death on the radio," he said. "It was horrifying and surreal and made me weep."

It also made him angry. Starting with the 1975 thriller *French Connection II* (a film in many ways the equal of William Friedkin's 1973 multi-Oscar winner, and in some ways even better), Frankenheimer's movies became infused with rage and disillusionment that was often difficult, if not impossible, for both audiences and critics to deal with. Many claimed that he had lost his touch as a director, but nothing was further from the truth. Watch *Black Sunday* and see how much of Bruce Dern's emotionally overwhelming breakdown scene you can look at, or test you mettle with the merciless heroin withdrawal sequence in *French Connection II*; even 1979's box-office disaster *Prophecy* (which is rumored to have been re-edited *without* Frankenheimer's participation or approval, though he bore the brunt of the blame when the film flopped) seethes with rage during its first forty-five minutes. (Many scenes in the film's second half were reportedly re-written and re-shot by a different director, and it shows in the inconsistent, embarrassingly sloppy visual and thematic composition.)

A few other films to mention: *Dead-Bang*—despite an awful script, this film should prove what a gifted director and solid cast can do with sub-standard material; *The Island of Dr. Moreau*—Frankenheimer came in on this one after the original director was fired and half the cast had quit, and considering what a debacle the production was when he inherited it (and his well-publicized difficulties with actor Val Kilmer), it's a wonder this film got made at all, let alone became as watchable as it is; *52 Pick-Up*—without a doubt the best film version of any Elmore Leonard novel, full of rage and cynicism and dark humor, with outstanding performances from the entire cast; and *Ronin*, another film wherein Frankenheimer was handed a paper-thin script (co-written by David Mamet under a pseudonym) but managed to instill the story with an immediacy and intensity that made its two-hour running time fly. Crackling performances, muscular editing, and two stunning car chases that forever raised the bar on that particular action-movie staple *should* have earned Frankenheimer an Oscar nomination for Best Director. (Despite winning a plethora of other awards, Frankenheimer was never even *nominated* for an Oscar, not even for *The Manchurian Candidate.*)

On a much more personal note, as a writer, Frankenheimer's films have had a profound and lasting influence on me. He taught me how to temper anger with dry humor, how to pace a story, how to visualize scenes, and, most of all, how to always give the story the spotlight. I was more saddened than I can possibly express by the death of this great American director on July 7, 2002. I think it might take a while for filmgoers to realize what a brilliant man they've lost, but realize it they will, as I did while viewing *Seconds* for the umpteenth time. This a film that remains a staggering and overlooked achievement, whose biggest surprise, perhaps, is the performance of the late Rock Hudson. In a role originally slated to be played by Laurence Olivier (whom the studio decided didn't have Hudson's box-office clout), Hudson displays a depth and power that viewers of *Pillow Talk* would never have thought possible. Hudson's face is a subtle prism of conflicting emotions; every joy, every sorrow, every triumph and regret is there, etched into his expressions like words on a headstone. When something hits at his core, you see it on his face—and not in any heavy-handed, watch-me-watch-me way; Hudson's performance is one of impressive constriction, understatement, and substance, heart-felt and affecting, and (like the superb performance of Tony Curtis in *The Boston Strangler*) a rare glimpse at a good but limited actor's one moment of true and undeniable greatness—which gives this film an added dose of bitter irony when viewed today: had Hudson lived, would he have wanted a second chance to prove his worth as an actor of substance and power? It's a saddening and frightening question—and those two words best serve to describe *Seconds*. It is an emotional film, certainly, but it is an also extremely terrifying one that grabs the viewer by the throat and never lets go, continually tying your gut into knots all the way to its tragic, relentless, and horrifying finale—a sequence that remains, in my opinion, the most terrifying finale ever filmed in a horror movie.

Seconds is available on DVD, and if you rent—or better, buy—it, make sure to listen to Frankenheimer's commentary. He not only offers a fascinating glimpse into the visual choices made by himself and Howe, but also offers an eloquent and frightening oral history of the Hollywood witch-hunts conducted by Senator Joseph McCarthy. With the exception of Hudson and Frankenheimer, *everyone* who worked on *Seconds* (both in front of and behind the cameras) had been blacklisted. Frankenheimer says several times—almost gleefully—that he purposefully hired the cast and crew *because* they had been blacklisted. His way of spitting in McCarthy's face. Bravo.

In the end, *Seconds* succeeds on every level: as an unflinching psychological study of its central character's disintegration, as a metaphor-rich cautionary fable about valuing what your life has rather than what it doesn't, as a science fiction movie, as a domestic drama, and, most of all—perhaps most importantly of all—as proof that a good horror film doesn't have to rely on cheap shocks, overdone special effects, and buckets of gore to disturb the viewer on a primal level.

I find a lot of comfort in watching *Seconds*—a film I've now seen easily thirty times. Disturbing, sad, cynical, angry, and existentialistic (in the dictionary sense of the word) as it is, this is one of the few films that still takes me out of the world while I'm watching it and leaves me feeling . . . well . . . *stronger* once it's over. It has helped me through some very bad times, and under the worst of circumstances . . .

. . . which brings me to the second incident that put me on the path to being a horror writer.

My father was a WWII veteran, 71st Infantry, Artilleryman. He fought in the battles of Regensburg, Straubing, Reid, Lambach, Weis, and Steyer; he crossed the Rhine, Danube, Isar, Inn, and Enns rivers; and he helped liberate the concentration camps of Strubing and Gunskirken Lager. He was a loyal soldier. He was born and raised in Ohio. He never made it past the eighth grade because he had to go to work to help support his ailing mother and three younger siblings after his father abandoned them during the Great Depression (he worked as a paper boy, ten different routes each day).

Near the end of the war, Dad was the sole survivor of a crash in Eberstadt, Austria—just beyond the village of Darmstadt—that killed all the men in his unit. While driving up an icy mountain road, the driver lost control of the truck and drove it over the side of a cliff. The truck plunged, upside-down, over 150 feet before landing in the ice and snow below, killing everyone except the driver and my father. He lay inside the wreckage of the truck for nearly two days, kept from freezing to death only because of the bodies on top of and below him. When at last the wreckage was discovered, it was by an SS unit that had been hiding out in the mountains, and who Dad's unit had been looking for. The first thing this unit did was pull all the bodies from the remains of the truck; the second thing was to defile the bodies; the third was to build a pile with the bodies; and the last thing they did, before they left, was to set that pile on fire. My father—who had been faking being dead the entire time—was right in the middle of that pile, and didn't dare move or speak for fear they'd discover he was alive and . . .

. . . and I'll just leave the rest of that to your imaginations.

The smoke from the fire was spotted by the Darmstadt villagers, who immediately came to the scene and put out the (thankfully) slow-burning fire (snow had begun to fall quite heavily, and while it did not douse the flames, it hindered their spreading a great deal). My father was discovered alive and was taken to Darmstadt, where he remained in their small hospital for several months before being transferred to one in Munich upon Germany's surrender.

He had broken nearly every bone in his body. He spent eighteen months in a full-body cast. (*Eighteen months.* Can you imagine what it must be like to not be able to move *at all* for a year and a half? My entire life, I don't think I ever saw him once sit still for more than thirty minutes at a time.)

After the war, he never received any kind of therapy to help him deal with it. As a result—and because he came from a generation whose members simply Didn't Talk About Such Things—he suffered from nightmares about the incident. He had a tremendous amount of trouble sleeping, and so took to having a few beers before bedtime to make him sleepy. As the years went on and the sleeplessness persisted, those few beers became a few *more* beers, then a few more beers with a couple of belts of whiskey, and he slipped quietly in full-blown alcoholism.

My father, for all his maddening habits and sometimes hateful fits of temper (especially when he was drunk), was one of the most decent human beings I've ever known. He sent all of his money home during the war so his mother could buy a house—a house that she would not allow him to move into upon his return because she thought of him as an embarrassment. This is the same woman who, when my father was a child, would beat him with the business end of her high-heeled shoes until he passed out from loss of blood. His back, shoulders, chest, and legs were a patchwork of scars she so generously gifted him with out of the goodness of her Christian heart. He had always been treated badly by most of the members of his family—the one member who loved him purely and unconditionally was his sister, Lucille, my Aunt "Boots," now fifteen years in her grave, God rest her selfless soul—yet he still loved them and sought their approval, especially his mother's. He never got it, and he knew it, and that made him one of the saddest human beings I'd ever seen.

The end of the summer of 1977 was, to put it mildly, not pleasant. Dad's alcoholism was at its violent peak, his self-respect was non-existent, and he saw no point to his life. He had worked for the Roper corporation for nearly twenty-two years when they decided to close down their Newark plant after the fifth labor strike, one that resulted in the worst riot of its kind in the city's history. Through a couple of (in my opinion) criminally deceptive clauses in the last contract they offered to their employees, most of the line workers were ineligible for full pension benefits—which wound up being beside the point because, somehow, the majority of the pension fund just disappeared, and what my father received as a severance package was $125 for every year of employment. Dirt money. Chump change. Money gone before it was got. And oh, yeah: kiss retirement before sixty goodbye, pal.

In the summer of 1977 my father had been at his new job at Larson's Manufacturing for a little over five years. He operated a sheet metal press, with lathe work on the side. His body was already showing the wear of a life that had been one struggle after another. He still couldn't sleep for shit. He couldn't concentrate. The mortgage—which should have been paid off with some of his pension money—was still looming over his head, and there was talk of layoffs at the plant.

His drinking that summer was the worst it had ever been. The nightmares were incessant. The pain in his body—from both his war injuries and those sustained from working the factory line for thirty years—was nearly unbearable, and the painkillers prescribed by his doctor barely helped. Add to this his heart and blood-pressure medication, plus a recent diagnosis of Type 2 diabetes, and the man never had a waking moment where he wasn't worried to death about something.

So he drank. A lot. He flew into violent rages that usually left my mother bleeding and me having to take her to the emergency room and lie to the attending physicians about how she came to be in such a state. I intervened as often as I could when Dad went into these rages. I've got some impressive scars to prove it.

In the summer of 1977, when I was seventeen, I came as close to hating my father as I ever had before. All I saw was a whining, violent, self-pitying drunk who blamed the world for his failures in life—and who saw his life as a wasted one.

On this day, the Fourth of July, my mother had taken my then-seven-year-old sister Gayle Ann to watch the big parade downtown. I had been out partying with some friends the night before, and had come home at four in the morning to crash on the sofa, not bothering to turn off the television, which was tuned to Turner Classic Movies.

I was awakened sometime around ten-thirty by my father falling on me. Drunk on his ass. He'd gone through all the beer and was putting a good dent in the contents of a whiskey bottle.

"Can't get to sleep," he kept slurring at me. "Can't get to sleep. C'mon, get your ass up and let's go make some breakfast."

I rose, groggy-eyed and cotton-mouthed, from the sofa, went into the kitchen, and—at Dad's request—microwaved a couple of TV dinners for breakfast.

I sat at one end of the kitchen table, Dad at the other. I began to eat. He started rambling on about the way his mother had treated him and my Aunt "Boots" when they were children; about the war and what had happened to him; about how he was too old and too tired to face another twenty-five years on another line at another plant. (He'd once told me he'd wanted to raise chickens for a living when he was a young man; how he wished he'd been able to do that. It was his dream, and it meant the world to him, and it just broke his heart that he and my mother never had the money to buy a proper farm for raising chickens.)

I remember all of this very clearly because, when he first began to talk, I looked up at him and saw the business end of a *Duetsche Werk* 7.65mm semi-automatic pistol pointed right at my face. I knew this gun well. Dad had taken it from where one of the SS officers who'd discovered the remains of his unit had dropped it in his haste to get away.

He ate very little of his TV dinner. But he drank the whiskey. Even used it to chase down some painkillers, as well as his heart and blood-pressure medicine—none of which were supposed to be taken at the same time, let alone with alcohol.

He began unraveling right in front of me.

And all the time that gun stayed pointed right at my face. He wasn't aware of it. I didn't dare make any sudden moves or loud noises for fear of startling him—his finger was on the trigger and the safety was off and the magazine, which he always kept fully loaded, was securely in place.

He began calling me other names—Stan, Willie P., "Slim"—all members of his deceased unit. He began talking about what had happened as if it were happening at that very moment and they were still alive to remember the experience with him. A couple of times he started crying and saying things like, "But I don't have any money for a hotel, Mom!" He began looking around the kitchen, whispering, "Shhh, shut your fuckin' mouth, Stan! Can't you hear 'em?"

It was at that moment that I did what was probably the first genuinely wise thing I had done in my life. Very quietly, with as even a tone of voice as I could muster (surprised I could find it in me to speak at all), I said, "Hear who, Frank?"

"Goose-stepping cocksuckers," he snarled, then jumped up from the table, threw his chair aside, and started toward the back porch door. He grabbed my arm on the way past and said, "We gotta get 'em first this time."

He pulled me out onto the back porch and forced me to squat down beside him as he aimed the gun. "The trees," he said. "They came out of the trees."

I remembered him telling me that earlier; how he'd seen the SS unit emerge from the snow-covered trees and move toward the detritus of his unit.

I don't know how long we stayed like that. Once I thought he was going to pass out, but just as I was stupid enough to reach for the gun, his eyes snapped open and he stood up and plowed four rounds into the sole tree in our back yard. The dog next door barked and damn near got its head blown off for the effort.

To counteract the wise thing I had done before, I did something supremely stupid—I tried to pull the gun out of his hand.

"The trees," he kept saying. "The trees."

And plowed off two more shots.

I didn't know it at the time, but one of those shots went through my right shoe and blew off part of my big toe (to this day, even in the worst of summer, I won't wear sandals because of that injury).

Finally, Dad hit me one upside the head with the butt of the gun and ran inside. By the time I staggered back into the house he'd reloaded the magazine, pulled out his hunting rifle, and was loading it.

I walked into the living room and said something to him—I don't remember what—but the sound of my voice startled him; he screamed, fell backward, and fired a shot that missed me by a good three or four feet but felt like it had come a helluva lot closer. I dropped to the floor in tears, hating myself for being so scared.

Dad crawled over to me and said that it was gonna be okay, we'd keep an eye on the trees, Mom would be proud of him because he got a medal and everything. (He received a Purple Heart and several other medals that left my grandmother notably underwhelmed. They now hang in my office.)

Dad rose up, pistol in one hand and rifle in the other, and walked out onto the front porch. By now a couple of our neighbors had figured out that something untoward was happening at the Braunbeck house and decided to come outside for a look.

One of them, a guy named Jess, walked right up to Dad and asked, "What'cha doin' there, Frank?"

Dad started to say something, then turned and looked at me, then turned back to Jess. Somewhere in there a shred of reason had returned to him. "Just showing Gary my guns. Boy don't know nothing about hunting . . . or sports . . . or anything interesting." Then he gave me a quick look over his shoulder—one filled with disappointment and a level of embarrassment that bordered on disgust.

Now, I'd always known that I wasn't the kind of son he wished he'd had—I was more interested in theatre and books and music and movies than I was in sports or cars or hunting or any of the other bullshit activities by which your value as a man is supposedly measured, especially in a hard-core blue-collar town like Newark—so this in itself was no revelation to me . . . but this was the first time that I realized that my father didn't much like me. Oh, he loved me, I knew that, loved me dearly, would do anything for me . . . I just wasn't the type of guy he'd choose for a friend.

I began shaking, feeling like a worthless piece-of-shit failure who was a supreme disappointment to his parent.

Much the same way, I imagine, Dad felt whenever in the company of his mother.

"Well, what say we get you back inside?" said Jess. "Can't stand all this excitement this early in the day."

Dad laughed, and turned to go back in the house, looking as if the madness had passed.

But did not let go of the gun or the rifle.

Jess and I sat him down at the kitchen table and I started pouring coffee down his throat. (Know what you get when you give coffee to a drunk? A wide-awake drunk. I didn't know that then. Important lesson. Teach your children well.)

He began to calm down. Jess said he'd see Dad later, and then left (to go home and call the police, I was soon to discover).

We sat at the table for a few minutes, neither of us saying a word. Dad began to drift off again. I took the gun and the rifle from him, setting them down on a chair in the front room. I came back into the kitchen to find him swallowing a handful of pills.

"You already took your medicine."

"Shut your mouth, boy. I don't need any shit from the likes of you."

The likes of you. Thirty-eight years later, that one still stings.

He rubbed his eyes, dazed and drained. I don't know that I've ever seen such profound loneliness on a human being's face.

I got him to his feet and started leading him through the front room toward the stairs. I noticed that my right foot felt really wet, like I was walking in thick mud. I looked down and saw a hole in my shoe. Every time I took a step, something dark squirted up through the hole and ran down the sides, leaving a little spatter-path on the carpeting. Mom was going to kill me, ruining her carpeting like this.

I had Dad on the second or third step leading to the upstairs and his bedroom when there was this loud *crack!* from behind, followed by an equally loud crash.

I turned around just in time to see the police officer who'd kicked open our front door come barreling in, decked out in full riot gear, wielding a pump-action shotgun.

Dad—who was still mumbling to himself—didn't seem to notice.

I propped him up against the wall of the first landing and went back down. My intention was to tell the officer that everything was all right now, that Dad was calm, that it was all over. But as I came off the last stair, the first genuine wave of pain from my foot registered with my brain and I lost my balance. I fell against the chair where the pistol and rifle lay. The officer evidently thought I was making a grab for a weapon, because before I knew what had happened, he slammed the butt of the shotgun into my chest, then shoved the business end right into my face as soon as I hit the floor.

It ain't like in the movies, folks; your first instinct isn't to deliver a Dirty Harry- or Bruce Willis-type smartass remark, one proving that you're made of steel and mere guns hold no fear for you: find yourself staring into the business end of a pump-action shotgun, and you'll know *exactly* what Nietzsche was talking about when he spoke of staring into the abyss.

The rest of it happened like this:

Dad came flying down the stairs and threw himself into the first officer. The shotgun discharged into the floor about a foot to the left of my head (I have a 22 percent hearing loss in my left ear as a result). Dad started screaming about filthy Nazi cocksuckers. By this time three other police officers were in the house, and all three of them did everything they could—aside from shooting him—to pull Dad off the first officer: they knocked him down; one of them pulled out his pistol and pointed it at Dad but couldn't get a clear shot because of the struggle; another one managed to get his club loose and clobbered Dad pretty good with it. Then, both officers fell back. One of them had what looked like a broken jaw. The other officer helped him outside where an ambulance waited. The third officer—the one who could not get a shot at Dad—radioed the rest of the outside units about the size of his dick and how his girlfriend was going to be glad it hadn't been shot off or something like that. I wasn't really listening.

I crawled toward the kitchen, pushing Dad's pistol and rifle in front of me. Don't ask me what the hell I thought I was doing, I couldn't tell you. Even now.

Two or three other officers came inside the house. They stood around Dad, looking down at him. I couldn't hear what was said, but their tones told me everything I needed to know: A) They were talking to him as if he were just another drunken example of the poor, ignorant, mean-spirited white trash they had to deal with every day, and, B) They weren't very happy that Dad had hurt one of their own.

Sometime in there, Dad was pulled to his feet. The officers laughed at him. Someone slapped on the handcuffs.

The circle of police officers parted. One of them noticed me on the floor in the kitchen and said something to the others.

I looked up and saw Dad looking back at me.

This is the part that I don't often talk about, because whenever I do, someone inevitably tells me that I must have imagined it, that I was in shock, that something like this *couldn't possibly* have occurred, blah-blah-blah, dozy-doe.

I was not then, nor have I ever been, one to "see things," to "imagine things," or to "hallucinate things."

I have never used this next incident in any story, nor will I ever, because no one would believe it.

I was on the floor, looking straight into Dad's face, and he into mine.

I was scared, I was in pain, and one of the officers had entered the kitchen and knelt down beside me, his voice ever so calm and patient as he tried to get me to hand over the guns.

The officer standing by the kitchen doorway looked at Dad, then looked at me, then shook his head and laughed.

I couldn't help what I did next; I laughed, too.

Then saw it register on Dad's face.

His son was laughing at him. Because these cops thought he was pathetic. Because he was an embarrassment. Because he was a failure whose life didn't amount to shit. Because he didn't matter.

I stifled the near-hysterical laugh as soon as it escaped me, but the damage was done.

Dad spluttered out one sob, just one, thick and heavy with humiliation.

Then his face turned into an expressionless slab of granite.

And *he* laughed.

Just once.

And snapped the chain holding the handcuffs together.

Just like that. Laugh. Snap. Like that chain was no more than a slightly thick stick.

I don't care if you believe that or not. I have copies of the police reports, and at least three of them mention being surprised that Dad was able to "... free himself of the restraints."

Before any of them had time to realize what had just happened, Dad slammed his elbow into the nearest officer's face and took his gun. The others started to turn toward the movement, a few drawing their weapons. Two of them jumped on Dad and he began to spin. That's all I saw before panic really got hold of me and I crawled and pushed for all I was worth.

Two shots were fired. One went into the wall over the kitchen entryway. The other one hit me somewhere between my lower back and the middle of my thighs. (All right, I'll just say it—I got shot in the ass.) I remember being surprised that it didn't hurt more. A few moments later, it registered, and then hurt like hell, and then made me angry. I rolled over onto my back and saw an officer pointing a gun at me. I offered up the pistol. It probably wasn't the thing to do, raising a gun toward a policeman in the middle of a situation like this, because he fired at me. This third shot is the one I'll always remember: I *felt* that son-of-a-bitch whiz by my temple.

At least two officers lay unconscious on the floor as others came inside, one of them leading an attack dog. Dad threw the gun in his hand. It hit the officer standing over me in the back of the head. Dad screamed: "You don't hurt my boy! Nobody hurts my boy! Not my Jeff!" At least, that's what it sounded like to me. (Jeff, had he lived, would have been my twin brother, but an accident at birth left him dead and me as the consolation prize. He now pops up as an alter-ego in some of my stories. I spell his name Geoff. Perhaps you remember him from a story in *Things Left Behind* called "Searching For Survivors," a story also known as "Safe," or the novel *Far Dark Fields*. The big event in that story and novel took place on the Fourth of July, and it wasn't until recently—believe it or not—that I actually made the connection.)

I tried to get up to stop Dad from making it even worse, but he'd come up behind the officer and yanked him off the floor. The officer pushed back against Dad and kicked out his legs. The toe of his boot got me right in the jaw. I lost three of my back teeth.

I resumed my crawling and bawling, pushing the guns along in front of me. Dad somehow managed to bulldoze his way through the officers clotting up the front room and threw the one he was holding through the front window. One of them screamed like I'd never heard anyone—man, woman, child, or beast—scream before or since. It is a sound I never want to hear again.

I was so terrified at this point that I was barely able to keep moving. I felt my bladder give way, and I wet myself, feeling humiliated and useless and cowardly.

Then it got worse.

As soon as the officer came crashing through the window, shots were fired into the house from outside. It looked like everyone hit the floor, searching around for weapons.

I thought Dad had been shot. He hadn't, but I didn't know that at the time. I called out to him and he shouted for me to get the hell out. The attack dog was barking and snarling.

Two windows exploded then—one in the front of the house, the other behind me in the kitchen. Tear gas. I remember choking and throwing up on myself. I remember Dad yelling for me to help him. I remember shadow-shape figures moving through the smoke, looking like something out of a science fiction movie because of the masks they wore.

I managed to make it down to the basement, guns and all. I didn't so much crawl down the steps as tumble face-first on my belly. I sat there in the semi-darkness and cried like a baby, while above I heard the sounds of Dad being wrestled to the ground by what sounded like an army. I looked up only once and saw another police dog being led by the small window that looked out from the basement onto the little sidewalk that ran parallel to the house. When I looked back down I saw that my hand was bleeding from where three of my fingernails had been crushed; the skin underneath them was swollen and dark purple. How it happened, I don't know.

(For those of you who are interested in final tallies, I ended this day with two cracked ribs, three crushed fingernails, a broken collar bone, three lost teeth, a dislocated shoulder, cuts on my head, arms, and chest that garnered a total of twenty-six stitches, a badly sprained left arm, powder burns on my temple, and two "official" gunshot wounds. I remember all this when I *think* I'm having a bad day now.)

I stayed down there for several minutes, until I heard the last of the officers leave the house. I pulled myself and the guns back upstairs and peeked out through the remains of the front window.

This is the important part; pay attention.

Both ends of the street had been cordoned off. There were three ambulances and seven police cruisers parked out front, bar lights flashing to beat the band. Neighbors lined the street on both sides the length of the entire block. The police officers could have put Dad in any one of six nearby cruisers—there was one right in front of the fucking house!—but they chose, instead, to walk him almost all the way down the block, parading him past the neighbors, to a cruiser that sat at the far end of the street. Dad was in a second set of handcuffs. He was sobbing. He had thrown up on himself. Vomit dribbled from his chin. He kept apologizing to every neighbor he was dragged past.

The worst of it, though, was that my Dad's pants had started to fall down in the back, revealing what some people laughingly refer to as a "workman's crack."

He was completely, totally, and utterly disgraced.

The two officers who were hauling him up the street were putting on quite the show, jerking him around and holding onto this beaten, weary, sad man as if he were still a threat. I hope they felt brave. I hope they felt proud of themselves, turning my father into a one-man freak show. I felt something crack inside of me, but had no idea what it was. It occurred to me then that I was armed. I almost raised one of the guns and fired a shot into the air just to watch these brave officers who had turned my dad into the centerpiece of a freakshow jump in panic. But I didn't. I simply dropped it onto the couch. And I continued to stare at my dad.

That moment is forever frozen in my memory, and I knew right then it was important for me to memorize everything I was feeling—the anger, the sick-making sadness, the horror, the pain, the helplessness, and the sudden, mystifying, overwhelming love I felt toward this man who once wanted to be a chicken farmer but had spent his life on the factory line, instead.

I wanted to mark this moment, and to remember it.

And the anger.

And the anger.

And the anger.

God, yes—the anger.

I stumbled over to the sofa and fell onto it. I could still hear the neighbors and the police all milling about, talking, some laughing, a few people crying. They didn't exist for me. All that composed my world at that moment was physical pain, humiliation, and anger.

I stared at the television set, which had been left on by Dad as he sat up drinking the night before and that I hadn't bothered to turn off when I got in. The movie I was looking at was *Seconds*, the scene where Will Geer, after listening to John Randolph's heartbreaking recitation of the things in his life that matter (". . . my boat . . . friends at the club . . ."), smiles sadly and says, "So this is what happens to the dreams of youth."

I lost it. The look on Randolph's face at that moment was so much like that on Dad's right before I started leading him up the stairs. I might as well have been looking at a black-and-white photograph of fifteen minutes earlier.

I looked away from the screen just in time to see the two police officers finally—*finally*—finish shoving Dad into the back of the cruiser.

So this is what happens to the dreams of youth.

I wiped my eyes and looked back at the screen, and, for a minute or so longer—until people remembered there had been a teenaged boy in the house when all the shooting started, and so started wandering in—for just a minute or so, I was pulled out of this world I really didn't want to be in, and was, instead, immersed in the story on the screen in front of me. Undoubtedly a large part of it was shock—everything within and without had gone numb—but a part of it was also because I *wanted* to be pulled out of the world, and I honestly don't know if anything but *Seconds* could have done it right then.

While I stared at the movie, I found myself humming, very quietly, a part of "The Rock" to myself, and somewhere in there I began thinking of each individual incident that had happened—to Dad during the war, to the police, to myself, to the Randolph character in the movie—as being an isolated musical theme that was trying to overlap with the others to create a cumulative, distinct, and final theme. I was grasping at straws, trying to find a goddamn *point* to all of this.

But I couldn't. I hadn't the capacity, the experience, the skill, intelligence, or wherewithal to string all of this together into a neat little final theme that would not fall shrill and tuneless on my ears.

But I wanted to have that ability, that intelligence and skill.

Life is material . . .

That was the catalyst that set me on the path to becoming a writer of horror fiction. I promised myself that I would always try to convey in my stories at least some small sense of what I felt at that moment during the summer of 1977 when I watched the police haul my father down the street. Horror is not merely creating unease or suspense, nor is it simply letting emotions, both light and dark, bleed all over the page or the screen. It should convey the genuine sense of tragedy that hangs over all our lives; it should scare us, yes, of course, no arguments, but there has to be an element of *genuine loss* connected to that fear—be it loss of life, limb, sanity, or loved one. Of all forms of fiction, horror shouldn't be satisfied with simply engaging the emotions—it should strive to make people experience every joy, every shudder, every tear and triumph; it must force them to assume the role of the story's characters, whether they want to or not, and live those characters' tragedies as if it were their own. I will not apologize for this, and if it makes me pretentious in your eyes, so be it. But I know that what I experienced that moment, looking through that window at my father as he was made a mockery of, is what all truly *pure* horror fiction should make its readers experience: the terror, tragedy, sadness, anger, and soul-sick absurdity of violence and grief, and how we struggle from womb to tomb to reconcile them with the concept of a just universe where, we're led to believe, the good are always rewarded and the wicked punished (insert rim-shot here). Sometimes a hand reaches out from the shadows to protect us, to lead us toward safety and acceptance; sometimes this same hand grabs our throats and begins to squeeze; and sometimes no hand reaches out at all. We're just left cowering in the basement, alone with the coldness and the darkness and the guns, bleeding and scared and helpless. True horror should leave you wrung out, physically and emotionally. The best of it can even change you.

Life is material . . .

I was changed that day, in that moment in the summer of 1977. It defined me as a human being, and that bleeding, frightened, pissed-off teenager defined me—and defines me still—as a writer of horror.

. . . you just have to live long enough to see how to use it.

My dad died of cancer on June 15, 2001, just a few days after his seventy-fifth birthday. Until he was moved to the nursing home where he died, he slept by himself in an old twin bed in my old room because my mom's snoring was too loud. There were no pictures hanging on the wall, no cases displaying his medals. There was a rocking chair in there; one he never used. It was weighed down by photo albums of the past that he never looked at. He had to wear Depends all the time because the radiation treatments he had received for his first batch of cancer had pretty much ruined his bowels and bladder. His clothes—all of them—were folded neatly into a pile that sat on a small table at the foot of the bed. He owned one pair of pajamas, one pair of slippers. Almost no one came to visit him at home during the last few years of his life, and he stopped keeping a phone in his room because when there was a call, it was never for him. When he died, it took my sister and me all of an hour to pack his possessions into boxes. He had never wanted much for himself, except to know that his hard work had counted for something. Anything he had, he gladly gave to his children. Up until the end, even in the nursing home, when Gayle or I visited, he asked if we need any money or anything. This from a man who couldn't find enough to pay for all of his prescriptions. His mother never came around to see him after his illness entered its final months. She said it was because of her health, yet she somehow managed to continue seeing her other living children several times a week.

When Dad died, he was sitting in a wheelchair waiting for the nurses to change his bed. He was parked at an angle by the door to his room—which meant that he was looking into the bathroom. He was alone, and sometime between the nurses' changing the pillow cases and unfolding a fresh fitted sheet, my father quietly, not wanting to bother anyone, died. Staring into a toilet. His mother did not come to his funeral, claiming health reasons (yet somehow managed to find the energy to visit with her daughters later that same day). Nine months after Dad's death, my mother passed away. Going through some of her things, I came across a letter that Dad had written to her when they were first married and both of them worked double shifts:

> "Dear Mary: I am so sorry that I did not have the money to buy you an anniversary present. I will make it up to you. I know I say that a lot. It always seems like I am making things up to people. But I wanted you to know how much I love you and am glad you are my wife. I'm sorry I don't have a present for you. Happy anniversary."

It always seems like I am making things up to people.

Someone should have made something up to him. Just once. To my mother, as well (who, I should add, grew up in the county children's home along with her four brothers, and she, like my father, worked her fingers and spirit to the bone to give her children a decent life).

So this is what happens to the dreams of youth.

There once was a young soldier who dreamed of becoming a chicken farmer, but he worked the line instead. I am that young soldier's only surviving son, and I am proud to have had him as my dad. He thought it was great that I wrote, and that I'd published books. He'd read a lot of my published work—at least, that work with typeface wasn't too small for his eyes, which were never what they used to be for as long as I knew him.

Ever since the deaths of my parents I have been slave to an obsessive need to make sense of human suffering, both within and without. I've always thought that Nietzsche's famous quote about what doesn't kill you only makes you stronger was intended to be ironic, if not outright tongue-in-cheek: makes you stronger to what end? So that next round you'll be able to endure more of whatever it was that damn near killed you in the first place? Suffering makes you stronger so that you can endure more suffering? Oooh—sign me up for that one. As much as I try, I see nothing noble in those who live lives of "quiet desperation." What I see is pain and isolation that empowers not the sufferers, but that which afflicts them. I want a reason for this. I want a reason for babies born with cancer, for the endless supply of thoughtless cruelties both little and large that we inflict on one another on an everyday basis, for old folks who are abandoned to die alone and unwanted and unloved; I want an explanation, please, for all of the soul-sick, broken-hearted people who become so hollowed by their aloneness that they turn on the gas, eat the business end of a shotgun, or find a ceiling beam that can take their weight. I want sense made of this. I want to know the reason why . . . and since none is forthcoming either from above or from those around me, I've decided to try and find the answer on my own. So far, the best—the only—way for me to work toward this is through writing horror stories. Now—aren't you surprised I don't get invited to many parties?

I take horror—though not, for the record, myself—damned seriously, and I have my dad and *Quadrophenia* and a certain film by John Frankenheimer to thank for it.

As a result of my attitudes toward the horror field, I tend not to find myself drawn to many of the more traditional books and movies that are so easily—even *too* easily—recognized as being part of the genre. *Of course* the movies in, say, Romero's *Dead* trilogy are horror films—and we'll talk about those shortly—but for my money, you have to expand not only your personal definition of horror, but your willingness to look for books and films that are not marketed as being the same. By looking outside of the narrowly-defined and popular misconceptions of horror, by moving past the obvious, you can often enrich your appreciation of those things that are good about the field and understand more clearly why the bad is so inarguably awful.

To that end, I want to look at some other "second chance" films that also qualify—strongly, in my opinion—as horror movies.

Just as complex as *Seconds*, though less overpowering in its execution, 1968's *The Swimmer* (directed by Frank Perry and written by

Eleanor Perry, based on the short story by John Cheever) was a labor of love for its producer/star Burt Lancaster. In it he plays a businessman who, at film's start, has decided to spend a bright summer Sunday afternoon making his way from pool to pool, swimming his way across suburbia to his own home. He lives in an upscale and trendy community where everyone knows everyone else in their chosen clique, so it comes as no surprise to anyone when Burt wanders into their backyards and tells them he is swimming home. They laugh. They make martinis. They talk about what a card Lancaster is and what a simply mah-velous party story his little escapade will make. It seems like another *Peyton Place* soap opera at first.

But then people start asking about his wife and daughters:

"I heard what happened . . ."

"I was so sorry to hear . . ."

"How are you feeling now?"

"I didn't think you'd want to be around anyone for a while, not after . . ."

What exactly did happen in Lancaster's life that has everyone treating him either with extreme caution or overzealous joviality? Where, exactly, is he coming from at the beginning of the film? Our first sight of him comes as he's running in his swimming trunks through the woods, already sopping wet, yet he tells the first back yard gathering he appears in that theirs will be his "first" swim on his way home. And why can't he tell anyone what he's been doing lately?

These key questions are skirted for the first half of the film, but it's the very lack of ready answers that provides a good deal of tension. Hints are dropped, concerned looks are exchanged, surreptitious gestures are made behind Lancaster's back. Soon, the viewer wonders about Lancaster's mental stability as, piece by piece, the horror of his life comes together like a jigsaw puzzle that's missing the last piece—which may be the reason *The Swimmer* is such a turn-off for many viewers: there is no direct and final answer to any of the questions, no last-minute revelation. But if you pay close attention, everything you need to know is there.

Lancaster gives a typically terrific performance, one full of both internal and physical catharses; every pool is a new baptismal fount where he washes away past sins, yet by the time he reaches the next pool, a different load of sins have made themselves known. You may not have a lot of sympathy for this character—he's shown to be a shameless opportunist, an adulterer, two-faced, and self-aggrandizing—but you will nonetheless be fascinated enough to follow him through to the genuinely shocking conclusion of his journey.

The Swimmer may be the closest American films will ever come to capturing the type of quiet dread so richly explored in the "Oxrun Station" stories of Charles L. Grant. Yes, it's difficult as hell in places, but it's also suspenseful, disturbing, and ultimately rewarding.

The next two movies have something in common the previous films don't share: both crippled their directors' careers for various reasons.

Sorcerer, made by William Friedkin after his triumphs and numerous awards for both *The French Connection* and *The Exorcist*, was his own *Apocalypse Now*: a film that went over budget and took three times as long to film as originally planned, but one denied *Apocalypse*'s subsequent fame, notoriety, and audience interest.

A remake of Henri-Georges Clouzot's *The Wages of Fear, Sorcerer* tells the story of four men, all wanted criminals, who flee to a nameless Third World country to escape punishment, imprisonment, torture, or death. When a devastating oil rig explosion offers the chance to make some big money very quickly (they have to transport old crates of leaking nitroglycerine over 200 miles of treacherous mountain road), each sees a chance to get out of this hell-hole country and forge a new life elsewhere, far from regrets and old enemies.

Screenwriter Walon Green (who co-wrote *The Wild Bunch* with Sam Peckinpah) foregoes a script filled with meaningful dialogue and concentrates instead on expressionistic imagery to tell large chunks of the story. This, coupled with Friedkin's flair for jittery realism, gives *Sorcerer* an effective and gritty documentary feel. There are three sequences in this film that remain, to this day, some of the most astounding ever executed in a fictional movie: a terrorist attack that makes you feel as if you're trapped in the middle of a Lebanon street war (part of which, Friedkin later revealed, *was* an actual street shootout that erupted while they were filming the fictional one); a riot scene of raw and terrifying violence; and a bridge-crossing sequence that should be held up to future directors as a quintessential example of how an expert filmmaker builds nerve-wracking suspense.

But, as in all these films, the final price of the second chance is extracted, and proves to be more than the characters bargained for. If nothing else remains in your mind after viewing this movie, the one indelible image that will haunt you is the gaunt, drawn face of the late Roy Scheider as small-time hood Jackie Scanlon; Scheider is the embodiment of weariness and regret who struggles against all logic and hope to find something worth going on for. Scheider gives a typically marvelous performance in a role that relies more on physicalization than dialogue to define and express the character and his struggle.

I greatly admire both *Sorcerer* and *The Wages of Fear*, but find my preference leaning toward Friedkin's film, if for no other reason than because *Sorcerer* takes the time to establish these men in their previous lives so the viewer can have some sense of what they've been forced to abandon. *Sorcerer* possesses emotional layers where *Wages* opts for the coldly intellectual, and though both films are potentially devastating to the viewer, *Sorcerer* remains the more humane and accessible of the two—that second word not being easily applied to the next "second chance" movie: Sam Peckinpah's *Bring Me the Head of Alfredo Garcia.*

Early on in *Garcia*, one secondary character remarks: "Be content with your lot in life, no matter how poor it may be. Only then can you expect mercy."

That line could have come from any of these films, and in each case would have been appropriate, but in *Garcia* it's doubly so, for no other American director has understood or been able to capture the Mexican "culture of poverty" as unflinchingly as Peckinpah. *Garcia* may not be Peckinpah's best film (it continues to appear on several "All Time Worst" lists), but it is without a doubt his most personal. From its lovely opening image (a young, pregnant Mexican woman resting by a river, sunning herself) to its harrowing closing shot (a smoking Gatling gun), *Garcia* is unique, for no other film of Peckinpah's has so seamlessly managed to contain every element this often-brilliant director was obsessed with exploring: love, betrayal, desperation, tenderness in the face of brutality, loneliness, helplessness, anger, the struggle of integrity vs. conformity, friendship, and, of course, the futility of violence.

Peckinpah was accused throughout his career of glorifying violence, but he insisted he was doing the direct opposite: showing how repulsive it was by dwelling on it so much. On no film was he more often accused of glorifying the violence he claimed to disdain than in *Garcia*.

The basic story goes like this:

The beautiful daughter of a wealthy and powerful Mexican land baron is seduced, impregnated, and abandoned by one Alfredo Garcia, a shameless gambler/drunkard/womanizer. The land baron, El Jefe, assembles his soldiers and declares his outrage at the loss of his daughter's (and subsequently the lessening of his own) honor, and shouts: "Bring me the head of Alfredo Garcia!" Like the Knights of the Round Table questing for the Holy Grail, El Jefe's army is off and running.

Into this scenario enters an American expatriate named Bennie (Warren Oates) who is biding his time playing piano in a sleazy Mexico City bar. He is approached by two gangsters he often works for as a bagman (Robert Webber and Gig Young), who have been authorized to offer him a substantial piece of change if he'll hunt down and decapitate Alfredo Garcia. Bennie, despite many indecent instincts he's been trying to kill, accepts the offer, telling them he can use the money to take himself and his girlfriend, Elita (Isela Vega, who remains the strongest female character to appear in a Peckinpah movie) somewhere far away and begin a new life.

Along the twisted way, Bennie proposes to Elita in what is arguably the most heartfelt and sadly moving scene Peckinpah ever filmed. The two run into and overcome several obstacles in their way (yes, I'm being deliberately vague here) before they find themselves at a rotting, neglected graveyard where the careless Garcia, shot by a gambling partner, is now buried.

The first half of this film has the loose narrative structure of an obscure European import—in fact, in places, it gets downright eccentric—but I still say this film was condemned only because it came from Peckinpah. Had it come from a director from New Zealand or France, critics would have drowned it in praise.

"Why does he think of this as a horror movie?" I hear you cry.

Because from the moment Bennie and Elita enter that wretched graveyard in the middle of the night, *Garcia* employs not only the classic visual elements of old horror movies (circling bats, wolves howling in the distance, misshapen shadows skulking in the background), but its heart and soul surrender to the horrific as well. The shadow-drenched grave-robbing sequence is truly nightmarish, and from that scene on, the film begins a fast and merciless descent through all nine circles of Dante's Hell as Bennie makes his way across country with Garcia's decomposing head inside a wet burlap bag that is perpetually swarming with flies.

"Just you and me, Al, baby!" says Bennie, who spends the second half of the film slowly going insane. Warren Oates (who was infuriatingly underrated for most of his career) gives a towering performance as Bennie, making the man at once repulsive, sympathetic, heroic, romantic, and tragic. His fascinating and complex characterization was easily the best American film performance of 1974.

Bennie's "relationship" with Garcia's head gets so creepy by the film's end that I refuse to spoil it for you by going into any more detail; suffice it to say that Bennie not only talks to Al, but often stops in the middle of a sentence to listen as Al gives him advice (and that's not even the weird part).

That Bennie is doomed from the moment he comes into possession of Garcia's head is a given, yet the viewer is perversely compelled to watch his slow and painful deterioration. Of all the "second chance" movies mentioned here, *Bring Me the Head of Alfredo Garcia* is the one whose heart, blood, and soul lie strongly within the field of genuine horror. (I am convinced that John McNaughton drew some of his visual and thematic inspiration for *Henry: Portrait of a Serial Killer* from the second half of *Garcia*. Watch both films back-to-back and you might think you've just watched the first two movies in an uncompleted trilogy.)

In the end, all of these movies seem to have the same philosophy about the second chance: you're better off where you are, for there is no mercy (a philosophy my dad would have agreed with—he wouldn't have *liked* agreeing with it, but he would have). If that doesn't qualify them as horror films, then maybe we'd all be better off reading Jackie Collins or citing reruns of *Alf* and *My Mother the Car* as examples of the well-told story.

First Intermission:
The Day the Movies Came Knocking at My Door, or, "I'm Ready for My Close-up, Mr. DeMille!"

At some point in their careers, most writers indulge, however briefly, in the fantasy of selling one of their stories or novels to the movies or television. Nothing wrong with that. If you sell an option for a year, you get some money from that; if you sell the film rights outright, you get a whole lot more money. My friend Brian Keene makes no bones about this subject; he readily admits that selling the film rights to *The Rising* was what enabled him to quit his job(s) and become a full-time writer who didn't have to worry about where the next meal for his family was coming from. Brian has also seen some dandy short films made that were based on a couple of his short stories.

Coincidentally, I happen to have a story about just such an endeavor. This essay was slated to appear in an online 'zine named *Cryptopedia* that, to the best of my knowledge, never published a single issue, much to my disappointment and annoyance.

Below, you'll find the essay in its entirety, as it was written when the rough cut was still being assembled. I'll have a few more—and more recent—comments at the other end.

As I write this, I am less than a week away from seeing the rough cut of the short film being made of my story "Rami Temporales" (originally appearing in *Borderlands 5*, known in paperback as *From the Borderlands*). The film, written and directed by Earl Newton, is now titled *One of Those Faces* (the story's original working title) and will be debuting the first week in September (about the same time the first issue of *Cryptopedia* hits your computer screen) on the *Stranger Things TV* website: (*www.strangerthings.tv*).

Oddly enough, I'm not nearly as anxious as I thought I'd be. Mostly what I am is inpatient, because I know what you're going to see when the film premieres is an exquisite, respectful, and pitch-perfect *adaptation* of my story, its spine fully intact, its emotional tone completely in tune with the original story, and its characters as fully realized as any author could hope them to be when seeing one's work make the sometimes-bumpy transition from one form of media to another.

How do I know this? Because from the beginning, Earl Newton has asked for my input on several of the script elements, and—much to my delight and shock—incorporated some of them into the final script, which I have read and admire tremendously. It's my story, but it's *Earl's* film; his interpretation, his vision (a horribly over- and misused word, but completely applicable here), his baby. And the story could not have been in better hands for my first experience with the world of independent filmmaking.

I want to discuss the adaptation process from the viewpoint of one who, after decades of hearing horror stories from others who have seen their work all but butchered when turned into movies, had prepared himself for the worst and was, for once, ecstatic to have been disappointed.

This whole thing started as an accidental mouse-click that became a whim and then a reality in almost as much time as it took for me to type this sentence.

Here's how it began: a few months ago, a friend of my wife's and mine, Lisa Dotzauer, came over and brought with her some CDs, most notably Zoe Keating's *One Cello X 16: Natoma*, which I immediately fell in love with. After Lisa left that night, I went online in search of other Zoe Keating albums (Lisa thought that she had recorded only one), found that she had two currently available, and purchased both of them. In the process, I did a search on her, found her website—*www.zoekeating.com*—and while exploring it accidentally clicked on a link to something called *Stranger Things Premiere.*

I was all set to go back to Keating's website when I noticed that the most recent update was an editorial by Earl Newton, *Stranger Things*' Executive Producer, so I clicked on it and was treated to a witty and even trenchant take on why it is that many people have become what are now deemed "webscabs"—individuals who use the Internet to "give away" their work in order to pique wider interest and gain a larger audience. Earl was funny, smart, eloquent, charming . . . and a goddamn *kid*—twenty-four, twenty-five tops. But his devotion to filmmaking came across loud and clear, so I figured, what the hell? I decided to take a look at the three films he had running on the site.

Here's what I expected to see: overly-stylized movies that more resembled music videos than actual films with stories and in-depth characterization; shaky, jerky, faux-Cinéma vérité camerawork that made the directors of *The Blair Witch Project* look as if they'd nailed the camera to the ground; and, of course, oh-so-trendy storylines about modern angst, always artsy, never touching upon anything like a genuine human emotion.

Here's what I *did* see: three actual *films* that were deeply concerned with the telling of stories about real people in fantastic—and even terrifying—situations, made by directors who knew not only *how* to use a camera but also—sometimes more importantly—how *not* to use it (in other words, there were no *Look, Ma, Ain't I Directing Good?* moments, those headache-inducing instances where the camera, for no reason other than the director *could* and thought it would look cool, gives us a moving shot from underneath a glass plate or shows us something from the perspective of inside a refrigerator or from the tip of a character's nose hair). No, I was watching films made by people whose primary concern was to tell a good story while drawing zero attention to the visual manner in which it was being told.

And the stories were *good*, compelling, suspenseful, funny, terrifying, and poignant. I am hard-pressed to decide which film is my favorite, because I like *Sacred Cow* and *Sins of the Mother* equally. The former is a wondrous yet nerve-wracking tale in the *Twilight Zone/Night Gallery* mode, the latter a tale that would have found a welcome home on the original *Outer Limits.*

Yeah, okay, he might be just a kid, but he was damned talented kid who worked with equally talented actors and crewpersons, one who knew to respect the story first and foremost, and whose influences were so similar to my own it was kind of creepy.

I then did something on pure impulse, and sent him the following e-mail:

"Dear Mr. Newton:

My name is Gary A. Braunbeck; my work has won the Horror Writers Association Bram Stoker Award 3 times, and the International Horror Guild Award, as well. I have published nearly 200 short stories, 10 fiction collections, and 9 novels. I am a former president of the Horror Writers' Association.

I only recently discovered *Stranger Things* and am just speechless—except to say I greatly admire it and would like to get involved, albeit peripherally, if you'd allow me the chance.

I have a particular short story entitled "Rami Temporales" (which appeared in *Borderlands 5—From the Borderlands* (Warner Books paperback title)) that I strongly believe would make a good candidate for a future ST episode.

I could not write a screenplay if my life depended on it (well, okay, *maybe* if my life depended on it . . . you get the idea . . .) but I'd very much like to send a copy of this story to you for your consideration.

If you'd care to check out my web page to peruse my credits for yourself, please do so at: *www.garybraunbeck.com.*

I thank you for your time and consideration.

Sincerely,

Gary A. Braunbeck"

Sending it onward, I resigned myself to never hearing back from him (which, with only two exceptions, has been the norm when it comes to follow-ups from filmmakers about optioning my work).

Two hours later I received the following response:

"Gary:

We'd be delighted. Send me a copy of your story and we'll be glad to take a look.

Have a great day!

Earl Newton
Executive Producer, Stranger Things
. . . Over 5000 fans and growing . . .
. . . one of iTunes' top 100 Best TV and Film Podcasts . . .
. . . Join the future of entertainment at *www.StrangerThings.TV*"

I immediately sent "Rami Temporales" Earl's way, and then decided, *This is probably as far as it will go.*

Once again, I was happy to be disappointed.

Roughly a week after receiving the story, Earl read it, liked it (". . . gave me a nice vibe . . ." were his exact words) and said that he'd consider it for a future episode of *Stranger Things.* He was in pre-production for his next film, *What Child is This?* and offered his apologies that it would probably be a while before I heard anything more. I was pleased that he was interested, and figured I'd hear from him again in four or five months, when the new film was completed and had premiered.

What happened next can only be called serendipitous, because it wasn't four or five months; it was four or five *days* when I next heard from him. In a nutshell: due to a family medical emergency, the leading man in the film for which Earl was in pre-production had to bow out, and as a result (the role had been written specifically for this actor) the film was in limbo and Earl—who likes to run a tight ship and keep to schedules as much as is possible in the world of filmmaking—was left without a new project . . . except for this odd little story that had landed in his e-mail about a week before.

Understand that Earl likes to keep the films fresh at *Stranger Things*, and the threat of viewers having to wait another four, five or six months for a new film was unacceptable. He had a crew, he had most of the actors, and he had an unplanned-for gap in his schedule.

Two days, three e-mails, and a ninety-minute phone call later, "Rami Temporales" was a go.

Earl was worried that, as the writer of the original story, I was going to object to the several changes that were going to have to be made in order to adapt it for the screen, that I was going to bemoan every cut, every alteration of lines, every change within a scene, and run through the streets crying at the top of my voice: *"Look what they've done to my song, Ma!"*

What he didn't know then (but does now) is that I have been a life-long admirer of the great William Goldman: his novels, his screenplays, and his non-fiction—particularly *Adventures in the Screen Trade* and its equally marvelous sequel, *Which Lie Did I Tell?: More Adventures in the Screen Trade.*

(Long parenthetical aside here: regardless of whether or not you're an aspiring screen writer, if you write fiction—be it for a living or not—you *need* to read these two books. Goldman illustrates in painstaking detail—in his inimitable style and with the tremendous wit and inventiveness he's known for—what happens to a script from its initial conception through the sales pitch and the assembling of a cast and director, then during production and post-production, and that moment when you realize that what's up there on the screen at the premiere bears only a 50 to 65 percent resemblance to what you started out with, *if* you're damned lucky. *Adventures in the Screen Trade*, in particular, contains a final section that is invaluable: Goldman reprints one of his short stories, and then walks you step by step through the process of its adaptation for the screen, including input from directors, composers, other screenwriters, and an assortment of other film professionals who point out what works and what doesn't, what needs to stay and what needs to go, and how they would go about approaching the project from their own unique perspectives—all of the things that can lead to massive changes from one's original story. I re-read both of these books every year, and continue to learn from them.)

So, armed with more than enough fair warning, courtesy of Mr. Goldman, I listened politely as Earl explained his initial concepts for adapting the story, all the time with a slightly nervous quaver at the edge of his voice, as if he were expecting me to cut him off with a, "*What the hell are you thinking, changing that? How dare you mess with MY WORRRRRRRDS!*"

To his surprise (it was about time for *me* to surprise *him*), I agreed with his initial concepts, in part because he completely grasped the spine of the story—its tone, its central theme, the motivations and backgrounds of the characters—but also because I knew that he was under a time crunch that would make even Roger Corman shudder and say, "Gee, I don't know if we can work *that* fast, fellahs."

In case you're not familiar with "Rami Temporales," it has become one of my most popular stories since its first appearance and has, in fact, brought many new readers to my work, for which I am grateful, because the story is a prime example of both what and how I write; it is the one piece to which I direct people who've never read my work before.

Without revealing too much about the piece, it concerns a middle-aged man named Joel who has throughout his life been approached by strangers who ask him for directions, to recommend a good restaurant, to beg spare change, and often to tell him stories, to share something that is troubling them. They approach him, specifically (even in crowds), because he has, as everyone says, "one of those faces."

The core of the story focuses on what happens when Joel meets an angel named Listen who knows *why* Joel has one of those faces and bargains with Joel to "give" his face to him. Listen has been charged with the task of reconstructing the Face of God, who, it turns out, once *did* have an actual face, but as His last act on the Sixth Day of Creation, broke that face into seventy-two sections and scattered them throughout time and the multiverse. (The reasons behind all of this are revealed as the story progresses.)

The story runs nearly 8,500 words, and when I read it to audiences at conventions (it's a great piece to read aloud), it takes roughly fifty minutes. Here is a brief excerpt from early on in the story; Listen is the first speaker:

> "Have you ever seen any paintings or drawings of Jesus?" he asked.
>
> "Of course."
>
> "Can you remember anything specific about them?"

I shrugged. "Beard. Hair. Flowing robes. Eyes."

"But the faces have always been different somehow, haven't they? The hair longer or shorter, the beard fuller, the cheekbones higher or lower, fuller or more drawn, even the hue of the skin has been different—yet somehow you always recognize the face."

"Okay . . . ?"

"Ever wonder how many different versions of that face exist in statues or paintings or sketches?"

"Thousands, I would think."

"Seventy-two, actually. Followers of the Prophet Abdu'l-Bahá believe that everything in nature has 'two and seventy names.' That's almost right. The thing that has always annoyed me about the various religions is that, with rare exceptions, their beliefs are too compartmentalized. *This* is what we believe in, period. I'll tell you a secret: they're all wrong—individually. The problem is none of them can see Belief holistically. If they were all to 'gather at the river,' so to speak, and compare notes, you'd be surprised how quickly people would stop setting off bombs and flying airplanes into skyscrapers. But I digress.

"Everything in nature *does* have seventy-two names. But certain of these things also have seventy-two forms. Like the face of Jesus, for example."

"You're telling me that Christ has been portrayed as having seventy-two faces?"

"No, whiz-kid, I'm telling you that Christ *had* seventy-two faces. Every picture you see is nothing more than a variation on one of them. Faces change over the course of a lifetime, dear boy. All in all, each of us wears seventy-one."

"I thought you just said—"

"—I *know* what I said, I recognized my voice. There is one face we possess that is never worn—at least, not in the sense that the world can see it. The best way I can explain it is to say that it's the face you had before your grandparents were born. *That* is the face I need from you. It exists *here*—" He cupped one of his hands and covered his face from forehead to upper lip. "—in the *Rami Temporales*."

"In the muscles around the eyes?"

"No, *those* are part of the *Rami Zygomatici*, an area controlled by the *Temporales*, which is a much larger and influential group in the temporo-facial division of—oh, for goodness' sake! Are you in the *mood* for an anatomy lesson? Are you worried that I'm going to pull out a scalpel and cut away? I'm not a graduate of the Ed Gein School of Cosmetology, so put that notion out of your head this instant."

I stopped at a red light on 21st Street. "Then I guess I don't understand what you mean at all."

"Perhaps we need to expedite things a bit. Turn left."

As you can tell from that excerpt, Listen's backstory concerning God's face is somewhat complex (as is the process that led him to find Joel, which—in a truly inspired move by Earl—was reduced from four pages of story to *one line* of dialogue in the film).

You can also tell that the story—like most of my work—relies heavily on dialogue, which is fine for the reading experience but can be deadly on the screen; you might as well film a play word for word.

This is where Earl really took over and made the story his own. Because he had to adhere to a one-week-to-ten-day shooting schedule in order to have the film ready for its August premiere, the finished movie couldn't run more than fifteen or sixteen minutes, so the dialogue had to be pared down to its core elements while still retaining the characterization necessary for the piece to remain emotionally true to the source material. If you'll take another quick glance at the excerpt from the story, you'll see that he had his work cut out for him.

Focusing on key story elements and on giving each character his or her own individual speech cadence, Earl's dialogue is reminiscent of early David Mamet or Harold Pinter in its intense focus and clipped directness, yet it still manages to celebrate each character's individuality (the following is taken from an early, unformatted draft of the script that has since been revised):

JOEL

```
Are there a lot of people like you?
```

LISTEN

Like what?

JOEL

All-knowing people. Omniscient.

LISTEN

I'm not omniscient, I'm just very well-researched. Do you know how many people you've listened to?

JOEL

No.

LISTEN

Seven hundred and twelve, if you include that man. Do you know what you are, Joel? You're a safety valve. People see you, and they know they can trust you with their pain. Do you think it helps them?

JOEL

I don't know.

LISTEN

In fourteen years, you've prevented forty-three rapes, one hundred and twelve suicides, thirty-three divorces, ninety-eight murders, and so many cases of spousal abuse I stopped writing them down. Do you know why?

JOEL goes to answer, nods his head softly.

LISTEN

Do you know why I want the piece back?

JOEL

To put it back together again, I guess.

LISTEN

Yes. Right now, the world is lost. It doesn't know where to look to. But once the pieces are reassembled...

JOEL

Things will be better?

LISTEN

Not immediately. Not soon. But yes. Better. It also means that, from now on...no one will tell you their stories anymore. You won't be a safety valve for anyone anymore.

JOEL

What happens to those people?

LISTEN

They just...do the best they can.

JOEL

What does that mean?

LISTEN looks at him, says nothing. But the meaning is clear.

By trimming the dialogue to its basics, Earl not only managed to retain the tone of the story, but also gave his actors a wide berth in which to create and enrich their characterizations. I have, to date, seen exactly six minutes of finished film, and the actors are nothing short of wonderful in their interpretations of their roles (more on that in a moment).

But this is only one element of the film and—as any director will tell you—while good dialogue is a necessity, it is hardly the primary concern when working in a visual medium. A lot can be expressed to the viewer with a simple look, a small, telling gesture, the lighting of a scene, or the visual composition of a single shot within that scene.

I have now learned this first-hand: adaptation is much more than just adjusting the dialogue or pruning story elements; it's an often exhausting process wherein the writer/director has to arrange and orchestrate every separate element in a shot so that each visual, each spoken word, each chord of music and subtle change in the lighting or ambient sounds creates multiple layers, each building upon what came before and reinforcing the base for what comes next—all the while knowing that if any single detail is out of place or just plain *wrong*, the shot will collapse, and so will the scene.

Think in terms of the work of Neo-Impressionistic painter George-Pierre Seurat and his masterpiece *Un dimanche après-midi à l'Ile de la Grande Jatte (Sunday Afternoon on the Island of La Grande Jatte)*, a work considered by many to be the greatest work of Pointillism ever created. Like the reverse of an Escher painting, Seurat's masterwork is stunning when viewed holistically, yet breaks down when viewed in closer detail (whereas Escher's paintings, such as *The Waterfall*, sustain close scrutiny, yet break down into chaos when viewed as a whole). *Sunday Afternoon* is composed—much like a newspaper photograph—of hundreds of thousands of layered dots that, taken individually, seem to mean nothing. It is only when one slowly steps back from the painting that the dots begin to merge into a breath-taking whole.

Every element in every shot of every scene of a film is composed much the same way when you've got a serious and dedicated craftsman at the helm.

I don't envy Earl the work he's put into this. The comparison to Seurat may seem a bit overreaching, but to this neophyte's eyes, that's how it appears. Everything I've seen of the film thus far—coupled with the numerous discussions Earl and I have had during the course of the shoot and editing—only reinforces my admiration for Earl and his actors and crewpersons; these are people who take their craft *very* seriously (but not themselves, thankfully), and no detail is too small to dismiss or employ off-handedly.

The look of the film is composed very much like an artist with brush in hand would do while standing before the canvas; if you look at any of the stills, each one of them could be pulled from the film, framed, and hung on the wall. To me, each shot is composed as if it were a single painting—or, to carry through on the metaphor, a point in space that combines and layers with other points in space to create an aesthetic whole.

Nowhere is this more evident than in the face of Laura Sebastian, the wonderful actress who portrays JoAnna with such honest emotion that there were times I felt as if I were intruding upon someone in the midst of her most intimate and vulnerable moments; her performance is *that* beautifully-shaded and realized.

Hold on a second, I imagine some of you are saying to yourselves. *Who's JoAnna? Isn't the main character's name JOEL?*

Ahem, yeah, well . . . about that; the main character's name *was* Joel, when the actor originally slated to play him was still attached to the project, but as with the leading actor in Earl's other film, real life family issue intervened, forcing the actor to withdraw from the film the night before shooting was scheduled to begin. (Believe it or not, things like this happen all the time, and a good filmmaker has to be prepared for all likelihoods; yet another reason I don't envy Earl.)

Laura was originally slated to play a small but crucial role at the beginning of the film, but Earl had worked with her before and knew she capable of carrying the film, so he called me up the morning shooting was scheduled to begin (from his car, on the way to the location) and explained the situation to me. I didn't even have to think about it. "That's fine," I said, "because ultimately the sex of the central character doesn't matter."

"I was hoping you'd see it that way."

And so Joel became JoAnna, and based on what I have seen of Laura's performance, this was the way to go. Laura has given JoAnna so many subtle character nuances it makes my head spin. There is a scene, about midway through the film, where she has a conversation with a heart- and spirit-broken homeless drunk in an alley. While telling JoAnna his sad story, the drunk offers her a drink from the bottle he's carrying. JoAnna accepts the bottle and begins raising it to her lips, but at the very last moment slips her thumb over the top of the bottle and *pretends* to drink, so as not to offend the man. It's one of several small but telling gestures Laura has given to JoAnna, giving her a nobility that never comes across as forced. As Listen tells her shortly after her encounter with the drunk, "JoAnna, you are a genuinely good person."

But she only half hears him; she's watching the drunk shamble away, and the look on Laura's face as she does this is one of such complete empathy that my breath actually caught in my throat; I was watching an actress who had become so submerged in the character she was playing that all that remained of Laura was her body: JoAnna was the rest, right down to the pain in her eyes.

(When you see the film—and I hope you'll take the time to do so—it might amuse you to know that, at the time they were filming this, a large bike race was about to begin, and if it hadn't been for a brass band warming up to welcome the competitors, Earl and company would not have known. Several hundred cyclists were within minutes of converging on the area, and Earl and his crew had to ask the brass band to stop playing long enough for them to get the scene filmed. Traffic was being re-routed to accommodate the cyclists, chaos and noise galore were about to fall on everyone's heads like a curse from heaven, everyone was tense and anxious because they had *one chance* to get this right . . . and there is this overwhelming sense of *isolation* throughout the scene, one filled with silences that speak more eloquently than my words ever could have. What is in the film is, I believe, the first take, and it is a glorious thing to behold. "Sometimes terror and desperation are the greatest motivators of them all," Earl later told me.

"This was guerilla filmmaking at its most raw and pressured. I don't know how we did it, but we did. These are the finest performances it's ever been my privilege to direct."

The casting of Listen I knew was going to be a problem before Earl even began the first draft of the script. In the story, Listen takes on the form of the late actor Peter Cushing (Joel's favorite actor) in order to immediately get Joel's attention. I knew there was no way Earl was going to be able to find an actor who both looked and sounded like Cushing, so I told him that Listen's age didn't really matter, but he'd have to come up with a way for Listen to instantly grab JoAnna's focus . . . and he did. I won't reveal Earl's ingenious solution, but suffice to say that it is so perfect I later found myself wishing I'd used something similar in the story.

Listen is played by a young actor named Toby Turner, who looks like a less edgy version of Jeremy Sisto. Toby's performance is one of quiet power; the face is young, but there are thousands of years of knowledge behind his eyes. I *believed* I was watching an angel.

The last major change—and the only time Earl and I almost got into a serious argument—concerns the location of the penultimate scene in both the story and the film. In the story, this climactic sequence takes place in a bright, green public park, which Listen explains to Joel is a "... place of power. A place where the forces of the Universe are intensely focused and can be harnessed by the faithful, filled with such power that you can feel the Earth thrum like some excited child who's filled to bursting with a secret their heart can no longer contain."

In Earl's film, the scene takes place in a dank-looking, cramped alley. (Keep in mind that *adaptation* has more than one meaning here; once the story has been adapted, then it becomes necessary for the filmmakers to adapt to shooting conditions, as well as time and budgetary constraints.)

I was not initially enthusiastic about this change of locale; if it could be said that I'd been "married" to any secondary aspect of the story, then having the climactic scene take place in the park was it.

A word of caution to all writers out there: *never* marry any secondary aspect of your story; defend the spine of the piece with all you've got, damn straight, but never commit your heart to anything that, in the end, can justifiably be categorized as "window dressing."

Which is what I had done with the park scene. I took a few seconds, counted to ten, then said to Earl: "Okay, you've got one minute. Convince me."

"Fine," he said. "Why does this 'place of power' have to be somewhere that's all sun-shiny and beautiful? Don't you think it would strengthen that aspect of the story if the place of power was somewhere dark, forgotten, and abandoned? Just because it's holy doesn't mean it has to be pretty. The whole story is built on contrasts—physical, spiritual, emotional, psychological and moral. Why *not* carry through on it with a visual metaphor for all the contrasts and inner struggles?"

I could not punch holes in his argument, as much as I wanted to. Because what he was arguing for was the right to present *his* interpretation of my story, and he should not have been put in a position where he felt he *needed* to defend his vision to me.

Plus, I agreed with his interpretation and his reasoning behind it.

"You're right," I said. "And by the way, I hate you."

"I know, dude. You're welcome."

And they got the sequence filmed before the cyclists showed up and the brass band let fly.

Which almost brings me to the end of this, my first experience with the process of not only seeing one of my stories adapted for film, but also of having had the rare opportunity to be consulted on several aspects of the process by the filmmaker himself. By the time you're reading this, *One of Those Faces* should be live at the *Stranger Things* website, so I hope you'll go over and see it, as well as Earl's other fine films.

I said "almost brings me" to the end because, in the weeks since I finished the original version of this essay you're reading, I have seen the entire rough cut of the film—which runs just under 15 minutes—and I could not be happier with what Earl and his cast and crew have done. Laura Sebastian's performance is quite remarkable, and each time I view the rough cut, I find a nuance that I had not noticed during the previous viewing. If you find that Laura reminds you of another actress, I guarantee you that it's Sigourney Weaver. There is a muted but omnipresent intensity about Laura's performance that often put me in mind of the redoubtable Ms. Weaver (Laura's physical resemblance to her aside). This is a performance that you don't so much watch and enjoy (though you will enjoy it) as study and appreciate. Toby's performance as Listen is one of tremendous subtlety (and I'd be lying if I did not say a part of me fears that in the eyes of some, it may be too subtle for its own good), but the key to Toby's performance is his eyes. Nothing else about him may seem ethereal at first glance, until you watch the eyes. Those things seem *ancient*. And the moment in the alley as he searches for the "place of power"—running his hands along a brick wall as if looking for the hidden switch that will open a secret passage—is one of my favorites in the film.

While the majority of *One of Those Faces* focuses on JoAnna and Listen, the actors who populate the supporting roles deserve their curtain calls, as well. Carol Kahn Parker, who portrays the woman who speaks to JoAnna at the beginning of the film, was, for me, absolutely perfect, not only because her face conveys years of worry, sadness, and struggle that have merged into a kind of grace, but because—and don't think this didn't freak me out a little—she looks *exactly, precisely* as the character in my head looked when I was writing the original story. Don Goodrum, as the alcoholic transient who talks to JoAnna in the alley about one-third of the way into the movie, gives the character a shabby dignity made all the stronger by the sound of his voice—a hoarse, sandpaper whisper, as if the character had spent the last few days screaming at the top of his lungs.

And without revealing anything that could possibly spoil either the movie or the original story for you, I can say that Earl has given his film a much more optimistic ending than the one found in "Rami Temporales." I found myself smiling from ear to ear the first time I saw it, and the more I re-watch the film, the more I like Earl's ending.

I would also be remiss if I didn't mention the wonderful, evocative score written for the film by Walter Muslo (www.cougarmediamusic.com), who was so inspired by the script that he wrote and recorded a theme song for the movie that you'll hear under the closing credits, sung by vocalist Kristin Crowe with a haunting, smoldering passion.

I plan on cherishing this, the first film to be made based on one of my stories, not only because the story could not have possibly been treated with more respect and care, but because it's the first time I've ever heard actors deliver lines of my dialogue (Earl uses some dialogue from the story almost word for word)—and you know what? It sounds damned nice to my ears.

As for my own personal future in movies, I find myself saying, "I'm ready for my close-up now, Mr. DeMille" a lot now when I'm alone. Psychiatrists have been consulted, and proper medications have been dispensed.

I could get used to this.

Re-reading the essay now, I find there's very little I can add in the way of postscript, except, maybe, for two items: A) The finished film was beautiful, and Earl and his cast and crew were so very happy to hear how much I admired their work, and, B) *One of Those Faces* went on to win *Stranger Things* the Parsec award—the highest award given to films made specifically for broadcast on the web. And it deserved to win.

Not that I'm, y'know, biased or anything.

2

For an Eye and a Tooth; Chowing Down; and The Emperor's New Clothes

"Violence, violence
It's the only thing that'll make you see sense."
–Mott the Hoople

EVERY YEAR THE TIRED OLD DEBATE OVER THAT OL' DEBBIL Violence on TV, in films, and in horror fiction erupts again, with proponents on both sides shrieking their intolerance of the other's views on the subject. The catalysts have ranged from the absurd bloodletting found in Brian DePalma's laughable remake of *Scarface* (with Al Pacino's brilliant three-hour impression of Charro) to the intentional over-the-top absurdity of Edward Lee's *The Big Head* and Robert Devereaux's *Santa Steps Out* to how many times Wile E. Coyote has plunged into that canyon in the Road Runner cartoons.

I think both sides of this argument would do well to consider something so obvious it almost depresses me to think it needs to be said outright: it's not the quantity of violence contained in television shows or movies or books—or, for that matter, even how graphically it is portrayed—it is the attitude *behind* the violence that should be called into question when someone is trying to determine whether or not something might be "harmful" to a viewer or reader. "An eye for an eye and a tooth for a tooth" might have worked well in the days of Saul and Moses, but the world has become less morally black and white since the stone tablets allegedly came down from the mountain. There has always been violence in the world, and there will always be violence in the world . . . and psychos with knives and rapists and sadists and pedophiles and bad folks with big guns *ad infinitum* and, eventually, like it or not, it will touch everyone in one form or another. I'm forty-three years old and have been (among other things) beaten up several times, stabbed twice, shot (see previous chapter), and not once did I blame the actions of my attackers on their having viewed *Dirty Harry* or *Taxi Driver* or *Friday the Thirteenth* or *A Nightmare on Elm Street* one time too many—or having spent too much time re-reading *The Books of Blood* or *The Regulators*, a novel that reportedly began life as an original film script by Stephen King that was to be helmed by director Sam Peckinpah. (Ain't it annoying, the trivial shit I know?)

I have been on the receiving end of violence more than a few times; I have also been on the delivery end of it; and I have been—like the character of Bonnie Winter in Graham Masterton's brilliant novella of the same name—among those whose duty it was to go in and mop up the aftermath.

Some of you may be familiar with my novella "Safe," which originally appeared in *HWA Presents: Robert Bloch's PSYCHOS*, and was also reprinted in *The Year's Best Fantasy and Horror*, as well as my collection *Things Left Behind* (under the title "Searching For Survivors"). The story concerns the after-effects of a violent mass-murder on a mid-sized Midwestern town; the core of the story details the night a skeleton janitorial crew goes into the house where the first of the murders took place and proceeds to systematically scrape, mop, wipe, and carry away every trace of the tragedy.

"Safe" took the better part of twenty years to get onto paper because it hit too close to home. I worked with a janitorial company for several years in the late 70s and early 80s, and one night I was awakened at two in the morning by a call from my boss asking me if I would volunteer to join a skeleton crew for an emergency job. The night would pay $300.00 for each crew member. At first, still groggy, I couldn't understand why anyone would turn down 300 bucks for four or five hours of work; then he told me why he had to call and ask for volunteers.

Three days before, a local man had snapped, killing his family and then himself. The family was a somewhat prominent one in town, and the surviving relatives wanted the house cleaned as thoroughly and as quickly as possible. Two of the family members this man had killed (with a shotgun) had been children.

I wound up cleaning the children's room. You cannot help but feel the sick-making silence and overwhelming loss of life when you perform a duty like this. Three times I had to stop work to go outside to either cry or vomit. But I got that room cleaned. I wiped away every trace of those children's existence. There was a lot of blood, as well as other liquids, all of them dried. There were also, in places, bits of tissue mixed in with that blood.

When it was all over, we collected our pay and went back to our homes. I fell asleep somewhere around 9:00 AM and didn't wake up until well after four. I had thrown my clothes from that night into the corner, along with the work boots I'd been wearing. As I was gathering everything up for washing, for some reason I checked the bottoms of my boots, and found a very small but—thanks to the mopping I'd done—still very wet and piece of human tissue wedged into the heavy treads. I got sick all over again. This was all that remained of one of those children. But which one? And from what part of them had this been blasted? Had they died immediately or had they suffered? All this came to me in a rush and I just imploded.

I tell you this because it's important that you know I am not one of those writers who employs violence in their stories simply because it's "cool" to wipe out as many people in as many grotesque and creative ways as possible. I have seen too much violence, as well as the consequences of that violence, to be so blasé and thoughtlessly off-handed about its uses and depictions in fiction.

If you haven't already guessed, this is a subject about which I feel passionately, because violence, regardless of your attitude toward it, is an indispensable storytelling tool to those of us who toil in horror and dark fantasy—a field in which the tales rely heavily on the exploration of, and connections between, violence and grief and how we as human beings try reconciling their presence and consequences with the idea of a just universe.

For the record, I am not one of the Happy People (an admission that will come as a great shock to readers of my fiction). I tend to define myself only by what I do: I am a writer, a storyteller, a professional teller of lies. For most of my life—as absurd as it may sound—I've never felt all that comfortable around people, which is why you don't see me at all that many conventions. As a result, I'm not all that close to anyone. What few folks can endure my company only feel comfortable approaching me as a writer—everything that is asked about or expressed, all opinions and philosophies and feelings that are shared, are almost always done in the sole context of what I do. Who I am doesn't enter into it, because I usually won't allow it to. I tend to keep people at arm's length, both emotionally and physically, and often wish that I possessed whatever mechanism it is that allows one to drop one's guard and welcome human intimacy without fear and suspicion, but the truth is, I don't trust happiness. I never have and probably never will, and that is very often reflected in my fiction.

It is also reflected in my tastes in fiction and movies. I find myself drawn most strongly to those stories in which the central character, while respected and even loved by those around him or her, remains at a distance from everyone and everything, an observer on the sidelines of their own existence; more often than not, these characters are also a bit monomaniacal, even obsessive, over one thing in particular: an object or concept or single-minded notion they believe is the only thing that gives their existence any meaning whatsoever. Add to this mix the threat of, or consequences from, violence, and as both a reader and movie watcher, I'm there.

So it should come as no surprise that I responded fervently to director Jim (*My Left Foot, In The Name of The Father*) Sheridan's 1990 film *The Field*, starring the late Richard Harris in what is surely his finest performance on the screen. He plays Bull McCabe, an Irish farmer who, for all of his life, has been tending a field that was passed on to him by his father, who was given it by his father, who was given it by his father . . . you get the idea. McCabe's dream—scratch that—his *sole purpose* in life is to pass this field on to his surviving son. (We learn early on that his other son committed suicide years prior to the start of the story.)

There's just one problem: McCabe's family doesn't actually own the field, but merely rents it. It's a matter of deep personal pride to McCabe that he took this field, once no more than a barren, dirty, rock-covered plain, and, with a tenderness and care most men reserve for the raising of their children, turned it into a piece of rich and fertile land that is not only stunning to behold but produces enough sustenance to keep his cattle fat and healthy.

The man who owns the field dies, leaving it to his widow. Upon learning that widow plans to move away, McCabe assumes that she will sell the field to him. Enter American businessman Tom Berenger, descendant of an Irish clan who fled the country during the Potato Famine. Berenger's company wishes to purchase the field for development, thus bringing industry and commerce to the area. McCabe swears upon the souls of his ancestors that "the Yank" (as he's called throughout the film, never being given a name) will not take what is "rightfully" his.

This doesn't even begin to set up the moral quagmire that the film grapples with. The widow does not feel a moral obligation to sell the field to McCabe—she'll sell it to the highest bidder. McCabe's son doesn't want to inherit the field; he wants to go to the city and make his own life, and so sets out on a campaign of terrorism against the widow so she'll sell to the American just to spite McCabe. McCabe, who sees the possibility of losing everything his life has been centered around, bullies the townspeople into siding with him. Add to this volatile brew the unspoken truth that McCabe's first son chose to kill himself rather than inherit the field and his father's way of life, and you've got a story where, from the outset, the question is not "Will it end well?" (you know it can't) but rather, "Who will suffer the least?"

Although it lacks some of the subtle moral shades that characterized the John B. Keane play upon which it is based, it's impossible to watch *The Field* and not be caught up in McCabe's passion, even when you begin to realize that his obsession with the field borders on psychotic. There is ultimately no Wrong or Right in the film, only a thick, murky grey area where the best you can hope for is to make a choice and stick with it and hope it's a good one.

About two-thirds of the way through, McCabe visits with the local priest, who has called a meeting between McCabe and the Yank. The scene is terrifying on countless levels (physically, morally, and psychologically) and culminates in what has to be one of the greatest single speeches in film history, in which McCabe, in order to make the Yank understand his love and loyalty to the field, recounts an incident from his childhood where he and his father had to choose between saving the life of McCabe's mother or tending to the field. They chose the field.

I don't "chill" easily, but this speech, brilliantly rendered by Harris, left me trembling. Violence, grief, obsession, confusion and self-loathing, passion and purpose, as well as fear of the unknown are all contained in this speech, and it is a testament to Harris' ability as an actor that he manages to convey all this, not in stops and starts, but in a hard, prism-like beam, delivered in a whisper that resounds stronger than countless roars. I defy you to watch this scene and not react.

In the end, though, understanding crumbles between the warring factions and leaves only violence. And when it comes, it comes down hard, culminating in a final sequence of inescapable tragedy that manages to be not only affecting but highly symbolic without resorting to heavy-handedness.

Although not billed as a horror film, *The Field* wrestles with issues and actions that are not uncommon to horror, and is, in that respect, a horror movie of the highest (though not most obvious) order. It should not be missed, if only for Harris' astounding acting. It reminds us that nothing in horror is so jarring as the genuinely tragic.

The genuinely tragic is the jumping-off point for director Alan Arkin's 1971 film *Little Murders*—a movie that serves to underscore the notion that it is not the violence, but the attitude behind it, that must be examined, and here the attitude hits decisively at the core of the American family.

Based on Jules (*Carnal Knowledge*) Feiffer's stage play, it chronicles the story of milquetoast NYC photographer Alfred Chamberlain, superbly played by Elliot Gould. Gould's character is passive to the point of catatonia, not defending himself from a beating by street thugs early on because, as he says, "There's no way to talk someone out of beating you up if that's what they want to do." Enter Patsy Newquist (Marcia Rodd), a hard-as-nails urbanite who tries to awaken in Alfred some sense of moral outrage at the wretched state of the world. The two fall in love, insomuch as they are able. (Alfred's declaration of "I really truly nearly trust you!" is the closest he comes to voicing his affection, and is the ultimate turn-on for Patsy.)

The New York of *Little Murders* is just as ugly as that presented in films such as *Death Wish* and *Combat Shock* (a.k.a. *American Nightmare*), but unlike those movies, this ugliness is tinged with a sense of absurdity, an onyx-dark humor that (intentionally) leaves the viewer unsure whether to laugh or cringe . . . so you do both. And, as if to underline the film's intent, director Arkin chooses to give it a music score—written by Fred Kaz—that sounds as if it was lifted from something that starred Charlie Brown and Snoopy.

After Alfred marries Patsy, the two move in with her family. Her father (Vincent Gardenia) is a button-down, extreme right-winger who makes George W. Bush look like a free thinker, while her mother (the marvelous Elizabeth Wilson) is a "take everything one day at a time" type who, when asked why she didn't flinch after nearly having her head blown off by a sniper, smiles and says, "I get shot at every day. Why whine about it?" These characters are the conclusive evolution of the jaded city dweller; violence and death are interchangeable with meat and potatoes in their lives, and are viewed in the same off-hand manner.

Little Murders defies easy analysis and must be seen to have its more trenchant moments fully savored. Every reel of the movie is saturated with violence, even when it occurs off-screen (which is often the case). With the exception of Patsy and her father, the rest of the characters are one step above zombies and remain so until the last fifteen minutes, when the depressing darkness of truth begins to overshadow the often sidesplitting comedy.

After a family member is murdered by a sniper's bullet—which comes through the window of the Newquist's apartment during dinner, and is reacted to by the mother in the same way most people would react to a fly—the Newquists turn their dwelling into a steel-doored fortress right out of a Batman comic book, but even this doesn't protect them from the encroaching insanity they try so hard to stay above.

A mind-blown detective (hysterically played by Alan Arkin) shows up to reassure the family that the NYC police department will protect them, but the detective himself is so burned out and rabidly paranoid that he only serves to amplify their fear, rather than alleviate it. (Don't misunderstand, the scene is so howlingly funny you might have to watch it twice in order to hear the parts you were laughing over.)

Finally, Alfred surrenders to the violence, bringing home a rifle that he proceeds to load in front of the family, then smashes out a window and begins shooting at passers-by in the street. This act is not presented as evil and deranged, but rather cathartic and healthy, for it snaps the family out of its complacency and bonds them together more firmly than any amount of love ever could. After each has had their turn at blowing away innocent bystanders, the family sits down to a nice American dinner while screams from the street filter in from the window and the wail of police sirens grows louder. Mrs. Newquist looks around the table at her smiling, happy clan, offers a benevolent matriarchal grin, and says, "You don't know how good it is to hear my family laugh again . . . for a while there I was really worried." The camera lingers on her sublime expression as the sirens scream and the madness outside covers everything like a shroud. If it weren't so terrifying, it would be funny—or is that, if it weren't so funny it would be terrifying? See it, and judge for yourself.

The point *Little Murders* seems to be making, in direct opposition to that made by *The Field*, is that when we resort to violence, we become not worse than those who direct violence against us, but sickeningly the same; there's no way to tell the difference. And where can we go from there?

If we are to believe the answer offered to that question in Sam Peckinpah's 1970 *Straw Dogs*, then where we go is deeper into the enjoyment of that violence, for it is only in the amount and scope of individual brutality that there can be found any hope of rising above the masses and establishing integrity of character. In short: if you're meaner than the meanest, that alone will redeem you in your own eyes—a theme that was both explored and eschewed by Peckinpah throughout his career.

Born in Fresno, California on February 21, 1925, Peckinpah grew up on a ranch in the California mountains. His father was a judge, and Peckinpah was a rowdy teenager who eventually enlisted in the Marines, though he never saw combat.

After his discharge, he discovered theater and eventually got his lucky break in the early 50s when respected Hollywood director Don Siegel hired him as an assistant at Allied Artists. Peckinpah began writing scripts (he helped rewrite and had a small role in 1956's *Invasion of the Body Snatchers*) and got his first job directing in 1958 when he did an episode of the television series *Broken Arrow*. His feature-length directorial debut was 1961's *The Deadly Companions*.

Peckinpah, with films such as *Major Dundee* and *Ride the High Country*, easily established himself as a great American director.

Critics were quick (before *The Wild Bunch*, anyway) to mention his name alongside those of John Ford and Howard Hawks.

Peckinpah hated it.

He hated it because in the "good old" Western, the only characters an audience was asked to sympathize with were, naturally, the good guys like Randolph Scott and Chuck Heston. When the so-called "bad guys" got blown away, it was supposed to make an audience cheer wildly.

Which, as Peckinpah was quick to point out, completely robbed the "bad guys" of any humanity whatsoever—after all, the "bad guys" in *Shane* and *Will Penny* were given full identities, so why couldn't this be a trend that could set itself firmly in the American Western?

Because no one is supposed to care about the bad guys.

So Peckinpah set out to make an "anti-Western," a film that, while it might be set in the West, horses and posses intact, had nothing else in common with the type of films he'd been making—and despising.

That film was *The Wild Bunch*. In it, audiences met the likes of Pike (William Holden in one of his finest hours) and his gang, a run-down, over-the-hill bunch of outlaws whom time and progress has caught up with. They were old, tired, anachronistic, and looking for a way out. Audiences learned to sympathize with these men as the film progressed, even side with them and, in the film's historic finale—almost folklore now—watch them die in blood-drenched slow-motion, every agonized twitch dwelt upon until their mangled bodies lay dead before the camera.

Here was Peckinpah's genius with his bloody ballet of death: he'd made a Western, all right, but he'd shown it from the "bad guys'" point of view, and no one cheered when they died. The black-and-white way of presenting right and wrong was forever destroyed, and the myth of the American Western was forever debunked.

Peckinpah was then asked why he chose to make the violence so bloody, and why he chose to film it in slow motion. His reply (which I am paraphrasing) was something along these lines: "I thought audiences should be given a good, clear look at what they've been cheering all these years."

That was in 1969. Vietnam was at its height. The Civil Rights Movement was the victim of more and more violent attacks. Students were being killed protesting. And a bunch of hippies had just gotten together for three days of peace and music at a place called Woodstock.

Things were nuts; and into this insanity Peckinpah unleashed *The Wild Bunch*, which many claimed was not so much an anti-Western as it was a thinly disguised metaphor for the dangerously unstable state of American society at the time. That Peckinpah had set his morality tale in the Old West and not on some college campus only served to give credence to this argument.

To which I say: "Yeah, right; whatever. Go back to your film school textbooks and leave me alone to enjoy the movie."

After enduring an endless series of attacks in the press and horse-shit intellectual "dissections" over the violence and themes in *The Wild Bunch*, Peckinpah followed it up in 1970 with the gentle, lyrical, funny, and uncharacteristically warm *The Ballad of Cable Hogue*, a bawdy, character-rich Western with Jason Robards, Stella Stevens, and a wonderfully daffy David Warner as a whacked-out backwoods preacher. The movie was a critical success, did lukewarm business at the box-office, and was just inoffensive and uncontroversial enough for people to stop worrying about Peckinpah—which I think is exactly what he intended, because he was about to unleash *Straw Dogs*—a film that not only escalated the levels of violence found in *The Wild Bunch*, but moved it into the modern-day world.

In the movie, Dustin Hoffman plays David Sumner, an American mathematician who, having received a research grant, moves to England with his ultra-sexy wife, Amy (Susan George, in what has to be one of the great smoldering-tease performances of all time). They take up residence in her former home, a remote village near Wales.

From the start, Sumner knows he's not welcome. Early on, he enters a pub to purchase a pack of American cigarettes and is met at first by condescending smirks, then, by the time he leaves, barely-disguised hostility—even after he buys a round of drinks for everyone.

In an effort to behave in a neighborly fashion, he hires a group of local men to re-shingle the roof of his house. One of these men turns out to be his wife's former boyfriend, Scutt, who, (and not to much surprise), still harbors a torch for her—and she for him.

Things get bad in a hurry. The men set out on what is at first a subtle campaign of terror (which is eerily echoed in *The Field*), intimidating Sumner at every opportunity. Somewhere in there one of them mutilates the family cat. But even after this, Sumner refuses to strike back, insisting that he is an intelligent and civilized man, and civilized men find other ways to work out their problems.

Failing to break Sumner, Scutt and the others change their tactics and invite him to go hunting with them—then, once he is safely isolated, humiliate him while Scutt makes his way back to the house and proceeds to rape Amy.

Viewing the movie again, you cannot help but be struck by the moral ambiguity of the prolonged rape sequence. In a time of ultra-lame-brained PC, filmmakers today are too nervous to try anything like this for fear of offending anyone. (An aside here: were Peckinpah still alive—and what a loss that he is not—and tried to release this film today, I am convinced that this sequence would either be heavily trimmed to make it one-sided, or excised altogether.)

In the scene, after the initial act of violence (a hard slap across the face that sends Amy slamming down onto the couch), Amy and Scutt set about wrestling with one another in a manner that, by turns, resembles both a rape and a mutual seduction of the soft-core S&M variety. Amy calls Scutt names while saying, "No, no!" over and over, all the time undressing him and wrapping her legs around his waist. Whenever he physically overpowers her, we see in her face that she loves it; and when she fights back against his brutality, this turns him on all the more. This is the kind of sex she prefers (that much is made obvious), the kind Scutt is best at, and the kind lacking in her marriage. In a way, it's the inverse of the ultimate rape nightmare, because the viewer is left uncertain of: A) who assaulted whom, or, B) if a rape occurred at all. When, later, Amy goads Sumner into making their sex more violent, the discomfort level is shoved up another fifty notches or so.

Throughout the film we get glimpses of a character named Henry Niles (the superb David Warner, brilliantly effective here in an uncredited role that he played for nothing as a favor to Peckinpah), who is basically the village simpleton, a gentle giant right out of Steinbeck's *Of Mice and Men*. Peckinpah deftly establishes, in a few brief scenes, the sympathetic connection felt between David Sumner and Henry Niles.

Later, when Niles accidentally kills a local girl, he seeks refuge at Sumner's home while a drunken band of heavily-armed men (Scutt among them) surround the house and demand that Sumner hand over "that idiot savage." Amy insists that they throw Niles out the door, but when a brick comes crashing through the window, Sumner turns to her and says, in a voice devoid of human emotion, "I will not allow violence against this house," and proceeds to defend his home against the invaders, accompanied by bagpipe music that blares from the stereo.

This last half-hour remains, in my opinion, unparalleled in its heart-stopping and perversely beautiful depiction of savagery as Hoffman's character gradually begins to enjoy the violence. Peckinpah's maverick and trend-setting use of the now-legendary (and often-satirized) "slow-mo" technique was never more effective or affecting than it is here; this astounding sequence has lost none of its power or vicious grace during the thirty-two years that have elapsed since its initial release. Employing everything from boiling liquids to splintered chair legs to a bear trap, Sumner—with an intensely calculated, automaton-like purpose—kills every single last one of the attackers. In the end, standing amidst the carnage, blood splashed across his face in ribbons, Sumner smiles. Even through the cracked lenses of his glasses we see the sparkle in his eyes as he says, "I did it. I killed 'em all." (This moment is in almost direct contrast to the closing moments of the novel upon which it is based, Gordon M. Williams' *The Siege at Trencher's Farm*. Though an excellent novel, it, like James Dickey's *Deliverance*, approaches the violence from an almost mythic viewpoint, and offers a sense of justice that *Straw Dogs* goes out of its way to avoid. Back to the bloodied Dustin now . . .)

Leaving Amy to weep and shudder over the body of her former lover, Sumner puts Niles into the car and the two of them drive out into the darkness. After they've been on the road for a few minutes, Niles turns to Sumner and says, "I don't know my way home." Sumner, his face illuminated by the dashboard lights, smiles, looks out the windshield with an expression like a serial killer on the prowl, and replies, "That's all right. Neither do I."

They vanish over the hill into the seemingly permanent night.

What one comes away with after viewing these films is a somewhat nihilistic view of human nature; the sense that we, as a race, are hell-bent on complete self-destruction and only bother creating music and art and temples so as to have an interesting backdrop for the blood-letting. It's a disturbing notion, but one that seems more a warning than a prophecy. It helps to think of these movies as being cautionary tales, which (in my opinion) is what enables the best horror stories to transcend the ghettoization imposed on the field by those who would have you believe that only works that concern themselves with what is true and fine and noble in the human condition are worth one's intellectual and emotional investment.

If that is true, how do you explain the controversy and animated discussions that *still* ignite when the subject of George A. Romero's *Dead* trilogy arises?

It can be argued that the *Dead* series not only challenges the notion of what constitutes cinematic art (witness the still-raging debates over the original *Texas Chainsaw Massacre*), but rends that notion to shreds, reconstructing it for a generation of horror fans who, like myself, were too young to be tolerated by the folks who survived World War II and weren't old enough to be embraced by the Woodstock Nation. We took refuge in the products of our and others' imaginations, be it a late night rerun of *Frankenstein* or *The Masque Of The Red Death* (or, nowadays, first-run showings of *May, The Ring,* or *28 Days Later*), telling ghost stories at sixth-grade camp (now: listening to Stephen King reading *Hearts In Atlantis* on compact disc or watching *Near Dark* on DVD), or huddling under the blankets at night with a flashlight and a pile of those nasty horror comic books our parents didn't want us to read (which have now become the Clive Barker/Peter Straub/Douglas Clegg/Anne Rice novels we proudly read in public). In short, the *Dead* films document (albeit covertly) the evolution of horror's moral and (you should pardon the word) aesthetic sensibilities.

Just so you know that I'm aware of something, allow me to quote the eminently-quotable Joe R. Lansdale; this is taken from his essay "A Hard-On For Horror" as it was reprinted in *Writer of the Purple Rage*: "I'm not saying that *Night of the Living Dead* and *The Texas Chainsaw Massacre* kept me awake at night pondering the meaning of it all. I have seen far too much attention given to the existentialist nature of these movies, and all I have to say to that is this: Bullshit, pilgrim!"

So understand that what follows—while heartfelt—might very well be just another steamy load of pilgrim bullshit.

Ahem.

Although the trilogy has been accused of dealing with everything from tribal mentality in the face of political paranoia to humankind's inability to seriously face its own encroaching mortality, the richness of the *Dead* films, for me, is in their exploration of the relationships that quickly develop among the human protagonists. In all three movies you have people who, under normal circumstances, would more than likely have nothing to do with one another, yet are forced to band together against a common enemy to survive. New enemies are made, to be certain, but so are new friends—and these latter relationships are always blood-brother/sister strong and undeniably compelling.

These movies are, first and foremost, scary as hell, fiercely executed to generate often dizzying levels of terror and revulsion, but Romero has never been satisfied with just giving his audience a good scare; he also wants to leave them with something to think about once the shock has worn off. He achieves this by offering zombie films that are also intelligent, literate, and populated (for the most part) by fully developed characters with whom the viewer feels an immediate empathy. Add to this already sublime mixture heavy doses of dry humor, and you've got a unique horror film experience.

One element in all three movies that has been almost consistently overlooked is their commendably unsentimental poignancy, the unflinching manner in which they present emotional pain that always reaches, and sometimes even surpasses, the level of physical pain so graphically portrayed on the screen.

Early on in *Dawn Of The Dead* is a scene where a woman who's holed up in her apartment opens the door to see her long-dead husband waiting outside. She embraces him, and he immediately chomps a large chunk out of her neck and shoulder. The scene is powerful and affecting not so much because of the gore (Tom Savini's makeup effects remain among the finest in the field) but because of the expression on the woman's face when she sees her husband: in a few golden seconds her expression goes from shocked to confused to relieved and, finally, joyful; the viewer gets a real sense of her loneliness and longing before her screams pierce the air. Violence and grief become two sides of the same coin; rarely is one present without the other. In the world of the *Dead* trilogy, where your "shadow at evening..." (the dead, who are, after all, ourselves) "... rises to meet you," that's precisely how it should be. The traditional funeral intonation may be "ashes to ashes and dust to dust," but here, where the zombies rule, our deepest fear (that all of us shall return to a state of dust one day) is held in their hands . . . and they shove the reality of death down our throats over and over again. (It occurs to me that an attempt to distill the true subtext of these film so that all of us will come away in agreement is a little like throwing a hundred strangers into a room and trying to get them all to agree on seeing the same image in a Rorschach blot. So, keep in mind that I'm speaking for myself and myself alone. One pilgrim's bullshit.)

In 1968, when *Night of the Living Dead* was released, such metaphorical notions were about as "different" as horror movies could get, and helped to establish Romero as a force to be reckoned with. He once told *Filmmakers Newsletter* that the movie was intended to be "an allegory, meant draw a parallel between what people are becoming and the idea that people are operating on many levels of insanity that are clear only to themselves. The zombies are us. We create them so we can kill them off, justifying our own existence—it's a kind of penance, self-exorcism."

To understand just how effectively Romero practiced what he preached, you would do well to remember that the Vietnam War was reaching its bloody height at this time. Had *NotLD* been released earlier or later than that painful, historic year of 1968, I think it possible that its sometimes diatribe-level symbolism would have been lost on its audience.

Another element that set *NotLD* apart from other horror movies of its decade was its then-radical use of a black hero *not* played by Sidney Poitier. In addition to Vietnam, the country was dealing with the violent opposition to the Civil Rights Movement. Giving an unknown black actor the lead in *NotLD* should have, given that volatile climate, signaled commercial and critical suicide for the movie. It's a testament to both Romero's integrity and the late Duane Jones' excellent performance that this did not turn out to be the case.

Romero stuck his neck farther out by having the script contain not one reference to Ben's being the only non-white among the main characters—and you can't help but wonder if this was Romero's way of paralleling the story with the Civil Rights Movement: a notion that, considering the violence that had befallen Malcolm X and was to soon befall Martin Luther King (not to mention the Watts Riots), makes Ben's death at the end of the film more tragic than ironic.

If you think social irony isn't present in these movies, take a look at the way people's attitudes toward firearms are explored over the course of the trilogy. In *NotLD*, guns are the source of salvation and power within the group—whoever holds the guns holds everyone's safety, and is subsequently the leader (a role that changes several times during the film).

In *Dawn Of The Dead*, guns—like the zombies—are rampant, and make their presence known almost immediately. Everyone has a weapon and an itchy trigger finger and is more than willing to shoot anything that moves—count how many times someone almost blows away a still-living character. Guns are almost glamorized here—a sentiment very much in vogue in a lot of the films of the 1970s. We're not supposed to blanch when a gun is pulled out, we're supposed to cheer. Pay attention to the sequence where the heroes, trapped in a large suburban mall, raid a gun shop and soon emerge looking like Pancho Villa's troops. This sequence contains some impressively intense editing, and is expertly calculated to make the viewer lust after the weapons just as much as do the characters. When the four of them run into hoards of the undead armed to the teeth, even the most passionate pacifists may find themselves shouting encouragement.

(An aside here: it was almost as if Romero saw the coming of the 80s' arrogant, flamboyantly materialistic way of life—"He who dies with the most toys wins"—and found it as ridiculous then as we do now. In one masterful sweep he offers the ultimate yuppie fantasy—a mall for the taking; then, after allowing us to experience the nirvana of having the most toys, he gleefully slaughters us and our greed before our own eyes, chuckling the whole bloody way.)

Then comes *Day Of The Dead*, wherein this underlying theme of guns equal power reaches its zenith. Trapped in an abandoned underground military complex, the protagonists find themselves at the mercy of two disparate but equally destructive forces—the zombies above and the macho bravado of the soldiers who have appointed themselves rulers below. Many have said (and I agree) that the dichotomy presented in *Day* quickly crosses the line into heavy-handedness: on one side you have the scientists, most of whom are presented as wise, resigned, level-headed thinkers; on the other side you have the MAs (Military Assholes), a bunch of swaggering, barking, arrogant, groin-kicking borderline psychotics who are an almost laughable embodiment of the Freudian theory of guns as penis extensions. There is no problem they won't solve by blasting it into oblivion. Early in the film, the leader of the MAs pulls an automatic pistol on the sole female scientist and threatens to blow her brains out because she won't sit down and listen to him rave on about why his way is best, thus almost totally reversing the attitude toward firearms: they are no longer instruments of salvation, but the implements of self-destruction and therefore evil. But a necessary evil, as the film's heart-stopping finale proves.

Day was released hot on the heels of Ronald Reagan's Star Wars ("Peace through strength") program, when the world's nuclear arsenal was at its peak and tensions between the U.S. and the (then) Soviet Union were approaching a boiling point (or so we were told) not seen since the Cuban Missile Crisis—which may help explain the film's disgust with and anger toward the military, as well as its barely-restrained bitterness toward humankind's hope for the future. This last element, perhaps the darkest and most genuinely affecting of the film, is all but negated by a trite, seemingly tacked-on and not at all believable "happy" ending that is made even sillier by its Eve-in-the-New-Eden symbolism, which is intended to echo the subtle power of the Pieta tableau early in the movie but instead trivializes it.

But let's get down to it: it's been twenty-five years since the third *Dead* movie was released, and thirty-five years since the original. Do the movies still hold up?

You bet your ass they do. Admittedly, the effects in *NotLD* pale in comparison to those found in the sequels (as well as director Tom Savini's exceptionally well-done but ultimately pointless remake), but the film still manages to retain a great deal of its power. This is one of the few movies in which the limited budget is actually an asset. The grainy, often jerky black-and-white photography gives a disquieting documentary feel to everything, especially in the middle of the film, after the survivors have barricaded themselves in the farm house.

If asked to name their favorite sequence in the original, a majority of people would probably pick the eerie graveyard opening. A good sequence, no argument there, but that scene has always struck me as somewhat self-conscious. Even when I saw it for the first time, lo these thirty years ago, I was painfully aware that I was watching a director trying to scare me—the kiss of death in any film that relies heavily on suspense.

My choice for the best sequence will always be the nerve-shattering race to the gas pump. When that truck blows up and leaves Ben stranded in the middle of the road with the zombies lurching toward him, it still ties my gut up in knots when I watch it today. The editing is inspired and muscular—Romero's trademark, as far as I'm concerned.

But let's face it; aside from that sequence and the little girl murdering her mother in the basement, the film isn't all that scary. Tense, yes; claustrophobic, yes; but for white-knuckle, sweat-inducing, Jesus-Am-I-Breathing terror, it leaves something to be desired. (And the peripheral ersatz-explanation of the "strange" radiation that may be responsible for re-animating the corpses just gets in the way.)

A lot of the film's original infamy came, of course, from the shock of seeing the zombies chowing down on the limbs and innards of their victims, but that doesn't happen until over two-thirds of the way through. Until then, we get a lot of panic, running around, and loud arguments—not to mention one close-up too many of the zombies, who look more like a bunch of folks after a three-day drunk than rotting corpses newly arisen from the grave.

I know this is probably blasphemous to those of you who would defend this movie with your last ounce of lifeblood, but it's the truth. There is more genuine terror in the last fifteen minutes of *Day Of The Dead* than there is in the whole of *Night*. This doesn't mean it isn't a good movie—it is easily that, and much more—it just isn't the scariest movie of all time, as some would have you believe.

Dawn Of The Dead, by far the slickest of the three movies, manages to strike a fever pitch of terror early on and sustains it for well over half the film, faltering only when the protagonists finally set up their little Utopia in a hidden section of the mall's upper floors. Romero spends quite a bit of time exploring the characters and their relationships (*Dawn* contains the richest characterization and best acting of the trilogy), but in the process the viewer almost forgets that the zombies even exist. I know this was the intent—we're supposed to be lulled into the same false sense of security and superiority that the characters are experiencing—but somewhere in here (I think it starts to happen right around the time the heroine, who is pregnant, and her hubby skirt around the issue of abortion) the pacing comes to a screeching halt and you begin to feel that you're watching a daytime drama. How much this "calm before the storm" section grates on your nerves may depend on which cut of the film you see—myriad prints run anywhere from 120 to 142 minutes. My vote goes to the 142-minute cut now available on DVD, wherein the length of the Utopian sequence seems to be just right.

When things pick up again, they do so with a vengeance; not only is the mall besieged by a group of the sleaziest bikers you're likely to encounter, but one of the three remaining characters is killed by the zombies, then resurrects and proceeds to lead the dead to the secret hiding place. (The other now-dead character, a SWAT team member who is bitten when his gung-ho mentality compels him to take an absolutely idiotic chance, is neatly dispatched by a bullet to the head from his friend's gun. We know from the start that this particular character is Dead Meat, because he cannot live in peace—he's used to violence and excitement and it's in the pursuit of these that his tragic fate is sealed—perhaps an augury of the antimilitaristic mentality to come in the third film.)

Finally, only two characters remain: Peter Washington and Francine Parker—the black cop and the pregnant woman, played to perfection by Ken Foree and Gaylen Ross. Ross, by far the most effortlessly sexy of Romero's heroines, manages to exude both Earth Mother pragmatism and innocent naiveté, turning her character into a fully-realized human being and not the whiny, self-righteous Grande Dame who pops up in the third movie.

Foree, an immensely likable actor (who was one of the many graces in the unjustifiably-maligned *Leatherface: The Texas Chainsaw Massacre Part III*), remains the most compelling hero of the series. There are endless levels of intelligence, compassion, and barely-restrained violence behind his eyes. Even in the scenes where he has little more to do than stand around while the other characters argue, you can't help but watch Foree, whose natural charisma dominates the proceedings, easily securing the viewer's sympathy. It is because of that sympathy that *Dawn* contains what may be the single most terrifying sequence in any of the films.

Foree's character, realizing that Ross' character has to get away, sends her to the roof to escape in a waiting helicopter while he distracts the zombies. Knowing this will cost him his life, Ross' character, Francine, begs him not to do it in a short but genuinely heart-wrenching scene. But Washington is burnt out; he can't stand the thought of living in this world anymore and would rather just go out fighting than fade away. (There's none of that noble warrior crap made trendy in later movies such as *Rambo: First Blood Part 2.*)

Francine gets safely to the roof as Washington leads the zombies deeper and deeper into the guts of the mall's work tunnels. Armed only with an automatic pistol, he manages to corner himself, waiting until the zombies are mere yards away, then presses the gun to his own head. The look on Foree's face at this moment will freeze the blood in your veins.

The zombies lurch and stagger toward him, and he begins to squeeze the trigger.

And then it happens. Like the Grinch finally realizing the true meaning of Christmas, we see the light of life not only ignite, but explode behind his eyes: this is a man who has decided he wants to live.

But he's got a long way to go to get to the roof, most of the zombies are closing in on him, and he doesn't have that much ammunition left in the gun.

Foree's mad dash to get to the roof alive is, hands down, one of the five or six most frightening and exhilarating sequences to ever appear in a horror film, and it manages to end *Dawn* on a slightly hopeful, if darkly cautious, note: if human beings can still find reason to not only go on living, but to choose to bring new life into such a world as this, can we really be doomed?

The ending is perfection, punctuated by a killer closing dialogue exchange. *Dawn* is the most successful film of the trilogy, the only one that—despite its scant flaws—gets better every time I see it.

Now for the fun part.

As much as I respect *Night*, and as much as I admire *Dawn, Day of the Dead* may be my favorite of the bunch. I know, believe me, that in terms of overall execution—the script, the acting, the action, even a lot of the characters' motivations—it is by far the weakest of the series. It is in turn terrifying, thought-provoking, shrill, muddled, philosophically top-heavy, laughable, tender, sadistic—and endlessly watchable. *Day* takes it rightful place alongside *Martin* and *Knightriders* as one of Romero's most thematically complex films, and I forgive it most (but not all) of its trespasses for that.

Day manages to encompass every theme previously explored in the first two movies, as well as introduce a few of its own: What is the true meaning of power? What constitutes genuine survival? How far will an individual's conscience allow him to go in order to protect himself? Is there any value to human compassion in a world spiraling downward toward self-destruction?

It reminded me of David Cronenberg's *Scanners*, insomuch as just when you think the movie is going to run out of ideas, it machine-guns nine more into your face. Unfortunately, these ideas are more talked about than illustrated—especially in the long, long, *long* initial confrontation scene between the sole female scientist and Captain Rhodes, leader of the MAs. This scene is overflowing with some of Romero's most brittle dialogue, but the actors give the words no texture whatsoever—Joseph Pilato, as Rhodes, screams continuously (I think he actually begins to foam at the mouth at one point) while the female scientist, Sarah (played by Lori Cardille) pouts and whines, only getting up some genuine backbone toward the end of the scene. One has to wonder why Romero—who usually solicits sparkling performances from his actors—allowed the thespians in this film to either badly overact or frustratingly under-act their choice roles. I am convinced that if the overall acting had been of the same high caliber as the dialogue and themes, *Day* would have fared better both at the box office and with fans of the series.

Oddly enough, the only character who emerges with a natural humanity (despite the philosophies espoused by the radio officer and black chopper pilot, who are so wise, warm, and fuzzy you just want to step on them), is Bub—a zombie who is in the process of being "domesticated" by a memorably daffy scientist named Logan (the late Richard Liberty, recipient of that year's Charles Laughton Award for Most Eccentric Performance). Bub is played by Howard Sherman, who is nothing short of astonishing in the role. Even through the layers of Savini's makeup, we can see every nuance of the dormant humanity that lies within. I don't know if it was Romero's intent to have Bub emerge as the most sympathetic character, but that's what happens. Add to this that, at movie's end, Bub is more than capable of organizing the zombies, and *Day* turns into not so much a movie as a long trailer for a possible fourth installment to the series (which reportedly, at this writing in August of 2003, will go into production as soon as Romero wraps his new movie, *The Ill*) (Yes, I know, the film was *Land of the Dead*, followed by *Diary of the Dead*, and the recent *Survival of the Dead*...I do try to keep up with these things, y'know). If some spark of distinct personality remains in each zombie—a theory grappled with throughout the movie—and if they can be re-trained to think, to read, to behave with civility in a societal environment, then is it so Out There to foresee a time when some zombie *gestalt* might occur and the few bands of humans left alive will find themselves facing an organized army that simultaneously wants to chow down on them but also learn how to live side by side?

In the end, I admire *Day Of The Dead* more for what it attempts to achieve than what it actually succeeds in doing. It is not so much about the ideas it explores, but those it leaves in the viewer's mind afterward.

But damn, can a lot be forgiven in light of those last twenty minutes. The chase/escape through the zombie catacombs displays Romero at full-tilt-bozo, and the ferocious editing contained in this sequence is hands-down the most muscular and agitating to be found anywhere in the series.

I truly hope that Romero does make a fourth film to bring the series full circle. Hopefully he will have the finances and capabilities to bring his vision to full life. The series should not end with a cluster of dangling, half-realized notions, fascinating though they might be. The series deserves one last grand hurrah, something that will leave its fans and admirers feeling the dead went out with a bang, not a sad, depressed, cynical whimper.

A final Big One before we get into the books and stories and writing.

Thus far, I have tried to avoid a simple, straightforward reprinting of any past film and review columns, simply because it is a format that, as I said earlier, grows wearisome and annoying in a hurry, but

I'm going to make an exception with this next section. For one reason, there is no way to break this particular column up into bite-sized pieces that can be sprinkled about elsewhere; for another, I want to offer up a coda with the luxury of 20/20 hindsight. I have, over the three decades since the following column saw print, changed my mind about certain things. The tone of this piece finds me in out-and-out smartass mode, and at the time of its appearance earned me so much hate mail I still sometimes start whenever someone at a convention mentions this column to me; some of that hate mail contained threats. I was "pissing on an icon"; I was "going after" Stephen King; I was "jealous and stupid," "elitist," "worthless," and of such a low nature that it would be doing the world a favor if "somebody blew your ignorant fucking head off your ignorant fucking shoulders."

We should all be exposed to such evangelical open-mindedness. Think of how it would broaden us.

I'm going to stop talking about the column and just let it speak for itself; I'll catch you on the flip side for the follow-up.

Bearing in mind that I was in my early twenties, full of piss and vinegar, and functioning under the delusion that the aroma of my bodily waste seduced the olfactory senses with the subtly sweet fragrance of exotic flora, I give you, from *Eldritch Tales #11*, the infamous column titled "The Emperor's New Clothes":

There is a moment in a certain motion picture when Richard Deacon (you'll remember him as Mel, the befuddled producer on *The Dick Van Dyke Show*), in the role of a shifty Hollywood producer, is negotiating with a certain female author for the rights to film her book; the author tells him that she wants to make sure the essence of her book is captured by the filmmakers, and to this Deacon replies:

> "Books, schmooks! Who do you know who reads books? Books are made for coffee tables or for something to look at while you're sitting on the toilet . . . but *movies*! Movies are for people with *vision*!"

Those of you who are late night flippers of the cable box will of course recognize this as a patch of dialogue from *The Happy Hooker*

Goes to Hollywood. I found it funny the first time I heard it, and I find it sharply perceptive now, something you'd never expect from a nervous-Nelly soft-core porno movie.

What? I hear you gasp, how *dare* he begin a column that deals with the five recent films based on Stephen King's novels with something from a low-budget, sleazy (but high-spirited) dirty movie?

Ah, mmm, well . . .

Considering what had been done with Mr. King's work in its voyage from the printed page to the big screen, that may be more appropriate than you'd care to admit to yourself, but . . . all right. Perhaps I'm being a bit too harsh here. Let's turn to the words of Mr. King himself.

From page 195 of *Danse Macabre*:

> "I am no apologist for bad filmmaking, but once you've spent twenty years or so going to horror movies . . . you realize that if you don't keep your sense of humor, you're done for."

From page 207 (damn my eyes, the same *chapter*, even!):

> "At this writing, three of my novels have been released as films . . ." (Referring, of course, to *Carrie, Salem's Lot,* and *The Shining*) ". . . I feel that I have been fairly treated . . . and yet the clearest emotion in my mind is not pleasure but a mental sigh of relief. When dealing with the American cinema, you feel like you won if you just broke even . . ."

Now, before going any further, let's play a game of Creative Cerebral Plagiarism: let loose the writer of your psyche and have him/her combine the three quotes you've just seen; if you can do this and form one fluent paragraph, you just might be able to put your finger on the reason why all of the five films based on King's work are so damned disappointing. (Also ask of this writer if he/she thinks Mr. King gives a golden rat's ass . . . the reply will most certainly be, "He's crying all the way to the bank.")

Since the majority of you who read this publication have without a doubt read all of the works in question, I'm going to dispense with too much Belaboring of the Point and tell you a fancy tale from the Igneous Age of Celluloid. Our characters are Mr. Stephen King (henceforth to be known as The Emperor), and the Film Producers With a Glorious Vision (from this point to be known as The Munchkins of Authority). It's called, surprisingly enough, "The Emperor's New Clothes."

Part One: Barking Dogs Never Ride Your Leg

Once upon a time the Emperor wrote a good book about monsters, the type that exist in your mind, the type that exist in The Seasons, and the type that are, sometimes, in your own backyard.

The Munchkins of Authority wanted to make it into a movie, but they didn't like the way it looked, so they dressed it all up as a new version of Jaws on land, with a little General Hospital thrown in for good measure . . .

Louis Teague's film version of *Cujo* isn't a total disaster, but it's in walking distance of the neighborhood. Here is where the point I made in an earlier column shows its flips side: with one notable exception, all the characters who played a major role in King's novel are here, right down to the Sharp Cereal Prof. (Yep, lotsa problems here!)

What came across as claustrophobic ingredients in a microcosm of fate and circumstances in the book, here emerges as a muddled, pointless mess. There is some splendid camera work by director Teague (especially in the last third of the film), a solid performance by Dee Wallace, and some damned impressive stunt work by three sheepdogs and two German Shepherds dressed in Saint Bernard costumes. (My favorite is the shot of the Shepherd, wearing only a puppet head, clawing at the windshield of the yellow Pinto from on the roof. Skinniest damn Saint Bernard I ever saw!)

Despite the whoops and hollers of fear from the semi-illiterate teeny-boppers who populated the audience at the showing I attended, there was not, in *Cujo*, one genuine moment of suspense. At one point I thought I could almost forgive this film all its faults if it would just scare me *once*! But, even if I found that one scare, I couldn't forgive this film its final, cheap, uninspired out-of-your-seat scare tactic borrowed from *Friday the Thirteenth*. The Up-With-Families happy ending completely destroyed any lasting effect the movie might have had (and need I remind you that it was that unexpected twist at the end of the book—Tadder's death—that gave *Cujo* it's real lasting chill; guess what? There *are* monsters in the world, Tadder!)

I do have to admit a certain begrudging respect for the makeup men who drenched the dog in mayonnaise and old mustard to give him a really decrepit, shambling-with-disease look. But, aside from the camera work and Ms. Wallace's performance, the thing that will stay with me from *Cujo* is the singular shot of the dog slamming itself head-first into the Pinto's driver door. I thought, "Gawd-damn! That musta hurt!" It's just a pity that the only beings who walked away numb from *Cujo* were the poor dogs who performed the stunts.

Part Two: Mr. Smith Goes to ComatoseVille

Then the Emperor wrote a book about a poor man who, after a terrible accident, wakes up with the gift of Foresight, sometimes Hindsight, but always something that only touches upon pain and human misery.

The Munchkins of Authority said to themselves, "Well, this one's pretty good as it is. Let's just get a big name this time and let them do it like they want . . . up to a point."

Under his own definition, King may very well feel that he "broken even" with Teag's version of *Cujo*; if such is the case, he must feel a small profit from David Cronenberg's film of *The Dead Zone*. *DZ* is, quite simply, a good movie drawing from a good book as its source. There is, however, only one reason that *DZ* is a good movie, and—guess what?—it ain't Cronenberg.

When Cronenberg is let loose with an idea of his own, even if it is an idea that fails (like *Videodrome*), one at least gets a sense of real passion in his work, even if it's a passion that gouts buckets of grue everywhere. Anyone possessing any doubts about this should pop into their local video store and rent copies of *Scanners* and *The Brood*. Even if you don't care for these two films, you'll have to agree that there is passion there.

One of the things many critics liked about *DZ* was Cronenberg's restraint as a director this time around. Well, droogies, I don't think I have to hammer this point too much; Cronenberg's "restraint" borders on the somnambulistic: at one point I was afraid the picture was going to put the audience into a deeper sleep than Christopher Walken had been in. It's been a long time since a director of Cronenberg's caliber made a film that is so devoid of passion.

Cronenberg does manage to inject *DZ* with his own darker form of excitement during the long sequence that involves the catching of the Castle Rock Killer; here, the power is derived from the anticipation of the final confrontation, one that ends in a cookie-whoopsing image of the killer going through death spasms in a bathtub, a long pair of sharp scissors jammed through the roof of his mouth and the center of his forehead. He jerks and convulses and spits out thick streams of dark blood. Just peachy. There isn't an audience anywhere (save NYC) that wouldn't feel their stomachs twist at this image, which Cronenberg lets his camera leer at for longer than is necessary.

Jeffery Boam is the credited screenwriter, though it was rumored that up to four different writers had a crack at it. Of all the films based on King's work, *DZ* seemed the one most intent upon the most literate form of condensing his novel to the big screen's hundred-minute format. There's nothing particularly wrong with Boam's script, but there's nothing particularly outstanding, either. It just breaks even.

That aside, you undoubtedly noticed that of all the King-based films, *DZ* seemed to stay around the longest. It was, as they say in Munchkin Land, a hit. There is a reason for this, and its name is Christopher Walken. Walken, who won the Academy Award for his wonderful performance in *The Deerhunter*, turns in a rich, flawless performance as John Smith, the protagonist of King's Rip Van Winkle terror tale. You like John, you care about him, and you feel his frustration and pain as he is forced to come to grips with a power he never asked for, but must live with, nonetheless. Every time John has a vision, it's an unnerving experience for both him and the audience, simply because Walken is so masterful at conveying compassion, pain, disgust, and fear; not individually, but in a swirling kaleidoscope of conflicting emotional reactions, all of them inexorably placing him in the middle of other people's lives with their pain, loneliness, fear, and sometimes their pettiness and perversions. It is solely because of Walken that *DZ* holds up all the way and manages to keep your interest focused when Cronenberg falls asleep and lets the film become stoic and unconvincing.

Martin Sheen is used to good sleazy advantage as Greg Stillson, as is Herbert Lom as Dr. Sam Weizak. In Lom's case, he achieves his convincingness not with sleaze, but with a tired, cynical type of compassion that is sparked by an occasional burst of good humor. However, were it not for Walken, their two good performances would have been lost amongst Cronenberg's celluloid sleeping tablet. One can only hope that, in the future, Mr. Cronenberg will keep himself to himself when making films; I'll take passion that fails over safe somnambulism any day of the week.

Part Three: Kiddies of the Porn

And so the Munchkins of Authority sat in their high offices and said to themselves, "We don't seem to be having a great deal of luck with these movies of his longer work; what say we try beefing up his short stories? He did write short stories, didn't he?"

One of the secretaries runs out to check, comes back a few minutes later and confirms that in fact The Emperor did, indeed, write short stories. None of the Munchkins of Authority had read any, however, but that would not stop them from taking a fine piece of his short fiction and dressing it in a sacrificial gown.

Fritz Kierch's film version of *Children of the Corn* appears in this section of the column under protest and only for the sake of continuity; it took a great deal of self-control not to place this sickening glop of cinematic afterbirth in the Tarnished Bedpan Award Winner's Circle (The Tarnished Bedpan Awards was a section in each column devoted to the absolute *worst* horror movies imaginable). I had a good deal of hope for this movie when I first saw it advertised. The best laid pans, et cetera . . .

An annoying pontificating pause here:

Stephen King's novels do not condense well. King is the master of intricate plotting in the horror novel and, even more than that, he understands and utilizes the importance of the minor character and the small, seemingly insignificant detail. A minor character, for instance, may do something that seems inconsequential at first, but stems from deeply rooted motivations in their systems that have taken years to manifest themselves. The mailman's forgotten trip to the Camber's farm in *Cujo* is a good example of this. Because of this, King's novels are rich in character, plot, and terror. There are a lot of heavy-handed episodes in his books, but there are an infinite number of subtleties also. It's these missed subtleties that so righteously muck up his books when brought to the screen. That's why *Children of the Corn* seemed such a good candidate for a film. Rather than screw up a full-blown novel, why not take a short story (though it borders on the novella) and beef it up a bit, say to ninety minutes, you'll get all the characters, detail, and terror, yet have some room to fill in some extra goodies. Sounds logical, right? Right. A good road to follow, right? Right. Easy path to success with, right?

Ahem.

Outside of the fact that this film (and I use that term loosely) takes every chance it can to gout grue and guts all over the floor, it takes a nosedive into idiot-pits yet undreamt of when it turns He Who Walks Behind the Rows into some sort of mythic super-gopher that burrows under everything in an effect that was used to much better advantage in John Carpenter's *The Thing*.

Kerisch and screenwriter George Goldsmith have taken a story that had "success" written all over it and turned it into another one of those horrid, tasteless, bucket-full-of-steaming-innards movies that only hold appeal to the idiotic, pre-pubescent teens with zits on their faces who to go these things with their boyfriends or girlfriends so they can act scared and/or grossed out so they'll have yet another excuse to grope each other's budding anatomies in the dark.

Children of the Corn could have been a decent film; there are one or two good images that are cut away from before they can work up any power, and the acting is just above that found in *Plan 9 from Outer Space* but not nearly at the level of something like *The Exorcist*, and Jonathan Elias has provided it with a much better musical score than it deserves. This movie only goes to prove that bigger isn't always better.

Part Four: Would You Buy A Used Car From This Man?

> *Then there was The Emperor's tale of love between a boy and his fiery red 1958 Plymouth; it was an intelligent, intense, and poignant tale of alienation, loneliness, and final revenge for all the wrongs done to an individual by the growing pains of youth.*
>
> *The Munchkins of Authority decided that no one could really take a story about a haunted car seriously—obviously, they didn't, and theirs was the opinion that counted—so they dressed it up in a stand-up comic's garb, complete with arrow through the head and whoopee cushion. Hardy-har. It is, as they say, to laugh.*

Christine is the biggest disappointment of all the King films, and there are two very big reasons behind this: first, but not the biggest, is that King's own agent, World Fantasy Award-Winner Kirby McCauley, was heavily involved in the production end of this film. One would think that, with such a literary man as McCauley helping to oversee the film, it would hold true to the vision that was presented in the book. Nothing could be more off-base.

The second reason is, unfortunately, director John Carpenter, who shows with *Christine* that he is not above compromising his craft for money. This film may be the sloppiest one he's ever made, and it pains me to say this because I've grown to respect Carpenter over the past few years, especially after *The Thing*. (For more on that, consult ET#9)

Christine is so self-enamored of its own smug-assed humor that after a while you begin to feel as if you're not being let in on someone's personal joke. The movie treads dangerously close to mocking

King's novel, which—even with its own good sense of humor—was a dark and saddening tale. Carpenter's film turns it all into one long punchline that is badly in need of a joke with which to be prefaced.

Not to be totally disheartened, there are some gems in this film as far as moments go. The opening sequence, where Christine is rolled off the Detroit assembly line, has some of the best tracking-cam work you'll ever see. With George Thorogood crooning "B-b-b-b-bad to the bone" under it all, it comes across extremely reminiscent of the opening sequence of Paul Shrader's *Blue Collar.*

Keith Gordon is wonderful as Arnie Cunningham, displaying (as much as the muddled script allows him) all the frustration and alienation that causes Arnie to be at first enamored of, and then possessed by Christine. It is only through Gordon's winning performance that Carpenter's film holds any lasting connection to the work upon which it was based.

Carpenter, who had been busy shooting *Firestarter*, scrapped that project in order to do *Christine*. The film came out astoundingly soon after the release of the book. Everyone swears that the film rights were purchased and the final script approved before the book was even released, but you should take those statements with a grain of salt; *Christine* was a rush job, and it looks it.

The car itself never really comes alive as far as character is concerned. In the book she was a fire-blazing bitch on wheels: possessive, jealous, and vengeful. Carpenter turns her into nothing more than an expensive central prop.

In the cheapest bit in the movie, Carpenter utilizes the same uninspired gimmick that Teague did in *Cujo*; I don't have to tell you what I'm referring to, do I? Didn't think so.

Under King's own definition of "The Horror Movie as Junkfood," I think that *Christine* fits in quite well: all taste with no protein. Dare I say that *Christine* runs out of . . . nah! Even *I* won't stoop that low.

All things considered, Mr. Thorogood's theme song was well-chosen.

Sorry, John.

Before going on to the final film, let's check back with The Emperor once more. He offers an analogy of all this that is better than any I could ever come up with, and I never try to improve upon perfection.

From page 210 of *Danse Macabre*:

> "You don't appreciate cream unless you've drunk a lot of milk, and maybe you don't even appreciate milk unless you've drunk some that's gone sour. Bad films may sometimes be amusing, sometimes even successful, but their only real usefulness is to form that basis of comparison: to define positive values in terms of their own negative charm. They show us what to look for because it is missing in themselves."

Beautiful. Just beautiful.

Part Five: Zen and the Art of Lighting a Gas Grill

And so The Munchkins of Authority chose The Emperor's tale of fire and love and pursuit. This time their boss, He Who Caters to the Distributors, told them to follow the book to the letter. The Munchkins bowed in obeisance to their boss while giving The Emperor's readers the finger. Then someone lit a match to see how high a flame would have to go in order to burn another person's ass.

If you follow such fine magazines as *Twilight Zone* or *Cinefantastique,* then you already know that, of all the King films, *Firestarter* was among the first to be started and the last to be finished. This undoubtedly gave you reason to be optimistic; with all the failures thus far, perhaps more care was being taken and the result would be a better finished product. ("Movies are for people with vision!")

Director Mark L. Lester's (*Stunts, Class of 1984*) version of *Firestarter* just misses being on target. There are many instances during the film when you want to jump up and shout, "GET YOUR ASS IN STEP!" in the hopes it will make everything synchronize. It doesn't, but you have to appreciate the effort, nonetheless.

The screenplay by Stanley Mann is pretty good as it goes, though I'd be willing to wager that a full 95 percent of the dialogue was lifted straight from the book. (King supposedly offered advice on the script, and I get the impression that if King had written the screenplay himself, it wouldn't have been much different than Mann's.)

Lester does a fairly competent job of stringing things along, but it seems more like a child following the instructions of a paint-by-number kit than a director trying to interpret something onto film. You also get the same feeling by watching this movie that you might get when listening to a live symphony where the orchestra, somehow, gets ahead of the conductor. Everything about *Firestarter* seems to be on the verge of connecting and turning itself into something pretty spectacular, but it never gets there.

What does recommend *Firestarter* is the acting. As I expected, George C. Scott's John Rainbird dominates the screen from the moment he first appears. It's nice to see that King's material is starting to attract such wonderful talents as Scott, Walken, Sheen, and Art Carney. Maybe someone will find a good role for Olivier in the film version of *Pet Sematary*, which will probably be out before this column sees print.

Scott, though badly miscast (Will Sampson should have played it) is chilling to watch as he struts around with his Neanderthal-like gait, smashing in people's faces and spouting existentialistic philosophy. It's only a pity that his makeup for the bad eye keeps changing from scene to scene.

David Keith is solid as Andy McGee, conveying all the panic and anger that is required for the role, though I got a little tired of the heavy-handed way he and Lester presented "the push."

Art Carney is just perfect as Irv Manders, and you'll find yourself wishing that he was used more in the film. It amazes me how, even in the worst of films, Carney seems able to submerge himself completely in another character—the whole point of fine acting. It's a pity he wasted so much time playing second fiddle to Jackie Gleason for all those years. He and Scott provide *Firestarter* with many memorable moments.

Then we come to Drew Barrymore's performance in the extremely difficult role of Charlie. In a surprising contradiction of Hollywood logic, the producers have cast an eight-year-old to play an eight-year-old.

Barrymore, who so charmed audiences in *E.T.*, here shows that she is a damn good little actress. There are times in the film when the script crams too many words into her tiny mouth and you get the impression of a child *trying* to act, but there are more than enough moments of real performing to erase the lesser ones. In a moment that will make you want to cheer, she turns to one of The Shop's members and says, "Get out of here you bastard or I'll fry you!"

I believed her. (Gulp!) And that's all you need here, just enough convincing moments to make you swallow everything.

Martin Sheen is back again, rapidly becoming the quintessential King villain: well-dressed, greasy hair that looks almost plastic, and a smile that Hitchcock would've loved. It's also good to see this fine actor pop up again in a King film. (In case you weren't already aware of this fact, the role Sheen plays—Cap—was originally going to be done by the masterful Burt Lancaster, who had to bow out when heart surgery needed to be performed.)

But, in the end, *Firestarter* never manages to get all its good elements in synch, something that will leave you disheartened and none the warmer. (Sorry, I couldn't resist just one comment along those lines.)

One last pontification and then we'll look in on *The Keep*.

King and his literary peers (Peter Straub, Charles L. Grant, Karl Edward Wagner, Ramsey Campbell, and Dennis Etchison, just to name a few of the biggies) all agree that the best type of terror (?) is the type that lingers in the mind long after the last page has been turned or the last reel has rolled through the camera. I don't think there's anyone who reads this publication who would argue with that.

When that statement is applied to the five films reviewed previously, it can be stated (without too much fear of protest) that there can be found more "lingering terror" in the grave-robbing sequence in *Bring Me the Head of Alfredo Garcia* than in all five of these movies combined. I don't possibly see how King could feel that he's "broken even" with this batch of movies. Perhaps he'll never see a really fine film made from any of his fine (and, in some cases, brilliant) novels. But something tells me that, in the end, and with all his seven-figure advances, Mister King probably doesn't much care how he is treated by Hollywood. And so, the big question: if Stephen King doesn't care, why should we?

Epilogue: The Nick-Nack Paddywack Burial Ground

So The Emperor left the golden land of Hollywood, none the worse for the wear, but richer. And, in the night, if you turn your ears toward the west and listen very carefully, you'll hear an ominous sound.

There! Hear it? That sound like desiccated flesh being set aflame? Not to worry, though . . .

It's only The Munchkins of Authority counting their box office receipts.

Man in the Low Castle

Director Michael Mann's version of F. Paul Wilson's *The Keep* shot in and out of theatres in less than twelve days, after an extensive publicity campaign. I'll not hold you in suspense about this: Gary A. (that crazy sonuvabitch likes *anything*) Braunbeck did not, overall, like *The Keep*, but that does not stop me from recommending that you see it in the event it pops up at the local drive-in or a cheap-seat matinee showing or on a pay cable film channel.

Michel Mann, who created one of the better (which I know isn't saying a whole hell of a lot) television detective shows, *Vegas*, had directed only two films previous to *The Keep*: *The Jericho Mile* and *Thief* (the latter being one of the best psychological studies of the criminal mind in a long, long time). He proved with his two films that he was a impressive technician and damned literate script writer. There was also a very muscular feel to both these films, an intense and often overwhelming power that left moviegoers breathless and stunned. Unfortunately, *The Keep* doesn't exercise these traits nearly as well as the other two films. What starts off brilliantly for its first thirty-five minutes quickly degenerates into a muddle of mixed metaphors, unconvincing characterizations, and buckets of quasi-mystical-super-psycho-gobbledy-gook. Mann stated that he was inspired by Jean Cocteau's *Beauty and the Beast* and he wanted to turn Wilson's novel into a seductive fairy tale of evil.

Mann has managed to give *The Keep* a wonderful look (it is undoubtedly one of the most beautiful *looking* films of recent years), and there are dozens of images that will stay with you long after the film has finished, but *The Keep* leaves you with a sense of being cheated, of being given a gorgeous package with nothing inside.

The film does have a few good moments during the first third: the Nazis' entrance into the town and then to the Keep itself moves along with the same feverish pace that marked the opening robbery in *Thief* (*The Keep* was shot in 70mm), and the Keep itself, though it differs radically in structure from the way it's described in Wilson's terrific novel, does have a murky, subterranean look that creeps up your spine.

One of the best things about this mish-mash of a motion picture is the stunning musical score provided by Tangerine Dream (who also provided *Firestarter* with an equally excellent soundtrack). If the name of this three-man group from Germany sounds familiar, it may be because they've done several soundtracks in the last few years, among them *Sorcerer, Strange Invaders, Strange Behavior*, and *Thief*. If you were a follower of the music column in Twilight Zone magazine, you probably didn't find Tangerine Dream listed anywhere, and more's the pity. Their particular brand of synthesized electronic wizardry is well suited to genre films, and it's good to hear them being utilized to such an advantage. Give them a listen the next time you read something by Charles L. Grant, and you'll see what I mean.

Finally, it should be noted here for the record that Michael Mann, though he's scored his first miss with *The Keep*, is a director who, if he can put aside his more condescending notions concerning the genre, may very well make a substantial contribution to horror/fantasy films one day. He possesses just enough scope of vision, cynicism, and hard-edged compassion to recommend him. Perhaps, after all, director Michael (and I couldn't resist this one) is The Mann Who Should Do King.

God save us from the echoes of our younger selves.

Is it just me, or can you still smell that column's stench hanging in the air? The over-use of exclamation points! The sudden attacks of

Capitalization Disease. The magnificently awkward, convoluted, self-conscious turns of phrase (". . . another one of those horrid, tasteless, bucket-full-of-steaming-innards movies that only hold appeal to the idiotic, pre-pubescent teens with zits on their faces who to go these things with their boyfriends or girlfriends so they can act scared and/or grossed out so they'll have yet another excuse to grope each other's budding anatomies in the dark"); what in the *hell* made me think I could ever make a living out of this?

Talk about your pilgrim bullshit.

This is not meant to serve as an apology. When I turned in that column, I thought it was a fairly good, clever piece of writing, and I think it still has a few things to give it merit or—believe me—I would not have reprinted it here.

A little background on how that column came to be written:

First of all, I was in my early 20s; secondly, I was drunk and upset most of the time, no more so than when I wrote it; third and lastly, my life and my budding career had come to a grinding, miserable halt and I was pissed off at everything. Not yet 25, I had already buried my first marriage and my only child and was making a vocation out of collecting rejection slips. In the meantime, I worked as everything from a janitor to a fry cook to a sometimes-actor and a the-less-said-about-it-the-better musician. I was as directionless as they come. Welcome to the beginning of your third decade, you pathetic loser.

Looking back on it, I fully admit there was an element of jealousy that colored my opinions (and if you're a professional writer who finds that you practically have to threaten editors and publishers with bodily harm before they pony up the long green you've been waiting months for, then you cannot possibly tell me that, on some level, you *maybe* begrudge King his phenomenal and well-deserved success; at least, not with a straight face, you can't).

I still maintain that this column was not an attack on King, despite some of the more sarcastic asides. It was, and remains, a badly-written assault on what I at the time perceived to be a batch of pretty mediocre-to-abysmal movies. (I can't help but add that, when the film version of *Pet Sematary* finally came out, it was even more horrendously awful than I'd feared it would be—though the production design and the late Fred Gwynne's pearly performance as Jud Crandall remain impressive, as does the heartfelt turn by Miko Hughes as the doomed Gage Creed.)

So, how do these opinions hold up at this end of the time-slip?

Not very well, overall.

I still stand by my comments about *Children of the Corn* and *Firestarter*, but find that I've softened my attitude toward *Cujo* considerably, *Christine* quite a bit, and have done a complete reversal on my opinion of *The Dead Zone*. This last, when viewed today, can easily take its place alongside *The Shawshank Redemption, The Green Mile, Stand by Me, Misery* and the unjustifiably-maligned *Hearts in Atlantis* and *Dreamcatcher* as one of the best adaptations of a King novel. Cronenberg has gone on to prove himself one of the few genuinely maverick directors working today, as such films as *Crash, M. Butterfly,* and the phenomenal *Spider, A History of Violence*, and *Eastern Promises* readily prove; his work on *The Dead Zone* is as pure an example of intense restraint as I've seen, and I couldn't have been more wrong in my assessment. Christopher Walken's performance remains one of the best he's ever given, and Tom Skerritt's understated turn as Sheriff Bannerman just gets better with repeated viewings.

The softening of my attitude toward *Cujo* is so intertwined with my reasons for disliking it the first time I still find it difficult to discern where one ends and the other begins.

Got another laugh-filled personal pause here, so whip out the whoopee cushions and that well-thumbed copy of *The Big Book of Fart and Booger Jokes*:

I once had a daughter. She died when she was very young. She had been sick from the moment she was born and never got better. She never learned to walk, never made a sound, never blew out the candles on a birthday cake. The only home she ever knew was the sterile room of an ICU. She was very tiny and she fought very hard. The last seventy-two hours of her life were agonizing, and when she died it was without the benefit of a warm, loving human touch lingering on her skin. Her mother, exhausted and sedated, was asleep on a couch in the hospital's lounge; I'd not eaten for almost a day and a half, and so had gone to the vending machines one floor below to get some coffee and a sandwich. The entire trip took four minutes. The coffee was lukewarm and weak, the sandwich stale and tasteless, and by the time I came back to the ICU, my daughter was dead and gone.

Her death was not a surprise. Her mother and I had known for a while that it was (as the tired cliché goes) "only a matter of time."

Not a surprise, but still the ice pick in my throat.

I remember seeing the curtain pulled around her incubator.

I remember the sounds made by the various machines hooked up to the other patients in the unit.

I remember wanting to cry but being unable to.

Then it was shuffling, being taken aside, muffled words from weary nurses, uncomfortable-looking orderlies, a gurney with a squeaking front left wheel, and the last sight of my daughter: bumps and curves and patches of pale flesh inside a translucent plastic bag, rolling away, away.

Her mother and I were both young and foolish and not nearly strong enough to handle this. Our relationship crawled along for a few more months, a joyless thing, back-broken and spirit-dead, before ending in infidelity, accusations and poison.

It's been almost twenty years since she died. I have since seen my writing career at last get on its feet, and finally gotten—albeit sporadically—the upper hand in the battle with my recurring bouts of severe depression.

Still, there are times—periodic though they may be, usually very late at night or first thing in the morning—when it all comes back, diminished not one whit by the passage of years, and I crumple. Simply crumple.

Don't believe what the pop psychologists or self-help books or daytime talk show hosts tell you about it: you *never* fully recover from the death of a child. The grief eventually works its way into the shadows, back there someplace, a whisper, an echo, a tendril of smoke perpetually curling in the air over a just-emptied ashtray... but it never completely goes away.

And the bitch of it is, you never know when it's going to come snarling to the surface, or what may cause it to rally and bear its teeth.

In my case, it was both the novel *Cujo* and its respectful—if not altogether successful—film adaptation.

In the novel, when Tadder dies despite all his mother has gone through to protect him, it drilled right into my core. Whether he intended it to or not, King's simple, elegant description of the boy's death and the emotional aftermath echoed what I was going through at the time. For that reason alone—even if I hadn't found the rest of the novel intense and compelling—*Cujo* remains one of my six favorite King books. The other five, if you're interested, are *The Dead Zone, Night Shift, Hearts in Atlantis, Roadwork,* and *From a Buick 8.*

From a Buick 8? I hear you cry. *It had no ending, it offered no explanations. How could you have enjoyed it so much?*

Funny story, that.

At the beginning of Peter Straub's wonderful novel *In the Night Room* there is a quote from philosopher, publisher, and journalist Roger Scruton that reads: "The consolation of imaginary things is not imaginary consolation."

Not to downplay Straub's redoubtable achievement with this novel, but Scruton's epigrammatic bit of wisdom knocked my socks off nearly as much as did the novel itself—and not to sound boastful, but I am not one whose sensibilities are easily affected; it takes *a lot* to genuinely move me. Scruton (*Bad Attitudes; A Dove Descending and Other Stories*) did just that.

To understand why this hit me as hard as it did, we're going to go back to 2002—October of 2002, to be precise—and join Gary during his stay in the nuthouse. (Okay, technically it was *not* the nuthouse, more of the pre-nuthouse holding facility, but why nitpick at this late date?)

Understand something before we move on: *none* of what follows is intended to be a ploy for sympathy; it's not a pity party, and it sure as hell isn't romanticized. I did not have then—nor do I now have—much sympathy for myself. I was weak, self-centered, and more than a little stupid. I could have turned to others for help, but I didn't; it was far easier to allow myself to implode. In short, I'm not attempting to make you feel sorry for me.

Okay, then.

Quick recap: the sixteen months between June of 2001 and December of 2002 were not, to put it mildly, blue-ribbon days for yours truly. During that time, I lost, within nine months, my favorite uncle (lung cancer), my grandmother (heart failure), my father (cancer), then my mother (emphysema). I'd moved to a new city, gotten divorced (my fault, all my fault), underwent surgery to repair nerve damage to my right hand, and somewhere in there went off my anti-depression medication—yes, I know, stupid, Stupid, STUPID.

The result of all of this is that one week before Halloween of 2002, I found myself in possession of a lot of seriously strong and potentially fatal medications taken from my parents' house. (My sister, Gayle, had enough to deal with, so I went through all the rooms and cabinets and drawers, shoving Mom and Dad's medications into a box, intending to dispose of everything when I returned to Columbus.)

Bear in mind that though I am far from the brightest bulb in the sign, I am not (under the right circumstances) without a certain cleverness when it comes to finding ways to self-destruct. I could not go for five minutes without thinking of my grandmother's lonely last years, or seeing my father's body, or the look on my mother's face when I told her that I had come to the hospital to take her off life support, or the deep, deep hurt in my soon-to-be-ex-wife's eyes the last time we had seen each other. I couldn't sleep. I wasn't eating. My writing production was down to practically zero because I couldn't concentrate on anything other than the People Who Weren't There Anymore, and my right hand was becoming more and more useless (this was before the surgery). I was surrounded by a circle of friends who were, on average, 15 years younger than me and with whom I ultimately had very little in common (I knew I was in trouble when I mentioned Harold Russell and not one of them knew who I was talking about). I allowed my world to become more and more circumscribed by the handful of rooms in my apartment. If I could bring myself to get out of bed at all, I spent a lot of time sitting in front of the television watching reruns of shows that hadn't been very good the first time, but that didn't matter because I wasn't seeing them anyway.

(An aside: some of you might be thinking, *Hey, wait a second—didn't you publish something like six books during that time period? How can you say that your writing was down to almost nothing?* Easy: all but one of those books had been written previous to the Fun Time, and since it takes about as long for a book to get published as it does for a pregnancy to come to fruition in the birth of a new life, I was lucky that I'd been so productive beforehand. You might have noticed that the past year has seen only *one* book from yours truly, and it won't be until March of next year before a new one appears. This is a direct result of my not having been very productive, and I'm working like a fiend to make up for that lost time. I wrote only a handful of stories during that sixteen-month period, and three of them—"Duty," "Patience," and "The King of Rotten Wood"—rank among the darkest and most hopeless tales I've ever produced. End of parenthetical aside.)

So it's October, roughly a week before Halloween, and I'm not really *here* anymore; some empty, cheerless thing that's wearing my face and using my body to get around has taken the wheel, and I don't feel like fighting with it. I have enough money to get a motel room for the night. I have more than enough medications in the proper dosages to ensure that the job will be done correctly (I've been researching this for several weeks). And I have recently purchased two packages of pudding cups so that there will be a way to ingest all these medications without causing myself to throw up. (The shuffling-off cocktail recipe ends here; just know that I had everything necessary to do the deed and knew how and when to take it.)

There's only one glitch: all of the motels within walking distance of my apartment (I don't drive) have no vacancies due to a Quarter Horse convention that's in town. So, much to my disappointment, I'm going to have to do the job at the apartment and hope that my two roommates will still be able to live there afterward.

I'm walking back to the apartment and realize I'm thirsty, so I make a short detour to the neighborhood Giant Eagle to buy a soda. I'm standing in line behind a couple with several children, and the youngest child—maybe three years old—looks back at me, then turns to her mother and tugs her sleeve and says, "Mommy, that man's crying."

Damned if she wasn't right. I'd had no idea, perceptive fellow that I am.

"Don't stare," says the child's mother, but the little girl looks back at me, still gripping her mother's sleeve, and says, "What's wrong, mister?"

"I'm sorry," I say to her sweet and concerned little face.

And then *she* starts crying.

Now *everyone* in this line and those on either side of us is looking over and trying to look like they're not looking. Me, I'm standing there shaking like an alcoholic in the grips of the DTs, my face soaked, crying so hard that snot is coming out of my nose in buckets, and a police officer is coming toward me.

Oh, good, I think. *Way to be inconspicuous, Einstein. Everyone's staring at you, you've got roughly two thousand dollars' worth of prescription medications in your bag, and now a cop's coming. This is going to screw up the shuffling-off schedule something fierce if you don't think fast.*

The officer asked what the problem was, and I managed to force a smile to my face and told him that I'd just come from a funeral and I was sorry, this just sort of hit me unexpectedly. He bought it, and I purchased my soda and walked back to my apartment, still shaking, still in sloppy tears. Pathetic.

I got back inside, walked up to my bedroom, dumped all the medications and pudding on the bed, and just sort of . . . imploded. I honestly don't remember much about the next twelve hours—I have vague impressions of peoples' voices talking to me, of someone holding my hand, of eating something, of sleeping for a while, of watching a movie—but when I finally came back to something like lucidity, I was being checked in to an emergency mental health facility here in Columbus. Two psychiatrists had been filled in on my recent history, both had talked to me (which I barely recall), and both had decided I was a danger to myself and to others, and promptly admitted me to the facility where I was kept in a snowy haze for about forty-eight hours by all the powerful sedatives that were at once pumped into my system.

I spent ten days there before being deemed stable enough for release. I won't bore you with the details of the intensive day-to-day routine of life in there, save for one thing—the book I had brought with me: Stephen King's *From a Buick 8.*

Understand that I had given up hope. I had no faith left—not in myself, not in humankind, not in love, friendship, integrity, this ethereal whoseewhatsit called God, *nothing.*

And my writing career? Forget it. I was more than aware that a lot of readers considered my stuff to be *too* dark, if not outright depressing. I didn't see my fiction becoming any more cheerful anytime soon, and as far as I could tell, the future was in no way bright enough to require my wearing shades.

Submitted for your approval: not a happy camper.

Still, I *had* already started King's novel, wasn't all that far into it, and God knows I didn't have anything better to do with my extra time, so during those free periods—few and far between that they were—I read.

And then something odd began to happen.

I started feeling . . . if not better, then no worse.

Don't go thinking this is leading up to my describing some thundering, overpowering, Wagnerian epiphany, because it isn't. I had no uplifting moment of realization; no heavenly choir began singing over too-loud, sentimental John Williams music as a beam of moonlight crept through the window and anointed my face and mind with the Silver Light of Truth and Inner Peace. I experienced no visions, no revelations, uttered no exclamations of "My God, the ghosts have done it all *in one night!*"

No, what happened was, simply, this: I became caught up in the story (which, for the record, may not be the best-written story King has ever told, but is, I think, the best-*told* story he's ever written). I wanted to find out what happened next. And because I read slowly, I was able to pace my reading so that I had only enough time to read a chapter or two in the afternoon, and the same later at night. (Sometimes less, sometimes more, depending on what feelings I had "shared" with the group during any one of the five daily sessions that were held—and those weren't counting the individual sessions.

(An aside: if you've read my novella *In the Midnight Museum*, Buzzland is based on the facility where I was kept for those ten days; the layout—including the gymnasium—is exactly as I described it.)

But here's the important thing: I had something to look forward to. What was going to come crawling out of the car's trunk next time? What was the deal with the lights and fireworks? Would the dog survive? (Dogs don't fare well in King's books.) Would King be able to pull off this round-robin of first person narrators? Inquiring minds wanted to know.

Okay—*I* wanted to know. And that came as something of a surprise to me. Because all of a sudden, I *cared* about something again. Admittedly, it wasn't myself, but why nitpick? Something within me still held onto enough wisps of hope that it allowed me to become immersed in a story. And that immersion, that curiosity, that wanting to know what happens next, began to spread over into the way I behaved toward the other patients, the doctors, the nurses, and myself. I started to actually talk *to* and not *at* everyone else. What did

I have to lose? If nothing else, I had *Buick 8* waiting for me at day's end.

Yes, I'm skipping over a lot of things—those times when I fell back into hopelessness, when something one of the characters said reminded me of something of my mom or dad used to say and I'd hurl the book across the room, only to retrieve it a few minutes later, smoothing out the cover and pages; those times I was too heavily sedated to focus on the words—because the point here is that as both a reader and human being I had found consolation in imaginary things, and knew it my heart that it was *not* imaginary consolation.

Looking at my trusty dictionary, I read the following about "consolation":

> **con-so-la-tion** *n.*
> 1. a source of comfort to somebody who is upset or disap pointed
> 2. comfort to somebody who is distressed or disappointed
> 3. a game or contest held for people or teams who have lost earlier in a tournament

Arguably, all of these definitions could apply (the third one falling more on the metaphorical side of the coin), but for the sake of this argument, we'll go with the first two.

I remember something comedian Red Skelton used to say at the end of his television show every week: "If by chance someday you're not feeling well and you should remember some silly little thing I've said or done and it brings back a smile to your face or a chuckle to your heart . . . then my purpose as your clown has been fulfilled."

That is the kind of consolation I'm talking about, and it is the kind of consolation that I found in reading King's novel at that time, and in that place. I honestly don't think any other book could have done this for me, under those circumstances.

What I came away with—aside from three different types of depression medications that I had to take twice a day—was the knowledge that good storytelling can be a source of great consolation, and that this consolation can give back a glimmer of hope to a weary heart. (Annoying update: it's now five antidepressants I have to take twice a day. I'm surprised I have a liver left.)

How many of you reading this have been lost in depression, or sadness, or lingering grief, or loneliness, or doubt, or any of the thousands of shadowed corners in the human heart where even the blackest darkness would look like a star going nova, and found some moment of comfort in a book or short story that you've read?

And, yes, you bet your ass that this can apply to horror fiction. I'm not talking about that old happy horseshit that says imaginary horrors help us to better deal with the real ones—we'll get into that at another time—but, rather, how the very act of reading something that raises anxiety or provides a good chill reaffirms the immediacy and necessity of your own existence. If some part of you is still willing to *choose* to be frightened, or disturbed, or repulsed, then this same part is embracing life by embracing fear. If you can still be scared, then you still think life has value and meaning; if you still think that life has value and meaning, then there is still hope in your heart.

What greater gift could a storyteller hope to pass on to his or her readers?

So, yes, the consolation of imaginary things is not imaginary consolation. Even if those imaginary things live in dark corners and aren't sometimes particularly pleasant or uplifting.

For as long as there is fear of the darkness, there will be hope.

Just look at what was done with *Cujo.*

Insert clever segue. Onward.

When I saw the film version of *Cujo*, I was actually quite pleased with the way it was unfolding (anorexic St. Bernard notwithstanding), and—as sadomasochistic as this is going to sound—I was looking forward to seeing Tadder's death and its emotional aftermath portrayed onscreen. I wanted to see if the moviemakers were going to get it right—and I wanted, if just for a moment, the audience to feel some small part of the crumpling grief I was still experiencing.

So imagine my reaction when "the Tadder" suddenly pulls in a wheezing, life-giving breath, opens his eyes, and begins coughing as Mommy and Daddy move together for a warm and fuzzy group hug as the picture freezes and slowly fades to black.

"Goddamn *cowards*!" I said loudly, much to the annoyance of the others in the packed theater and to the embarrassment of my mom, who'd come to see it with me. "Goddamn spineless, wimpy, gutless cowards!"

Mom smacked my arm. "It's only a movie, Gary. Calm down. And watch your language. We're in public."

Here's where the old debate between novel vs. film adaptation comes seriously into play.

My mom—who had not read the book—was pleased that Tadder did not die; in fact, she smiled and got a little teary-eyed, she was so happy. That stuck with me, and over the years when I talk to others who have seen the movie but *not* read the book, the majority of the reactions have been positive; they like it very much (anorexic St. Bernards . . . cha-cha-cha).

Re-watching the movie, I realized that Teague and screenwriter Don Carlos (*Impulse*) Dunaway were not attempting to *dramatize* King's novel (as I had unreasonably expected), but rather re-interpret it as a dark fairy tale with a happy ending. If you watch the movie—and you don't have to watch it all that closely—there are several hints throughout that Tadder is going to make it and that Mommy and Daddy will be reunited. With the sole exception of the makeup used on the dogs, *Cujo* succeeds in what it sets out to do, and to that end must be respected. What is there is simply a solid, if not particularly distinguished, movie.

I have warmed slightly more to *Christine*, as well. It still isn't a very good movie, but the tongue-in-cheek supporting performances of Robert Prosky, Harry Dean Stanton, and the sly cameo work of Roberts Blossom as George LeBay give the film an effortless, understated black humor that the rest of the movie strains to achieve. And Alexandra Paul is just gorgeous. (Gimme a break; I've loused-up two marriages. Any fantasy helps.)

As for *The Keep* . . . well, F. Paul Wilson's understandably low opinion of this film is well known, and almost every fan of the book agrees. However, despite all the pissing and moaning and assorted brouhaha, it's not a lousy movie; it is *one half* a lousy movie, one half a stunning and sure-handed adaptation of the novel. Its gorgeous photography and production design still hold up, as do the fierce performances of Jurgen Prochnow and Gabriel Byrne. The confrontation scene between the two near the three-quarter mark in the movie is almost up there with the Burt Lancaster/Fredrick March scene from *Seven Days in May*. Both actors are on fire and the dialogue crackles.

I suppose it's only fair I offer some comment about the performance of Ian McKellen in the pivotal role of Dr. Theodore Kuza. This was McKellen's American film debut; he was just coming off his award-winning triumph playing Antonio Salieri in the Broadway production of Peter Shaffer's *Amadeus.* In the play, McKellen had to portray an old and crippled man who, before the audience's eyes, is transformed into a healthy, vital, younger man, before returning at play's end to his former old and crippled state. To stretch his acting range for his American film debut, McKellen took on the demanding role of an old and crippled man who, before the audience's eyes, is transformed into a healthy, vital, younger man before returning at film's end to his former old and crippled state. McKellen—who, for the record, is one of the four or five finest actors alive—was a bit too histrionic here, playing Kuza as if he wanted to make sure ticket buyers in the loge seats would be able to read his every expression. The performance is far from an embarrassment—McKellen is incapable of giving a bad performance—but it lacks the subtlety and richness he has since brought to his subsequent roles, particularly his excellent portrayal of Gandalf in Peter Jackson's magnificent *Lord Of The Rings* trilogy.

Michael Mann has since gone on to prove himself a great director, with films such as *Manhunter, The Last of the Mohicans, Heat, The Insider,* and *Ali.* He is arguably the successor to John Frankenheimer, and I maintain to this day that a Stephen King novel adapted and directed by Michael Mann would be a wonder to behold.

Before moving on to the next section, I want to offer a short list of other movies that, though not marketed as horror films, nonetheless fall easily into the category and should be required viewing for any serious student of the field. Don't be surprised if you haven't heard of most of them, just know that they are all available on either VHS or DVD, so you don't have much of an excuse not to seek out at least one of them.

The Offense: This 1973 film, directed by Sidney (*Network, The Hill, Dog Day Afternoon)* Lumet and written by John (*Murder by Decree*) Hopkins (based on his stage play *This Story of Yours)*, is one of the most nerve-wracking and emotionally devastating studies of moral and psychological deterioration ever filmed. Sean Connery, in hands-down the most intense, multi-layered, and moving performance of his career, stars as Detective Sergeant Johnson, a bitter, angry, hard-drinking London Police Force detective whose tenuous grip on sanity is finally pushed past the breaking point during his interrogation of a suspected child molester (the late Ian Bannen, who matches Connery every step of the way in an equally powerful performance). Decades of dealing with rapes, murders, beatings, and other serious crimes he's had to investigate have left a terrible mark on Johnson's psyche. His rage and disgust have been suppressed for far too long, and during the course of the interrogation he reveals that the state of his own mind is just as bad, if not worse, than that of the suspected child molester's.

The Offense does not unfold in a traditional linear fashion; there are flashbacks, flash-forwards, and scenes that appear as brief fragments reflecting the crumbling state of Johnson's mind. (I firmly believe that writer/director Christopher Nolan had to have found at least part of the inspiration for *Memento*'s structure from watching this film.) The sequence where Johnson breaks down in front of his wife and delivers a shattering, stream-of-consciousness monologue (wherein he begins mixing up the specifics of various cases until they all become one massive, bloody pile of bodies) was and remains Connery's finest moment on the screen. The entire cast is first rate, Lumet's direction is tense and claustrophobic, and Hopkins' brittle, literate dialogue is some of the best you'll ever encounter. When anyone asks me to name the five most terrifying movies I've ever seen, *The Offense* is always one of them.

The Tenant: Based on the superb novel by Roland Topor, this 1976 film remains one of Roman Polanski's most personal movies. Aside from directing, Polanski (*Chinatown, Rosemary's Baby, The Pianist*) also co-wrote the script and stars as Trelkovsky, a bookish clerk who comes into possession of an apartment whose previous tenant, a woman, committed suicide. As an ever-increasing series of bizarre events sends Trelkovsky into a downward spiral of sleeplessness and paranoia, he begins suspecting that his landlord and neighbors are trying to turn him into the previous tenant so he, too, will commit suicide.

Polanski offers a subtle and sly performance as Trelkovsky and is given solid support from Melvin Douglas, Shelley Winters, and the luminous Isabelle Adjani, whose sexy, shaded, off-putting portrayal of

Stella (the parallels to *A Streetcar Named Desire* are deliberate) make her one of the most fascinating female characters ever to appear in a Polanski film.

The rich, deep-focus, brooding photography by Sven Nykvist (*Fanny and Alexander, Crimes and Misdemeanors, Chaplin*) is a real asset, employing negative space to great advantage, especially during the second half of the film when Trelkovsky's already too-insular world begins shrinking even further.

The only shortcomings in this otherwise excellent film are some ill-advised dubbing by American actors of the French cast's voices (not all the French actors were dubbed, which creates at times an annoying inconsistency), and a tendency in Polanski's and Gérard (*Dario Argento's The Phantom of the Opera*) Brach's script to, in places, make literal those elements of Topor's novel that should have been left unexplained. But even these problems do not fatally detract from one's enjoyment and appreciation of this tense, haunting film, one whose closing sequence ranks just below that of *Seconds* in its power to shock and terrify.

Child's Play: Not the 1988 Tom Holland movie that shoved Chucky, The Doll From Hell, up our noses and down our throats, but the 1972 Sidney Lumet film based on the stage play by Robert Marasco (*Burnt Offerings*). Child's Play—one of the best stage-to-screen translations made during the 70s—tells the story of a new gymnastics instructor (Beau Bridges) at an exclusive boy's prep school who's drawn into a feud between two of the older instructors and soon discovers that things at the school are not as staid, tranquil, and harmless as they seem.

The instructors are played by James Mason and Robert Preston, both cast effectively against type: Mason, usually the strong and confident intellectual, is an open nerve, a man whose grip on his self-respect and faith in his fellow human beings is being systematically chipped to pieces, causing him to question not only his worth as a teacher, but his sanity; Preston (the one and only Prof. Harold Hill of *The Music Man*), typically the boisterous, good-natured, fast-talking rascal you can't help but like, here is as eerie and intensely low-key a psychotic as filmgoers had met until the appearance of Hannibal Lecter early in the next decade.

Drenched in quiet dread and oppressive atmosphere, *Child's Play* also boasts a memorably creepy ending that culminates in a final, understated, chilling image whose unapologetically dramatic presentation only serves to empower rather than detract from the film's lasting effect.

Okay, time for a quick recap:

If you're doing research and want to know what it feels like to be shot, stabbed, beaten up, not invited to many parties, and generally have most people cross to the other side of the street when they spot you coming their way, then I'm your guy.

If you're hoping for one last non sequitur personal tidbit to close this section, here it is: I worked for a short time as a clown for children's birthday parties. Hand to God, I did. My professional name was Rags. I wanted to call myself Scuzzo the Marginally Humorous or The Banal Mr. Wiggles, but was worried folks might get the wrong idea about the nature of my show.

If you're looking for horror movies that fall well outside the often short-sighted boundaries of the popular definition of the field, then here's a roll-call of the movies I've been attempting to foist on you:

Bring Me the Head of Alfredo Garcia; 1974, directed by Sam Peckinpah
Child's Play; 1972, directed by Sidney Lumet
The Field; 1990, directed by Jim Sheridan
Little Murders; 1971, directed by Alan Arkin
The Offense (a.k.a. *The Truth Or Something Like It*); 1973, directed by Sidney Lumet
Seconds; 1966, directed by John Frankenheimer
Sorcerer; 1977, directed by William Friedkin
Straw Dogs; 1970, directed by Sam Peckinpah
The Swimmer; 1966, directed by Frank Perry
The Tenant; 1976, directed by Roman Polanski

Onward . . .

Second Intermission:
A Matter of Life or Death

THERE'S A DARK SIDE TO PROFESSIONAL WRITING THAT FEW people have dared address. I'm talking about the single most dangerous foe to the writer's resolve, the thing that can stop even the most dedicated wordsmith dead in his or her tracks, an element of the publishing business that renders all of us absolutely powerless when faced with it.

No, it isn't the dreaded book signing that finds you sitting at a table for ninety minutes, during which time the only person to approach you and the unsold stacks of your new book is someone asking for directions to the bathroom. It isn't having someone discover you're a horror writer and asking (almost as if compelled to do so by a congressional Decree): "So, do you know Stephen King?" And, no, it isn't that utterly radiant, mettle-testing moment when you open that first royalty statement to discover that your book has, in the course of one year, sold only one-third of its print run so obtaining that more pricey loaf of bread is going to have to be put on the back burner once again. Yes, all of these can test you, no doubt; they can chip away at your confidence if you let them, and they can make you a real buzz-kill who doesn't get invited to many parties, but I'm not here to discuss my dreadful personality problems.

No; the single biggest foe to the writer's resolve, confidence, and determination is (insert ominous chord here): the Horror of the Used Book Store.

We all shop at them. We're writers, for pity's sake. Our major source of income is our writing, so none of us can afford to shell out thirty bucks for each new hardcover or eight bucks for each new paperback on a consistent basis. We go there to find a bargain, or perhaps to locate a book that's been hard to find or out of print for several years. While we're doing this, we remind ourselves that the First Sale Doctrine, codified in Section 109 of The US Copyright Act, allows the original owner of any book to transfer ownership of the physical copy in any way they choose, so, technically, there's nothing legally or morally wrong with our purchasing any books here.

Besides (we tell ourselves), stores like this make books affordable to folks who otherwise wouldn't have the money to buy them. So it's all good . . . until we find ourselves face to face with copies of *our own books.*

Don't shake your head at me; if you've ever published with a mass market house, odds are you've found yourself in this situation. And what is the writer's first reaction? *But, my work is* eternal, *it speaks to the deepest pain of the human condition; my books are to be* treasured, *to be passed down from generation to generation, not end up here!*

The first time I discovered copies of my novel *In Silent Graves* on the shelf at a used book store, I felt a slight twinge of disappointment—who wouldn't? We all hope that our books will be things that readers will want to keep around to read again someday, but here we are, faced with the bald hard truth that not everyone who buys and reads our books is going to want to keep them. I at least had the pleasure of knowing that the three copies I found on the shelf had been well-read, as evidenced by the wear on, and cracks in, the spines.

A while back, I was in another used book store with a friend of mine who also happened to be a writer, and he pointed out to me that another copy of *Graves* was on the shelf. I was really into this by then, I'd adopted a *healthy* attitude, and I wanted to see how well-read the copy was, enjoy the sight of those cracks in the spine, hold it in my hands knowing that whoever had owned it before read the living shit out of it before selling it here.

Well, guess what? (Here's the moment that really tests the mettle.)

It hadn't been read. It hadn't even been opened, as far as I could tell. It still had the Walpurgis-Mart sticker covering the bar code on the back.

"What is it?" asked my writer friend.

"This hasn't even been read," I whispered.

"You don't know that," he replied. "Maybe the person who sold this is an anal-retentive basketcase like you; they take care not to damage the spine when they read a paperback. Maybe they're just very careful with their books."

"And maybe they just didn't read it." (Outwardly, I'm doing the Healthy Attitude Shuffle; I'm very calm and cool and collected. Inwardly, I'm jumping up and down and throwing a fit and threatening to hold my breath until my face turns blue.)

"Okay," my writer friend said, "then you gotta tell yourself that there was some earth-shaking emergency that *forced* them to sell this book. They lost a job. They lost a limb. Their workman's comp ran out. *They had to do it to put food on the table for their family, man! You know they had to do it to put food on the table! Dear God, why* else *would they part with one of your books? IT WAS A MATTER OF LIFE OR DEATH!*"

"So what you're telling me in your own subtle way is that I'm overreacting?"

"God, no! You're a *hero*, Gary, a lifesaver!" He threw his arm around my shoulder and began talking very loudly, attracting the attention of anyone within fifteen feet of us. "Because of you and your book, somewhere in this city tonight, a man's family is *not* going to go to bed hungry. They can afford Grandma's medication for another month. Little Charlotte can get that knee surgery so that her dreams of the Bolshoi Ballet needn't be forever buried, thus turning her into a bitter, heartbroken, empty shell of a human being before she turns thirteen! And it's all because of *this* book on this shelf. I . . . I . . . I'm sorry, I'm . . . I'm getting emotional, tearing up, verklempt, even. So moving, it is. I so rarely get to witness acts of decency and heroism. It reaffirms my faith in humanity. We must all hold hands," he cried out to the terror-stricken customers. "Indeed, we must *all* hold hands and sing out our joy at being here to mark this resplendent moment in human history. Come, sing with me, all of you: '*WHEN YOU WALK THROUGH A STORM, KEEP YOUR HEAD HELD HIGH, AND DON´T BE AFRAID OF—*'"

"So what you're telling me in your own subtle way is that I'm overreacting?"

"Nah. They probably got through the first twenty pages and decided it was too much of a downer. You gotta admit, this thing ain't gonna make *anybody's* list of My Top Ten Favorite Chuckle-fests."

"I feel so much better now, thanks."

"Hey, take your pick: they did it to put food on the table, or they did it because they thought your book sucked the dimples off a golf ball through forty feet of clogged garden hose."

We're writers. We exist because of fantasy and delusion and our ability to convey them on the page. And when you have to rely on your writing as your major source of income, any delusion helps, especially if you *know* it's a delusion.

So I helped a stranger put food on the table for his family. I feel good about myself.

Hey, I'm a writer. Delusion is my business.

Part Two:
Proud Words On Dusty Shelves

"Persons attempting to find a plot will be banished.
Persons attempting to find a moral will be shot."
–Mark Twain

Statistics; Subtext; and Why Horror Will Never Be Considered Serious Lit-rah-chure, No Matter How Much We Stamp Our Feet and Threaten to Hold Our Breath Until Our Faces Turn Blue and We Pass Out From Lack of Oxygen, Which, If We'd Been Using it Properly in the First Place, Would Have Gone to Our Brains and Made Us Realize that We Need to Make Our Writing More Than Merely Competent, Only Now We're All Passed Out on the Floor and Have Wet Ourselves and Little Kids Are Sticking Uncomfortable Things Up Our Noses and Who's Going to Take Us Seriously After That?

I REALIZE THAT THE UNCLEAR NATURE OF THE ABOVE TITLE might be a little bewildering, and for that I apologize, but if you'll just stick with me, I promise you I'll do everything I can to clear up the confusion and make this section's schema a bit less nebulous.

Here's a real interesting pair of statistics for you to mull over before we get any farther along:

In 1978, according to study done by the University of California at Berkley, only 9 percent of this country's then 200,000,000-plus population bought books; of that 9 percent, only 2 percent bought more than a single book a year, and the other 7 percent bought only the flavor-of-the-month popular bestseller.

In 2000, this same study was conducted again, and on the surface the results seemed more optimistic: that 9 percent from 1978 had risen to a whopping 11 percent, and the 2 percent who bought more than one book a year had risen to 5 percent. Looks good at first, until you consider one itsy-bitsy teeny-weeny little fact: the population of this country in 2000 was nearing 300,000,000.

Grab a calculator and do some quick math; g'head, I can wait.

Uh. Huh.

Factoring in the rise in population, you have just discovered that not only have the stats from 1978 *not* improved, they have actually worsened by a margin of something like seven-tenths of 1 percent. Which means that the other 6 percent of that 11 percent are still buying, as their sole literary indulgence each year, the latest Grisham, Collins, or current self-help-trend manifesto typed out (notice I didn't say "written by") whichever self-proclaimed expert the vapid, glassy-eyed hosts of daytime television talk shows are told by their focus groups will nab the biggest audience.

Excuse me while I go whip up a Bailey's and Drano® cocktail.

Yeah, I'm overstating things just a smidgen (but only just) in order to make a point: horror fiction is still the deformed drooling bastard child who picks at its scabs and who Literature keeps locked up in the cellar when company drops by, but for all our complaining about its being the last "ghetto" of fiction, has anyone given serious thought to the single greatest reason why?

I refer you back to the subtle and evenhanded title of this section.

Horror will never be taken seriously by a majority of readers or the so-called academicians who would have you believe that unless you can savor the metaphoric layers and protests against the restraints of language throughout something like Joyce's *Ulysses* or marvel at Tolstoy's groundbreaking use of the verb "to be," then you're Missing The Whole Point of Reading. None of them—readers, teachers, scholars, your sweet Aunt Eunice, *nobody*—is going to let horror out of the basement until horror writers do one simple thing: stop being, at best, merely competent.

. . . he said with some truly loopy syntax, thus nearly defeating his own point.

Ahem.

No, I am not claiming the right to pontificate from some higher ground because my own writing is so without flaw that I can say, "Listen to me because I and I alone am correct." God knows my own work has more than its share of problems: my attempts to consciously create atmosphere are sometimes laughably bad, my aversion to having so-called villains in my fiction creates grey areas that alienate many readers, and you can count on one hand the number of simple sentences found in any single story of mine—my tendency is to use the longer, sometimes circular, always complex breed of sentence because it enables me to establish both tone and rhythm . . . and sometimes indulge it a little too long; case in point: this sentence you just read.

Understand that everything that follows is prefaced by these unwritten words: In my opinion.

All clear? Good.

Onward.

Many horror writers cry that it's the Curse of Categorization that keeps horror trapped in the literary cellar, and readily point to the publishers on whom they are all too willing to lay blame. Here's a Muppet News Flash: it isn't only publishers who categorize our fiction; it's also the readers, the editors, and even (sometimes especially) the writers. No one here is blameless, regardless of how much chest-thumping and eloquent self-serving grandstanding is done to prove the contrary. There is a market for horror, so there exists a genre label for horror, because there are writers of horror who want to sell their work to horror publishers in order to reach the horror-reading market. (Can you say "Ouroboros Syndrome"? Good, I knew you could.)

All this brouhaha over labeling and categorization is just a rubber sword wielded by writers of limited talent and imagination to make themselves and their work seem more polished and important than either really is. With a handful of exceptions—Harlan Ellison, Dan Simmons, and Peter Straub, to name three—I find those who bitch the loudest about their fiction being categorized are usually those whose work is the most limited in its vision, scope, execution, and expertise. They aren't getting a wider audience because their work doesn't *deserve* a wider audience . . . and in some cases doesn't even deserve the limited one it already has.

All of which is a smokescreen, because nowhere in this self-manufactured "controversy" is there directly addressed the question of quality in the field, of which there remains a noticeable lack.

Face it; the majority of horror published during the standards-free *tsunami* of the 1980s was worthless. I it lacked depth; it lacked thoughtful characterization; it lacked even a nodding acquaintance with the concept of "theme," let alone an ability to have its plot stick to the ground rules established in the story—if, indeed, the effort to establish same had even been made. It seemed that any idiot with access to a typewriter (who'd also read all of Stephen King's books and seen every *Friday the Thirteenth* and *Nightmare on Elm Street* movie) decided that, in order to become a published horror writer, all you needed to do was take a graphic description of a day's work at the local slaughterhouse, set it in a remote town, throw in a couple of sex scenes, add some dialogue here and there to give the impression something worthwhile is actually happening, then slap it all together as thinly-veiled *homage* to Freddy or Jason or that chick who vomits pea soup in *The Exorcist* and—*voila!*—you have a saleable horror novel.

And here's the thing: it worked. That *was* all you had to do in order to sell a horror novel in the 80s. (Slightly overstating again to make the point—but only slightly.)

Where'd I set that Bailey's and Drano® cocktail?

Many lament that we are still paying for the cornucopia of conscienceless crap that littered bookshelves back then, and they're right, we are. We're still paying for it because we *should* still be paying for it. The majority of horror in the 80s was a supreme embarrassment to the holy craft of storytelling; there was no excuse for it then, and there's even less of an excuse for it now, three decades later, when the field is finally enjoying the start of a resurgence in popularity. Unfortunately, many of the new breed of horror writers cut their literary teeth on that cornucopia of conscienceless crap for which we're still doing penance, and despite their potential, enthusiasm, or varying levels of skill, you cannot build a literary foundation on the influence of that which the field is trying to overcome.

A well-respected and excellent writer I know who used to write horror under a pseudonym during the 80s once said the following to me: "I did it because it was decent money, it didn't take long, and I sure as hell didn't have to worry about whether or not the book had any kind of *value*; people just wanted a lot of violence as soon as possible, not too much thinking, and as much shock value as I could deliver in 300 pages. It was nothing more than bloody junk food. I never blew a brain cell on it."

To this writer's credit, the novels written under the pseudonym were much better than their above words would lead you to think; in fact, they were some of the better horror novels being produced at the time. That might seem to denote that horror wasn't as bad as

I've made it out to be; the more likely subtext is that this writer had personal standards that so far surpassed those of the field that even their "bloody junk food" writing outshone everything around it.

Nothing that I have said up to this point has been said while wearing my writer's cap; I am in full reader mode for this central section, and if my tone comes off as arrogant or know-it-all, there is what I feel to be a pretty good reason: I am a merciless reader. I have zero tolerance for sloppy, uninspired, hollow-cored storytelling, pedestrian prose, or characters whose sole purpose is to wander onstage, do something stupid, and then be graphically slurped by the glop. I may occasionally slip on my writer's cap for an aside here and there, but the bitchy guy you're dealing with now is Gary the reader.

Let me tell you *why* I rank among the most unforgiving of readers:

I read *very* slowly.

Where most people I know ripped through Stephen King's marvelous *The Girl who Loved Tom Gordon* in three hours, it took me three days. The upside to this—and what makes me a sloppy writer's worst nightmare—is that, because I read so slowly, I notice more detail than most people and have a greater awareness of the micro-writing. Not a bad thing at all.

The downside is that I can't read as many books in the course of a week or month as I would like to. I envy people who read two, three, four books a week. I wish I could devour literature the same way, but I can't.

When I was in the second grade at St. Francis de Sales School in Newark, Ohio, our English teacher, Sister Mary Elizabeth, required that we read aloud on Mondays and Fridays. Coming from a hardcore blue-collar background, reading was not something that was encouraged in the Braunbeck household. Not that my parents *dis*couraged it, but because both of them worked long hours at hellish factory jobs, they were either too tired or too busy with things like bills and home repairs to find time to read much. Neither of them completed high school, and neither of them ran in social circles where "intellectual" pursuits such as reading were the norm.

No, I'm not blaming them; far from it. Mom would always buy me a book if I found one I wanted, and Dad was more than happy to read to or with me. (Aside: Mom was a big Mickey Spillane fan, and read his books whenever she could, but the only two books I ever saw her re-read were Blatty's *The Exorcist* and F. Paul Wilson's *The Keep*, which she thought was "one of the best books I've ever read. I hope he writes another one.")

Okay, so I'm sitting there in English class one Friday, and we're taking turns reading paragraphs from some book—I wish to hell I could remember its name—about this kid named Johnny who works odd jobs so he can earn money to go to the movies because he likes to imagine that he's the cowboy hero or brave fighter pilot or smart detective.

Gets to be my turn, and I'm reading along—slower than the other kids, but smoothly, nonetheless—when I encounter a word I'd often heard but had never actually seen in print before: "aisle."

I stopped, stared at the word, and tried to figure out how to pronounce it.

Sister Mary Elizabeth made quite a show out of my inability to read this word aloud, so finally, embarrassed beyond belief, I gave it a try.

What I said was something akin to "A-sell."

Everyone laughed. Sister Mary Elizabeth told me to try it again.

A-sell. Again.

I couldn't figure out any other way to pronounce it.

Sister then pulled several other books from the shelf and opened them to selected pages, thrust them under my nose, and ordered me to read about twenty-five different words at her random choosing, all of which I'd *heard*, none of which I had ever seen in print before, among them "redundant," "envelope," "digestion," "automatic," and—my personal favorite to this day—"repetitive."

I missed every last one of them.

And everyone got a dandy guffaw out of that.

Most of the kids who attended St. Francis came from fairly well-to-do families, families who financially contributed heavily to both the church and school, who held positions on the school board or church board, and who got to wear dresses and ties to their jobs and sit behind desks.

I was one of a small handful of kids who came from, well, not-so-well-to-do families, and there was a marked difference in the way we were treated—both by our fellow students and many of the teachers.

If one of the rich students was having difficulties, well, then, hire a tutor, arrange for special sessions with teachers after school, cut them as much slack as possible.

But if one of the poorer students was having trouble . . . tough shit. Their families were barely making the quarterly tuition payments, so it wasn't worth anyone's time to give them any extra help.

Three days a week, I was provided with a free lunch because my parents couldn't afford to pay for an entire week's worth. Somehow, Sister Mary Elizabeth managed to work that into her scolding of me in front of the class that day, as well as several observations about the limited selections available to me for my wardrobe.

"Go sit out in the hall, you're holding everyone else back, you dumb-bunny."

Dumb-bunny. Never forgot that one, either.

So I went out into the hall and sat there.

Which is how I came to find myself transferred to the "special" English class the following Monday.

Here is what the "special" English class consisted of:

Some assistant coach (or Darrell Sheets, the marvelous, kind man who was the school's janitor) sat at a table in the cafeteria while the rest of us—there were five—were seated at another table. On this table was a stack of children's books. Twenty of them, in fact. I remember this because these books never changed. Ever.

These were books written for children at the kindergarten/first grade level.

This is Dick. This is his sister, Jane. Dick and Jane are playing with their dog, Spot. "Run, Spot, run!" See Spot run. Run, Spot, run.

Goddamn page-turners were these books.

From grade two until grade five, that is how I spent my English classes; down in the cafeteria, sitting at a table with four other "special" students, reading the same twenty books over and over. (We were not allowed to bring our own books; we had to read only those that were deemed to be "within" our "ranges of comprehension." At least at the beginning of every year they gave us twenty different books from the year before. Our big exam was to read two of them aloud at the end of the year.)

As a result of this and the lack of reading time/assistance at home, I read at a first-grade level until the sixth grade. Even then, I was way behind the other kids. (The "special" program had been 86'd at the end of my fifth grade year because they could no longer find anyone to babysit us.)

I somehow managed to bluff my way through sixth grade English—I squeaked by with a C—but even that summer, I found that I was still having trouble reading books that, by all accounts, I should have been able to breeze through four years before.

I was given a reading comprehension test at the start of my seventh grade year.

I was reading at a third-grade level . . . and just barely, at that.

But I got lucky. My English teacher that year was a terrific guy named David Kessler who had been made aware of my "learning disability" and who, even though he wasn't allowed to give me any extra help either in or outside of class, did provide me with books designed to help me read better. I guarded these books as if they were my life savings. Whenever either of them could, Mom and Dad helped me, or one of the neighbors if I offered to cut their grass. But mostly I had to do it on my own.

By the time I left the Catholic school system at the end of my eighth grade year, I was reading at the fifth-grade level.

For me, it was a personal triumph.

I haven't bothered getting myself tested in decades, because whatever level I'm reading at right now is the level I will read at until I take the Dirt Nap.

But there remain times . . .

There were several sections in Dan Simmons' brilliant *The Hollow Man* that I had to re-read more than once before fully understanding what I was reading. As much as I admire and enjoy the work of Joe Haldeman, Harlan Ellison, Joyce Carol Oates, and Gene Wolfe, there are times while reading them that I feel genuinely stupid, as if I'm standing there in front of Sister and the class trying to decipher "aisle" once again.

It took me three days to read a short novel that most people read in three hours.

To this day, I remain angry about that.

To this day, I still have trouble reading at times, and always will, and that has caused some measure of enjoyment to be subtracted from my life, and that saddens me whenever I think about it for too long.

Because the ability to read is one of the most precious gifts we possess, and few things piss me off more than to meet someone who has the ability to read—odds are, at a level higher and faster than myself—who chooses not to because reading is "boring" or "a waste of time."

One of those few things that *does* piss me off more is to have my time, trust, and skill as a reader taken for granted by sloppy writers who think that "bloody junk food" is the best they need strive toward, and as a result waste my time, insult my intelligence, and needlessly slaughter acres of trees whose continued existence the rest of us could use to help us breathe easier.

Okay, I can go on tossing out generalities until we're all lulled into a coma. It's time to get specific.

Instead of citing dozens of examples of bad writing in horror, I'm going to illustrate what I find to be right with the current state of horror fiction by examining one short story that encapsulates the absolute best craftsmanship to be found in the field when the writer is willing to take chances.

I'm kind of a snob when it comes to fiction—horror or otherwise—and don't mind admitting it. This gets me into a lot of trouble when it comes to reading for pleasure, something I have less and less time for these days. I often make the mistake of applying (sometimes consciously, mostly not) my own storytelling standards to the work of those I read, and that's just silly (as well as being a habit I am fighting to break); if everyone wrote the same kind of stuff I do, and wrote it the same *way* I do, variety would be the stuff of fairy tales. And everyone would be depressed and grumpy all the time.

But every once in a while I start to ask questions about the fiction being produced in the horror field, simply because I'm still stubborn enough to want to see the field expand beyond its popular definition.

Take, for instance, a certain type of story, one that I have come to call the After-the-Fact story. I have not seen many After-the-Fact stories written in the horror genre; mostly, they've stayed in the neighborhood of you-should-pardon-the-expression literary fiction. So, why haven't we seen more of this type of story in horror?

After-the-Fact stories are tricky little bastards because the main action of the story has already happened *before* the first sentence.

After-the-Fact stories do not employ flashback, nor do they resort to the obvious mechanism of having a character offer a quick recap of what happened before the reader came into it. No, in these stories, you're presented with a situation that, nine times out of ten, is in no way connected to what actually happened; you have to piece together the events by what is said and done by the characters. They're a little like walking into a room just after someone's had an argument or gotten a piece of bad news; even though you know something's just happened, no one will tell you what it was, so you have to figure it out for yourself by observing the effect it's had on those around you. You have to pay attention to the detritus, because that's all you've got to go on.

A classic example is John Cheever's story "The Swimmer." (Yes, *The Swimmer* again. I return to this incredible piece of work in the hope it will motivate you to track it down and read it, along with Cheever's other stories.)

Repeat after me: on the surface, it's about nothing more than some rich guy in suburbia who's spending a Sunday afternoon running from neighbor's house to neighbor's house to use their swimming pools. "I'm swimming my way home," he tells his friends and neighbors, all of whom laugh and remark on what a card he is as they go about mixing their martinis and discussing events at the country club. Occasionally someone remarks, in passing. "He's looking better, don't you think . . ." or "I'm really surprised to see him out like this, after, well . . ." Then the main character comes over to them and that line of conversation is dropped. This goes on for a while, each successive neighbor becoming more surprised and anxious at seeing him, offering more whispered comments when he's out of earshot—"didn't realize he was back . . ." etc.—until it becomes obvious that something fairly awful has happened to this guy sometime before the story began, and though Cheever never once directly states what happened, everything you need to know is there.

The first time I read "The Swimmer," its sudden shocker of an ending seemed to come out of left field, so I went back and re-read the story, much more slowly than the first time, and realized that Cheever had, indeed, dropped a ton of clues. Unfortunately, the majority of them were hidden in the detritus, given only through subtext.

Raymond Chandler (creator of Philip Marlowe, the hero of such classic novels as *The Big Sleep* and *The Little Sister*) once gave the best example of what constitutes subtext that I've ever encountered (and I am liberally paraphrasing here):

> A man and woman, both middle-aged, are waiting for an elevator. It arrives, and the man helps the woman get on. For the first several floors they are alone, watching the blinking lights. They do not speak and stand well apart from each other. The woman wears a very nice dress. The man wears a suit, tie, and hat. The elevator stops—not their floor—and a young woman gets on; she smiles at both the man and the woman, who smile at her in return. The man removes his hat. The ride continues in silence. The elevator stops, the girls gets off, the man puts his hat back on. A few floors later, the man and woman get off and walk together toward a door at the end of the corridor.

It was usually at this point that Chandler would ask the listener: "What's written on that door?"

So I'll put the question to you: what words are written on that door that our middle-aged couple is heading toward?

How the hell am I supposed to know? some of you may cry. No one in that freakin' elevator said *word one* to anyone else, and on the basis of all the *nothing* that happened during that boring, boring, *boring* ride, I'm supposed to guess what it says on that stupid door?

Yes, you are.

Because an awful lot happened during that elevator ride: A) the man and woman never spoke to each other, even while they were alone; B) they also made it a point to stand well apart from each other, even though the man helped her get on; C) when the young woman got on, the man, obviously out of respect and courtesy, removed his hat; D) once the young woman disembarked, he put the hat back on; and, E) the man and woman got off on the same floor, and are heading toward that door together.

Still say nothing happened and that you have no clues to go on?

Detritus. Subtext. The unspoken information that is conveyed to a reader through a character's behavior, actions, speech, or lack thereof. In acting, it's referred to as nuance. It's subtle, but its implications are quite direct if you care enough to pay attention.

That is, in my opinion, what the horror field has lost over the last few decades: a willingness on the part of both writers and readers to (respectively) employ and appreciate the quieter, more delicate, and less obvious details of character and scene that can make fiction so much richer and rewarding.

Last chance: take a guess what it says on that door.

Try: *Marriage Counselor.*

That was an After-the-Fact story. Tricky little bastard, wasn't it?

There's usually very little action in these stories; nothing much seems to happen at the core—it's what's on the periphery that you have to watch out for yourself.

A handful of other After-the-Fact stories you'd do well to search out and read include Ernest Hemingway's "A Clean, Well-Lighted Place"; Eudora Welty's "A Worn Path"; Raymond Carver's "What Do You Do in San Francisco?" "Popular Mechanics," and "Why, Honey?" (these latter two being arguably horror stories); Carson McCullers' "A Tree, A Rock, A Cloud"; Michael Chabon's "House Hunting"; John O'Hara's brilliant "Neighbors" (a horror story if ever there was one); and a personal favorite of mine, Russell Banks' "Captions"—perhaps in its way the most extreme After-the-Fact story I've yet encountered—wherein Banks details the agonizing disintegration of a married couple's existence through captions taken from newspapers or written underneath pictures in photo albums.

You've undoubtedly noticed that the above list contains no horror writers. There is a reason for this: not many have attempted an After-the-Fact story. Maybe it's because the structure of this type of story seems too self-consciously "literary" to them; maybe it's because horror readers have become far too accustomed to having everything spoon-fed to them and don't think they should have to work a little while reading a story, and so horror writers just automatically assume that All Must Be Revealed as quickly and in as simplistic of terms as possible. I don't know; I'm guessing here. But I've been going through my books, searching for at least six examples of a successful After-the-Fact story in the horror field, and here's what I came up with:

"Sitting in the Corner, Whimpering Quietly," by Dennis Etchison
"Petey," by T.E.D. Klein

"Red," by Richard Christian Matheson
"Snow Day," by Elizabeth Massie
"Taking Down the Tree," by Steve Rasnic Tem
"The Geezers," by Peter Straub

And that was nearly it (even with this small a list, Klein's, Matheson's, and Tem's stories almost offered too many concrete hints to qualify).

I thought perhaps more Peter Straub—"Bar Talk," "The Veteran," or "A Short Guide to the City" (all from his magnificent collection *Houses Without Doors*)—could be used to beef up the list, but that would have been stacking the deck (pardon my mixed metaphors). Straub's work is the result of an exceptionally well-read literary background, so of course the sensibilities of his work are informed from countless sources, resulting in fiction that is challenging in its approach to structure and subtext—no more so than in the "Interlude" fictions sprinkled throughout *Houses*.

So no additional Straub; it wouldn't be playing fair on my part. Same goes for Stewart O'Nan, whose wonderful collection *In The Walled City* contains not one, but two After-the-Fact stories: "Calling" and "Finding Amy." (I exclude O'Nan because, though he does sometimes dabble in the horror field, he is not primarily considered a horror writer.)

So I came up with six stories, four of which (though superb) just barely made it onto the list. I'm sure there are other After-the-Fact horror stories out there that I missed, but my guess is, not that many.

Okay, there are two more, but I'm saving them for a few more paragraphs. Sneaky little bastard, aren't I?

Horror may be trying to outgrow its popular definition, but it's still suffering from a case of arrested literary adolescence—and I'm not one who apologizes for using the term "literary" when talking about horror. It can be among our most literary forms of storytelling, emphasis on *can be*. We still need to take chances, even if we fall flat on our faces in the attempt.

Now I want discuss these two stories, one of which I am going to break down piece by piece so you can see how it was done. The other is for you to read and solve on your own. After all, what good is it to show you how to solve a puzzle if you're not then presented with another?

The first story is "Gone," by one the field's leading practitioners, Jack Ketchum. It can be found in his short story collection *Peaceable Kingdom*.

"Gone" was the recipient of the 2000 Bram Stoker Award for short story, and rarely have I outright cheered such news as I did that announcement. Make certain you've read it before continuing, because what follows is going to include so-called spoilers. Don't say I didn't warn you.

I'll state for the record that I am a great admirer of Jack Ketchum's work (one of the stories in my upcoming collection, *Destinations Unknown,* is even dedicated to him); I am not, however, a fan. If you don't understand the difference, then you've just been skimming, and shame on you. Me works hard to be entertaining and illuminating.

I've never met Jack Ketchum. I've been at conventions that he has also attended, but have never been introduced. I only know him as, A) a writer, and, B) a mid-sized, lean fellow who looks like the less-stable twin Willem Dafoe keeps chained up in the family cellar. Everyone I know who's met him says that he's a terrific guy, and I do not doubt this; I am not here to discuss him as a person, but as a storyteller.

(Sidebar: I have since met Jack several times at various conventions, and he *is* one of the sweetest human beings you could hope to cross paths with. Funny as hell and courteous almost to a fault. If you ever chance to meet him, beware: his bear hugs can crack your spine.)

Ketchum's work never fails to solicit a strong reaction from me. (The worst thing anyone can say about a writer's work is that it left them feeling indifferent. You can't say that about Ketchum's work, and bravo to him for that.) The best of his work is literate, stylish, oft-times feverish in its emotional intensity, and unflinchingly brutal in its depiction of the violence we either inflict on one another or, through inaction, allow to be inflicted upon others. Nowhere is this sentiment more beautifully expressed than in the closing passages on his introduction to *Peaceable Kingdom*: "And that, finally, is my wish for us all, concealed or obvious somewhere in each of these stories—*they shall not hurt or destroy*."

How the hell could I *not* admire the work of a fellow writer whose core agenda is so close to my own heart? Ketchum's overall body of work functions at extremes: from the visceral, no-holds-barred horror of novels such as *The Girl Next Door* and stories such as "The Passenger" to more gentle but no less affecting works such as *Red* and "Mother and Daughter." (*Red* was later turned into an excellent motion picture, featuring a powerhouse performance by Brian Cox and a fitting cameo for Ketchum, who is undeniably as charismatic on film as he is in person.)

"Gone" remains for me one of the most elegant, chilling, and genuinely disturbing he's written.

In it we meet Helen Teal, nee Mazik, a divorced woman whose house has, for the past five years, been shunned by the neighborhood children on Halloween. The other neighbors think of Helen as being a bit unstable, but if this is the case, she's got good reason: her three-year-old daughter was snatched from a parking lot five years before, sending Helen into a downward spiral of depression and drinking that drove away her husband and left her branded as that "lady down the block" by everyone.

This year, however, Helen has at last begun to get a handle on her depression, and has turned on the porch lights, stocked up on candy, and—as the story begins—is waiting for the first of the trick-or-treaters to come to the door:

> Seven-thirty and nobody at the door. No knock, no doorbell.
>
> What am I? The wicked old witch from Hansel and Gretel?
>
> The jack-o-lantern flickered out into the world from the window ledge, the jointed cardboard skeleton swayed dangling from the transom. Both there by way of invitation, which so far had been ignored. In a wooden salad bowl on the coffee table in front of her, bite-sized Milky Ways and Mars Bars and Nestle's Crunch winked at her reassuringly—crinkly gleaming foil-wrap and smooth shiny paper.
>
> Buy candy, and they will come.
>
> Don't worry, she thought. Someone'll show . . .

Already you can recognize the familiar, sure-handed use of cadence—one of Ketchum's stylistic signatures—easing you into the one-set, four-character narrative (and take note of the splendid imagery, particularly the way the candy bars "winked at her reassuringly." This is the Good Stuff.)

As Helen waits (and waits . . . and waits . . .) for the first of the trick-or-treaters to come knocking, she broods about the loss of her daughter and how she herself has "gone from pre-school teacher, homemaker, wife, and mother to the three *p's*—psychoanalysis, Prozac, and paralysis."

Almost ready to give up, Helen is preparing to make herself another strong drink when three children—dressed as, respectively, a witch, a werewolf, and an alien, all of whom identify themselves as brothers and sister and are *not* from the neighborhood—come to the door. Seeing them gives Helen hope:

> She felt a kind of weight lifted off her, sailing away through the clear night sky. If nobody else came by for the rest of the night that was fine too. Next year would be even better.

Having been frightened of so much as looking at another child in the years since her daughter's disappearance, Helen revels in the presence of these children, happy that she feels no sadness or regret from enjoying their brief company; a quietly moving sequence where the compassion of and for this character shines through.

Then, just as the children are readying to leave, one of them asks Helen something:

> "Excuse me?"
> "You're her?"
> "Who?"
> "The lady her lost her baby? The little girl?

Helen answers that she is, and the children apologize for having asked, wish her a happy Halloween, then turn and walk off the porch.

What follows the children's exit is one of the most well-crafted and well-executed sentences Ketchum ever wrote, one where the unspoken subtext starts as a paper cut and ends as a dagger in the gut:

> They turned away and headed slowly down the stairs and she almost asked them to wait, to stay a moment, for what reason and to what end she didn't know but that would be silly and awful too, no reason to put them through her pain, they were just kids, children, they were just asking a question the way children did sometimes, oblivious to its consequences and it would be wrong to say anything further, so she began to close the door and almost didn't hear him turn to his sister and say, *too bad they wouldn't let her out tonight, huh? too bad they never do* in a low voice but loud enough to register but at first it *didn't* register, not quite, as though the words held no meaning, as though the words were some strange rebus she could not immediately master, not until after she'd closed the door and then when finally they impacted her like grapeshot, she flung open the door and ran screaming down the stairs into the empty street.

Note how Ketchum once again uses the repetition of "and" to great advantage in the early portion of the sentence to build the tension, then switches to "but" to achieve the same effect, resulting in a passage where the two words are repeated with the panicked near-stutter of a crime victim trying to describe what just happened to them to a confused police officer.

Had Ketchum chosen to end the story with this powerful passage, the story would still rank as one of his best, but an argument could be made that the knife needed to be twisted, quickly, just once, to make sure Helen's pain is driven into the reader's core. The forty-four words that comprise the coda of "Gone" are not only well-chosen, but build upon the previous revelation, ending the story with a coda that is both chilling and heart-wrenching:

> She thought when she was able to think at all of what she might say to the police.
>
> Witch, werewolf, alien. Of this age and that height and weight.
>
> Out of nowhere, vanished back into nowhere.
>
> Carrying along what was left of her.
>
> Gone.

It rarely gets any better than that, folks. "Carrying along what was left of her. Gone."

Some writers would kill for an ending that concise and affecting.

Oddly enough, "Gone" is a story that many of the Ketchum fans I've spoken with like well enough in a lukewarm kind of way, but don't think of as being among his best. After much prodding, pushing, and pouting on my part, I've managed to get them to admit to me what it is about the story that leaves them shrugging.

At least one-third of the Ketchum fans I have spoken with are wary of "Gone" for one simple reason: they don't understand the ending. And I purport that if readers of this story are left scratching their heads after the last six paragraphs are read, it is not through any fault of Ketchum's. Everything you need to know is there, very clearly, done with amazing subtlety and grace, but *there*, nonetheless; you may have to read the closing passages slowly, with a greater attention to detail than you've become accustomed to, but everything you need to know about Helen, those three kids, and the fate of her lost daughter is right in front of you. If, after re-reading "Gone," you still don't get it, it's not necessarily all your fault; it's not that you're some stuttering kid standing in front of his second grade class trying to fathom how to pronounce "aisle" or "repetitive"; it's not that you're stupid or a slovenly reader; it's because, since the 1980s, a growing majority of both horror writers and horror readers have become deadened to, respectively, the use and presence of subtext in the field. Writers avoid it because they have come to think that every last detail must be described and every last question answered or else it's a cheat to the reader; readers tend to be mystified by it because they've grown habituated to not having to *think* about anything while reading.

Which has the makings of genuine disaster all the way around, because subtext, like hesitation, is one of the greatest tools available to writers of dark fiction.

What do we know about what's happened in "Gone"? A) That this is the first time in five years (since her daughter's disappearance) that Helen has turned on her porch light to draw trick-or-treaters for Halloween; B) she's been waiting for hours because the neighborhood children have been avoiding her house at the urging of their parents; C) when finally some trick-or-treaters do arrive, they are not from the neighborhood; D) even though they are not from the neighborhood, one of them knows to ask if Helen is the "lady who lost her baby"—not only that, but knows that the "little baby" was a girl; and, E) as they are leaving, one of them comments, in a low voice, how it's "too bad they wouldn't let her out tonight . . . too bad they never do . . ."

Subtext. What is conveyed through action and situation but not outright stated.

Now do you know what happened?

The three little trick-or-treaters not from the neighborhood came to Helen's house *specifically*; they came there specifically because they *knew* Helen's missing daughter, who either lives with them, or with someone who lives near them, or is being held prisoner by the people they live with; whatever the case, these three kids are terrified to tell Helen anything because of what might happen to them or Helen's daughter if they do.

This is what turns "Gone" into the stuff of classic tragedy. Helen's closing the door before the kid's words finally register is akin to Romeo walking past the nurse who carries Juliet's note, and, like with Romeo, by the time Helen realizes what it means, it's too late; the kids are nowhere to be seen, "Carrying along what was left of her." (Take note of Ketchum's choice of the word "along" rather than "away"; "away" implies that they took something that was offered; "along" suggests something that was taken by force. Adds a whole new dimension to an already multi-dimensional story.)

It's not hard to imagine Helen, after this night, doing a Miss Amelia from *The Ballad of the Sad Café* or a Miss Havisham from *Great Expectations* and forever sealing herself up in that house, boarding up the windows, remaining alone with her grief and regret, never venturing out into the world again—an added dash of profound sadness that only serves to amplify the initial horror of her loss.

I'll say it again: subtext. Just because Ketchum doesn't spell it out in exact terms doesn't mean it isn't there.

Subtext.

We need to get it back into horror; the sooner, the better.

Because until we do, until we avail ourselves of those storytelling tools that have so well served the work of such writers as John O'Hara, Raymond Carver, Carson McCullers, Eudora Welty, Charles L. Grant, M.R. James, Kate Wilhelm, James Agee, Jack Cady, James P. Blaylock,

Tim Powers, and others, until we are no longer satisfied with the "bloody junk food" we developed a taste for in the 80s, until we as readers and writers say that we are no longer content with stuff that simply gives us a good scare, then horror is going to stay locked up in the literary basement, picking at its scabs and drooling on itself and wondering why in hell no one seems to care about it.

Thus raveth Zarathustra.

Now, for the second story, the puzzle you have to solve on your own: my story "Need," which originally appeared in the *Corpse Blossoms* anthology a few years back. I hope you'll find that I practice what I preach once you reach the ending.

Need

> "One can go for years sometimes without living at all, and then all life comes crowding into one single hour."
>
> –Oscar Wilde, *Vera, or The Nihilists*

The letter, written on official department stationary, tumbles across the autumn sidewalk, skimming the surface of a puddle (soaking only the middle of the page, smearing certain portions of certain words) before the wind propels it against the base of a lamp post where it flutters, trapped, neither the wind nor the puddle nor the letter aware of their part in this brief mosaic nature is forming to amuse itself. A nearby rat, searching for nest material, sits up on its hind legs and regards the paper, then slowly moves toward it. The rat doesn't care about the needs of wind or paper; it is not aware of its own determined part in this mosaic; it only cares about its own need, for which this sheet of paper will do very nicely . . .

"I've got a special dessert for you guys tonight."

The two children look at each other and smile. It's been a long time since they've had a meal this good—hot beef tacos and now Mom says she's got a "special" dessert.

When the children don't say anything, their mother shakes her head and laughs. Now the children are very excited—Mom hasn't laughed in a long, long time.

"Well," she says to her son and daughter. "Aren't you even going to ask?"

"What're we having?" says the little girl.

Mom leans back in her chair and folds her arms across her chest, then looks at the ceiling. "Oh, Jeez, I don't know if I'm going to tell you or not, seeing as how you weren't interested enough to ask me in the first place."

The children give out with groans of disappointment and frustration—groans they both know Mom is expecting—and their mom laughs again.

"Okay," she says, leaning forward and gesturing for them to lean closer.

Mom whispers—like it's some kind of a big secret—"Chocolate mousse."

"*Chocolate mousse!*" they both shriek, delighted. This is their absolute, hands-down, no-question-about-it favorite dessert in the whole wide world.

"But only," adds Mom, "if you guys have another taco."

The children tell her how much they love her, grab up another tortilla, and spoon them full of the sliced beef for the tacos.

. . . now Charlie's going on and on about how no decent woman would whore herself out like that because that's what it amounted to and how that spineless scumbag was more concerned about his parents' money than he was about being a man and owning up to responsibilities so as far as he's concerned you don't talk about it with him, not ever, and Henrietta nods her head and smiles at him but not too widely, too wide a smile and he might think she's humoring him (which she is but mustn't let him know it) and get even angrier, and Charlie, you never have to do or say much to get him started on one of his rants, like today, all it took was Henrietta's letting slip with a mention of "the whore's" name (Charlie only calls her that, "the whore") and off he went, asking how could she still *talk* to that whore every week, and he was still going on, so Henrietta nods again and waits for him to storm over to the other side of the room (Charlie likes to cover a lot of ground while he's ranting), and when he does, when he heads toward the other side of the living room, Henrietta sits forward to look like she's really paying attention, like she's really interested, and as she does she slips one of her hands down into the space between the sofa cushions because just maybe Charlie or her lost some change down there, and it won't kill her, walking to the Bridge Club meetings instead of taking the bus for a week, she could use the exercise and at least the weather's been nice and as Charlie turns to make his way back her fingertips brush across the surface of something that might be a couple of quarters, so she continues smiling (but not too widely) and nodding her head because as long as Charlie makes eye contact he won't be paying any attention to her hand . . .

Inter-Office Memo
From: Paul Gallagher, Principal

Darlene:
I know you meant well, I really do, but several of the other teachers have expressed concern to me over your actions during 2nd Grade class pictures last Tuesday. You did not have permission to take that girl off school grounds, let alone to the mall. We have a lot of children from poor and disadvantaged homes in this school, and anything that even remotely smacks of favoritism is frowned upon, not only by myself and the other teachers, but the School Board as well. Your actions—caring though they might have been—can be looked upon as "playing favorites." It is not our responsibility to make sure the poorer students have decent clothes to wear for their class pictures, and it is certainly not your responsibility to buy them (though I've seen the pictures, and the little girl looks like an angel).

In the future, please keep your more dramatic humanitarian impulses in check. You're new here, and I'm sure you'll learn how things are done in due time.

Albert Morse sits on the front porch of his house on Euclid Avenue. He's enjoying the warm weather and thinking that he needs to trim the hedges this weekend. Just because the house isn't in the best neighborhood is no excuse to let it all go to hell. The house is paid for, and Albert takes a lot of pride in that. He and Georgia have made themselves a nice home here, one that the kids and the grandchildren love visiting. At the end of the day, what more could a man ask for? Work your whole life away on the factory line, retire with a good pension and good insurance, own your own home, have the family over for dinner and holidays.

Why the city decided to build those goddamned government-subsidized apartments across the street was a mystery to him, and an even bigger pain in the ass some days. Not a day goes by when someone who lives on Welfare Row doesn't drag their business into the street.

Like now, for instance; that young girl at the row of mailboxes, screaming "*Fuck!*" over and over again because of something she just read in a letter. Can't take your drama inside, no; you've got to play it out here in front of God and everybody like your problems are so much bigger and more important and painful than everybody else's.

Albert watches as the young woman continues screaming "*Fuck!*" over and over, louder and louder, until finally she breaks down into violent, wracking sobs. She wipes her arms across her eyes, shakes some hair from her face, reads the letter again, and then just tosses it away before starting in with the "*Fuck!*" and the sobbing again, right there in the middle of the damn sidewalk. She continues screaming and sobbing until a school bus stops at the corner; as soon as she sees this, she turns around, pulls some tissues from her pocket, wipes her face and nose, and turns around, puffy-eyed and smiling as a little boy and girl run from the bus to her side. She kneels down and hugs them, then holds their hands as they make their way back inside, behind closed doors, where any decent human being ought to damned well keep their troubles.

Georgia comes out and hands Albert a glass of fresh iced tea. "Just got off the phone with Cal. He and Rhonda are bringing the kids over for dinner Friday night. Cal says he wants to take us all out to see the new Disney movie."

"That sounds like fun," says Albert, taking the iced tea but staring at the letter the young woman had tossed away.

"What was all that racket a minute ago?" asks Georgia.

"Some gal over there," replies Albert, nodding toward Welfare Row. "I swear, honey, some of *trash* they allow to live there . . ."

"Don't get yourself worked up," says Georgia. "You don't need to go and get all upset about the way they act."

Albert shakes his head. "It just . . . it just makes this seem like such a rotten place to live, and it isn't, you know? Or it *shouldn't* be." He discovers that he can no longer see the letter; the wind must have blown it somewhere. "I swear, the *trash* . . ."

"I tried so *very hard*," says the drunk as he's escorted from the bar by Sheriff Ted Jackson, who's been through this routine enough to know that this particular drunk doesn't require handcuffs.

"I *tried*, I really did," says the drunk.

"I know you did," replies the sheriff, as he always does. He looks over his shoulder and sees Jack Walters, owner and proprietor of the Wagon Wheel Bar & Grille, standing in the doorway, shaking his head in pity. Jackson nods to him that everything is all right, just business as usual, and Walters gives the sheriff a mock salute before turning around and going back inside.

The drunk stumbles, almost falling, but catches himself on the trunk of Jackson's car. "It wasn't my fault. It wasn't." He reaches out and grabs Jackson's collar. "You know that, right, Sheriff? You know that it wasn't my fault."

Jackson removes the drunk's hand from his collar and gently guides him into the back seat. "You need to sleep it off, Randall. We've got your usual bed ready, and in the morning, we'll get you fixed up with a nice hot breakfast, okay?"

"Nobody calls me that," says the drunk. "I mean, she used to, once . . . like it was a pet name, you know? But nobody calls me 'Randall.' I always hated that name. I should have said something once I was goddamn old enough. Fuckin' sissy-assed name like that." He curls up into a fetal position on the back seat and begins sobbing. "I should've said something about that. I . . . I should've done a lot of things, you know? If I'd've stood up to my folks, then maybe . . ." He leans over the seat and vomits into the plastic bucket Jackson had put there earlier, in anticipation of the usual pattern. Once he finishes vomiting, he wipes his mouth, sits up, and hands the bucket to Jackson, who empties it in the gutter.

"I'm gonna quite wasting my time and get on with my life," says the drunk.

"I know you are," replies Jackson, as he always does, as he always has every few weeks for the last couple of years after Walters calls to say, "Same old song and dance, my friend."

Jackson closes the door, stuffs the bucket into a plastic trash bag, then, as always, tosses it into the trunk of the cruiser, thinking as he does that all the money in the world—and God knows that the drunk's got enough money, having inherited it from his parents—can't do a damn thing to make the nights less lonely.

From the back seat the drunk's sobbing grows louder and more violent; the spasms wracking his body shake the entire cruiser, and Jackson cannot help but feel a morbid kind of awe. While there is the usual excess of self-pity in this puking, slobbering booze hound, there's also a depth of genuine anguish that Jackson cannot ignore—which is, he supposes, why people put up with this sort of behavior from the drunk.

There is some grief you never recover from.

`to inf-rm you that, up-n revie-, the Cedar Hill Dep—tment of -ealth and H-man`

Having completed the required six weeks of training, this Wednesday is Daniel's first night working the Cedar Hill Crisis Center phone lines without backup. It is a little before 8:00 PM when his phone rings for the first time. Taking a deep breath, he answers, and after identifying himself and telling the caller whom they have reached, listens as the voice on the other end says: "How can you go on living when all there is to look forward to is more yearning?"

The caller hangs up before Daniel can say anything.

He notes the time in his log, and in parentheses adds: *probable crank call.*

Still, the question finds him again, as it will continue to do over the course of the otherwise uneventful evening, as well as a few mornings later when he happens upon the article and photos on page two of *The Cedar Hill Ally*; it comes back to him again and again as it will for the rest of his life, never leaving him, never losing him, no matter how much he tries to hide from it.

Detective Bill Emerson stares at the stack of mail on his desk, none of which is addressed to either him or anyone else at the Cedar Hill Police Department. There's the usual monthly detritus you expect to find in the mail—phone bill, gas bill, electric bill—only all of these envelopes are emblazoned with the words Final Notice stamped in bright red ink.

Emerson cracks his knuckles, then runs a hand through his thick grey hair, noting that he needs to get a trim. Between his bushy hair and equally bushy moustache, it's no wonder some of the other officers call him "Captain Kangaroo" when they think he can't hear them.

He riffles through the mail once again, tossing the bills to the left, the junk mail to the right, and everything else in the center. He's been doing this off and on for the last two days, his variation on walking a labyrinth for the purpose of meditating on a problem, and, as always, he comes back to the business-sized brown envelope that weighs more than all the rest and has way too much postage on it.

They should have used Priority, he thinks. *Four bucks and it's there in three to four days.*

He checks the postmark date against the report. Five days. Even with all the extra postage, it had taken this letter five days to reach its addressee. If they had used Priority, it would have only taken three to four, and that might have made all the difference in the world.

He drops the letter on top of the center stack, unconsciously wincing at the muffled *thump!* it makes when it lands, and stares at it.

He's still staring a few minutes later when his partner, Ben Littlejohn, comes in with dinner in the form of four cheeseburgers and two orders of fries from the Sparta. It smells great—The Sparta makes the best cheeseburgers in the free world, period—and Emerson looks up as Littlejohn sets the food on the corner of the desk.

"Still haven't opened it?" he asks Emerson.

"And your first clue was . . . ?"

Littlejohn wags a single finger back and forth. "Ah-ah, save the snappy banter for the rookies, not me." Littlejohn looks at his partner for a long moment, then says, his voice softer: "You want me to do it?"

"No. I was first on the scene, I found it. It should be me."

Littlejohn parks his ass on the edge of Emerson's desk and starts removing the cheeseburgers from the bag. "So . . . *when* are you and Eunice going to take that vacation she's bugging you about?"

"To London? Don't start, I'm warning you. She has talked about nothing *but* going there since she saw that damn *Notting Hill* movie. I rue the day Julia Roberts and Hugh Grant were born, because it set into motion the events that would lead to the making of that movie. My life has been endless misery since. Did you know they serve their beer room temperature there? Can you imagine that? No wonder we broke from the Crown."

"Uh-huh. Open the goddamn thing already, will you?"

Emerson picks up the brown envelope, noting again its weight, then looks at his partner. "You're a radiantly compassionate fellow, you know that?"

"I'm an intensely *hungry* fellow who's not going to be able to enjoy his dinner until whatever's in that envelope is out of our lives, and since that isn't going to be anytime soon—seeing as how you've put off opening it for almost two full work days—I'll settle for our knowing its contents."

"You should have seen it," whispers Emerson.

Littlejohn leans forward, rapping his knuckles on the desk to break Emerson's morbid reverie. "I *did* see it, Bill. I was only two minutes behind you."

"I know that, I'm not completely dim." He taps the envelope against his hand in a soft, steady tattoo that after only a few seconds annoys even him, but he doesn't stop. "Have you ever heard of something called 'The Observer Effect'?"

"That's a physics term, right?"

Emerson nods his head. "If I understand it correctly—Einsteinian whiz-kid that I am—it says that a person can change an event just by being there to watch it. They don't have to take any kind of physical action or what we think of as active participation, just *being there* changes it."

Littlejohn's expression grows concerned, albeit cautiously. "Okay . . . ?"

"It was *different* after you came in. When it was just me, there was a . . . I don't know . . . almost a *peacefulness* there for a few seconds. But then you came in, and I saw your face and you saw mine and when we looked at it again, it was just . . . ugly and pathetic and sad." Emerson feels that last word fall from his mouth and land at his feet like a dead bird dropping from the sky.

"Bill," says Littlejohn, "I'm asking you now as your friend, not your partner, okay? I'm asking you to please, for everyone's sake, open it."

Not taking his stare from the cheeseburger bag, Emerson picks up the letter opener, slips it under the flap of the envelope (Scotch taped, three times), slashes open the top, and removes the two sheets of paper inside.

The first sheet is blank, a twenty-pound standard weight of recycled typing paper that has been used to make sure someone couldn't hold the envelope up to the light and discern its contents.

You used a brown *envelope; no one could have seen through this, anyway.*

Unfolding the second sheet, he watches as the bills tumble down on the desk: two twenties, a ten, a five, and three ones. He reaches down with his other hand and arranges the bills side by side.

He looks at the letter, reads what it says—words written in a slow, unsteady hand (*probably arthritis*, he thinks; *a lot of older folks have trouble with that and can't write as neatly or steadily as they used to*)—but it's not the words that cause his throat to tighten, though they are bad enough. No; it's the two quarters, three dimes, one nickel, and four pennies that are taped across the bottom of the page (three pieces of Scotch tape, just like the envelope).

He blinks, pulls in a breath that is heavier and thicker than it ought to be, and hands the sheet to his partner.

"Fifty-eight dollars and eighty-nine cents," he says. "Who the hell sends someone fifty-eight dollars and eighty-nine cents? *Eighty-nine cents?* Why not just make it sixty dollars even?"

Before Littlejohn has a chance to finish reading the letter or respond to the question, Emerson speaks again:

"I'll *tell* you who sends someone fifty-eight dollars and eighty-nine cents; someone who only *has* fifty-eight dollars and eighty-nine cents. Someone who has to go through their purse or wallet, and then the pockets of their coat—hell, they probably even pulled the cushions off the sofa to see if any loose change had fallen down there, just to make sure they could send every *penny* they possibly could. *Anybody* could send you sixty bucks, but only . . . only someone who *cared* enough to scrape together all the money they possibly could would send you fifty-eight dollars and eighty-nine cents."

He realizes that he is almost on the verge of tears but doesn't care. "*Eighty-nine cents!* I'll bet that old woman had to walk to the store instead of taking the bus to make sure she could get that eighty-nine cents in there. Jesus H. Christ, Ben—*why* didn't she use Priority? That might have made all the difference in the world!" Emerson presses the heels of his hands against his eyes, takes a deep breath, then releases it slowly before wiping his eyes and lowering his hands, which aren't shaking nearly as much as he feared they would be.

"That was very moving," says Littlejohn. "Look at me—I am visibly touched."

"I'm turning into an old woman, aren't I?"

"No, you're just maybe possibly arguably a little too you-should-pardon-the-expression human for this job sometimes."

"And my cheeseburgers are probably cold."

Littlejohn shook his head. "Nope. I had them wrap everything in heavy-duty aluminum foil, just in case we didn't get to the food right away."

"I really *am* predictable, aren't I?"

"Let's call it 'dependable' and remain friends, shall we?"

"You're too good to me."

"I get a lot of complaints about that."

Emerson unwraps the first cheeseburger, starts to bite into it, then pauses and says, "Why didn't she use Priority?"

It is a question that will find him again and again throughout the rest of his life, never losing him, even when he tries hiding from it.

Edna Warner stands in line at the grocery store and thinks to herself, *The damn meat's gonna start thawing if she takes any longer.*

The young woman in front of her is riffling through a small stack of food stamps. The cashier exchanges a quick, exasperated glance with Edna, one that says, *I'm really sorry, ma'am, but there's nothing I can do.* Edna smiles in understanding, though it's a forced smile. Why did it seem she *always* picked the slowest line in the store? Just her luck, getting stuck behind a welfare case who doesn't have the sense to have her food stamps out and ready.

She takes a tissue from her purse and blows her nose, quietly, as a courteous lady is supposed to do. *Why* she felt compelled to stick her head in the pet store earlier would probably always remain a mystery to her, but that puppy in the window had been so *cute*. It never occurred to her that the pet store would also have cats. Edna is severely allergic to cats, couldn't even be near someone who *owned* the terrible things because people who owned cats always had at least a *little* shed fur on their clothes, and that's all it took to make her allergies go crazy.

Luckily, that was a few hours ago, and she's had a chance to take some non-drowsy allergy medicine, so now she's feeling much better, for which she is grateful. The last thing she wants is to be all stopped-up and red-nosed when Joe gets home from work. He always says it's hard for him to eat at the same table with her when she's like that, eyes all puffy and nose running like it was trying to win some kind of race.

Sometimes, her Joe can be awfully high-maintenance.

Edna busies herself with looking over the headlines on the tabloids in the rack by the checkout lane; this star has gained weight, another one has entered Betty Ford, someone else is having an affair. It's actually quite funny, when you think about it, how these newspapers try to make stars' lives seem even more dramatic than the characters they play in the movies; as if splattering all their troubles on the front page will make them seem like regular folks. *We have problems just like the rest of you,* these stars' faces seem to say.

Sighing, Edna checks her watch and sees that she's been standing here for almost five minutes. The young woman in front of her hears Edna's sighing, and smiles at her in apology. Edna is at first embarrassed to have been found out, then struck by how sad the young woman's smile is and—*Lord!*—how tired she looks. There are dark crescents under the young woman's eyes that stand out against her pale skin and make her smile seem even more cheerless. For a moment, Edna almost feels bad for having drawn attention to the awkwardness of the situation—*the poor thing looks like she hasn't slept in days*—then thinks again of the pot roast in her cart and how she hopes it doesn't thaw too much before she can get it home and into the freezer. If it thaws too much, she'll have to make it tonight, and Joe wouldn't like that; it's only Thursday, and Joe likes to have pot roast on the weekend. Feed him a too-heavy meal during the week, and he complains about how it keeps him awake and feeling tired all the next day.

Still feeling the young woman's eyes on her, Edna busies herself with the contents of her vinyl coupon holder, making sure that all the ones she'll need are in front, ready to go so that the cashier can scan them without delay. When she's sure the young welfare woman is no longer looking at her, Edna sneaks a peek at what she is buying. Edna's father always used to say, *You can tell a lot about a person by the contents of their shopping cart*, and over the course of her fifty-six years, Edna has found a lot of truth in that observation.

So she looks.

There is a coloring book with a torn cover and a bottle of over-the-counter sleep aids (both of which the young woman pays for with a handful of singles and change from her pocket), six cans of cat food (sliced beef in gravy), a quart of milk, a box of instant pudding mix (chocolate mousse, actually), a packet of taco seasoning (mild), and some frozen tortillas (corn).

The first thing that crosses Edna's mind is that she's not sneezing.

The second thing that crosses Edna's mind as she stares at the items is a commercial from the 1970s with that old gal—what was her name? *Clara Peller, that's right!*—where three old ladies are looking at a hamburger that's mostly all bun and Clara Peller starts squawking, "*Where's* the beef?"

Edna doesn't know why that, of all things, crosses her mind at that moment, but Clara Peller's famous question will find her again, during dinner, as it will find her again and again, for the rest of her life, never losing her, even when Alzheimer's disease begins fragmenting her mind in another seventeen years: to the attendants on the ward at the nursing home where she will die quietly in her sleep, Edna Warner will always be known as the "Where's-the-Beef?" Lady.

man Serv-ces has, aft-r conside-tion of yo-r individ-l case (#AB765-17) determi-d

In the basement of St. Francis Church on Granville Street, the Monday night Alcoholics Anonymous meeting is winding down, and Chet Beckman—twelve years sober, known to his friends as "No-Skid" because he's got the best record of any bus driver for the Central Ohio Transit Authority—is adding an extra spoonful of sugar to his coffee when one of the other fellows in the group says, "Where's that guy who was here last week? That fellow whose family . . . oh, what was his name?"

"Randy," says Chet, sitting back down and stirring the creamer until the coffee takes on that soft golden color that means it's just right. "And they weren't his family except in his head, and my guess is he's down at the Wagon Wheel getting stewed to the gills."

The fellow who'd asked the question seems genuinely disappointed. "How can you *know* that?"

Chet sips his coffee and smiles; it tastes perfect. "I can know this because Randy comes in here about—what?—every three or four weeks after he's gone on a real bad binge, and sits there and says 'I'm gonna stop wasting my time and get on with my life.'" Chet takes another sip of his coffee. "He's been doing that for damn near two years, and the pattern never changes, no matter how many sponsors we sic on him or how many quit or how many he fires. Hell, *I* was his sponsor for a while, when it looked like he might actually get past what happened."

"It sounded to me like it wasn't his fault, hear him tell it."

"That's what he keeps telling us when he bothers to show up. 'It wasn't my fault. It wasn't my fault.' You ask me, he keeps repeating that because he's hoping that if he says it enough, he'll start to believe it." Chet shrugs. "Hell, maybe that wouldn't be such a bad thing, you know? Him starting to believe it."

The fellow who'd asked about Randy leaned forward. "Sounds to me like maybe you don't agree it wasn't his fault."

Chet sits back in his chair and regards the other fellow carefully. It doesn't do to get tempers flaring at these meetings; a bad argument's all the excuse someone needs to fall off the wagon, and this other fellow, the one who asked about Randy, he's only been sober five weeks and has got that desperate, anxious way about him that says he can go either way in a heartbeat. The first six weeks are always the hardest, and that sixth week is always the killer. Half the people AA loses they lose during the sixth week of sobriety, so Chet considers his words very carefully as he replies.

"Did you see that news story the other night about that avalanche they had in Colorado? The one that killed them two skiers?"

The other fellow nods his head.

"See, here's the thing about assigning blame to anyone or anything," says Chet, taking another sip of his perfect, golden-hued coffee. "I kept wondering—I wonder about shit like this sometimes when I can't sleep—I kept wondering, what if the snow itself could think like we can? I mean, imagine that every snowflake in that avalanche was able to think. Do you suppose any one of them would feel responsible for those skiers' dying, or would they just tell themselves 'It wasn't my fault'?"

The other man thinks on this for a moment, then shrugs. "I don't guess I see your point."

"So what's responsible for that?" asks Chet. "Is there any one word that I just said that's responsible for your not understanding me, or was it *all* the words?"

The other man shakes his head. "You're fucking with me now, aren't you?"

Chet shrugs, deciding that he's had enough coffee for tonight.

that you no longer qualify --r ben-its as outlin- under O-io Co-e --- and

"Would you look at *this?*" shouts Steve over the roar of the garbage truck's compactor.

His partner, Marty, pulls the wax plug out of his left ear and shouts back, "What?"

Steve points to the contents of one of the trash cans they're emptying along Welfare Row. "This one bag came open. Take a look at this."

Marty peers over the edge of the trash can, looks at Steve, then back down at the contents.

The compactor finishes chewing up the last batch of trash, and howls loudly as it moves back into place for the next load.

"Looks to me like somebody's got insomnia."

Steve shakes his head. "That's more than insomnia, bud. There must be—what?—forty empty bottles in here. Fuck, that's enough to knock out Godzilla for a week."

"Is there anything else in there? Anything that might be salvageable? A busted radio or something we could maybe hock?"

Steve rummages through the rest of the contents. "Nah, ain't got shit."

"I guess that DVD player yesterday was a fluke, huh?"

"We were in a better section of town."

"Oh."

They toss the contents into the back of the truck, toss the cans back to the curb, and run to grab the next ones.

`all monies and oth-- of ----- sha-l be immediately discontinued. If you h-ve`

The rat finishes shredding the paper for its nest, not caring that a large section of it has been caught by the wind again as is tumbling its determined way toward another role in a different mosaic that nature will soon form because of the need to amuse itself. The rat carries away the last of the shreds, knowing now that its nest is complete, is warm, is safe.

"So . . . how was dessert?"

"It was really *good*" say the children.

"It was different than last time," says the little boy. "It was kinda . . ."

". . . kinda *crunchy*," says the little girl.

"Yeah," says the little boy. "Like there was sand in there. It made it a lot thicker."

Their mother brushes some hair from their faces. "But it was good, wasn't it?"

"Oh, yeah!" they cry in unison. "It was yummy. And we ate it *all!*"

"We sure did," says their mother.

"And you made so much of it!" says the little girl, laughing and yawning at the same time. "You never eat dessert when we have. You're always saying . . . oh, what do you say?"

"That chocolate goes right to her hips," says the little boy, who's also laughing and yawning at the same time.

Their mother laughs, as well. "Well . . . tonight was special."

". . . sure was," says the little girl, fighting to keep her eyes open.

"That was the best dinner yet," says the little boy.

She kisses them both on the forehead, then the cheek, then hugs them and tucks them in for the night. She turns off the lights and sits on the floor between their beds, her right hand stroking her daughter's cheek, her left hand touching her son's shoulder.

She remains like that until they are both asleep.

She lowers her head and pulls in a deep, wet breath, then listens to their breathing.

She sees the coloring book lying on the floor at the foot of her daughter's bed. The two of them had been coloring in the pictures. They hadn't finished the last one.

It looked very nice. They played well together. They were each other's bestest friend.

They had loved the coloring book.

She listens to their breathing as she studies the colors, how well both of them stayed within the lines.

Later, she goes into the bathroom and runs hot water into the tub, lights a candle, unfolds the plastic bag, and measures out the duct tape.

"Goodnight," she whispers in the direction of her children's' room. "Sleep tight. Don't let the bedbugs . . ."

She begins to undress, feeling groggy.

Would you believe that one review of *Corpse Blossoms* actually called this story *sentimental?* That astounds me. It always does. Every so often I will come across a review of one of my novels or stories wherein the reviewer accuses the piece of being sentimental. While that used to frustrate me no end, I've learned now to be amused when this happens (after all, who the hell wants to waste their time reading a horror story that bothers to create an emotional core?) because I remember the words of Oscar Wilde: "A sentimentalist is one who wishes the luxury of exploiting an emotion without paying the price of actually *experiencing* it." Honest emotion can only be labeled "sentimental" when it's glaringly obvious that the writer is manipulating you in order to achieve a single, desired effect, one with no room for variation or for being left open to individual interpretation.

I've been very lucky in the course of my career in that readers and many of my fellow writers feel I have a certain knack for creating emotionally rich, compelling, three-dimensional characters. When not being accused of sentimentality, I'm often asked how I manage to do this, so I thought I'd go over some of the methods I employ for characterization, and then—to illustrate how I try to apply these methods—deconstruct a scene from my story "Union Dues" that numerous readers have told me is one of their favorites.

Please bear in mind that these methods are those that work best for *me* and are not being offered as absolutes or—God forbid—a template that will guarantee you'll get the same results. There *is* no such template; creating a multi-layered, believable, sympathetic character is, like everything else one learns about writing, a matter of trial and error.

It is also a deeply personal matter, one that demands the writer be completely honest with him- or herself when creating a detailed map of a character's emotional landscape. If you, as a writer, can find it in yourself to face the honest feelings in your own heart and convey those feelings through those of your characters, you will achieve that rare feat in horror: to create a truthful sense of a character's grief or joy, triumph or remorse, courage or cowardice, loneliness, redemption, any and all of the above, and then lead them and the reader through the very worst of it, transforming them through acceptance, and leaving the reader with a deeper appreciation for their lives and everything that is a part of those lives.

I know that sounds like a tall order, so let's make it even more impossible and bring in this thought from the late novelist John Gardner (*Grendel, The Sunlight Dialogues*): "You must write [each story and novel] as if you are trying to convince someone not to commit suicide."

There is, believe it or not, a point of reconciliation between the somewhat detached compassion in Gardner's directive and the facade of nihilistic darkness in horror fiction, and it hinges almost solely on the ability of the writer to unblinkingly convey honest feeling. (This point of reconciliation can be summed up in—curiously enough—thirteen words, and we'll get to those later.)

But first, let's talk a little bit about acting.

Lauren Bacall tells a marvelous story about her acting debut opposite Humphrey Bogart in 1944's *To Have and Have Not*. Bacall had never acted before, but her head was stuffed full of these overly-glamorous preconceptions about how "stars" behaved (gleaned from devouring an endless diet of film fan magazines of the time), so when the moment came for her to make her entrance in her first scene and utter her first line, Bacall danced through the door into the room where sat Bogart (the perennial cigarette dangling from the corner of his mouth), made a wide, elegant sweep of the room as if modeling a dress on a fashion runway, and then all but swooned at Bogart's feet before delivering her first line as if she were singing an aria.

With the exception of director Howard Hawks, everyone on the set either burst out laughing or—following Bogey's example—groaned and rolled their eyes heavenward. Bacall, mortified, began to flee the set, but was stopped by Hawks. Bacall asked him what she'd done wrong, and instead of listing the at least 3,240 things she'd screwed up, Hawks told her to look at what she was wearing (an old blouse and slacks), pointed to the door she'd waltzed through just a few moments earlier, and said: "Think about where you're coming from—not just about from where *in the house* you're coming from , but also from where in your *life*. And then ask yourself how and why all of it has led you to walk through this specific door at this specific moment and enter this specific room. Because it's all connected, and you need to make sure that we can *see* all of that before you even open your mouth." Sixty-five years later, Bacall still insists that those instructions from Hawks remain the single finest piece of direction a young actress could have hoped to receive at the very start of a career.

Hawks' words remain as wise today as they were in 1944. It's not just the things he told Bacall, but also the things he *didn't* tell her; like why, for instance, her character wore an old blouse and slacks, or had chosen those particular shoes, or how she knew it was safe for her to be alone in a room with a man she'd never met until this moment.

Being a fervent believer in string theory, I cannot help but smile at Hawks' having told Bacall that "it's all connected," because those three words should be framed and hung over the desk of every fiction writer. From the smallest of gestures to the most grandiose of Shakespearian soliloquies, nothing happens within the microcosm of a story that is not somehow connected to everything that came before or that will follow. I came to this realization not through writing, but during my time as a professional actor.

For the better part of a decade—between the ages of nineteen and thirty—I worked as an actor, mostly summer stock and dinner theatre, with extra work in a movie and television miniseries, and was actually *paid* to pretend I was someone else. During those years, I worked with an assortment of other actors, all of whom had their own approaches to interpreting the particular roles in which they were cast.

The late Laurence Olivier was a self-proclaimed "technical" actor—he worked from the outside in. He would find a walk, a speech pattern, various mannerisms, etc. through which the character would reveal itself to him. While rehearsing a Noel Coward play in which he played a prissy English lord, Olivier was having difficulty getting a handle on the character. This semi-famous story reached its happy ending when Olivier, passing by an antique store, happened to glance in the window and see a walking stick for sale. He went into the store, picked up the walking stick, and the moment it was in his hand, he *knew* the character. (The walking stick, by the way, was described by Olivier as "one of the ugliest, most ostentatious things" he'd ever seen, but he knew that his character would think it was classy and tasteful.)

I worked with a lot of technical actors. I was one myself. I also worked with a lot of Method actors. Method actors are an ongoing gift to the world from Constantin Sergeyevich Stanislavsky, an actor, writer, and director from Moscow who created an approach that became the vanguard for tackling the psychological and emotional aspects of acting: the Stanislavsky System, or "the Method."

Method acting requires that, if an actor is to portray fear, he must remember something that once terrified him and use that remembered fear to instill reality and credibility into his performance. The same with joy, lust, anger, confusion, etc. Stanislavsky's Method also requires that the actor know *everything* about his or her character, usually by having the actor write a short "inner history" for the character, details of their lives that, while never used on stage, will nonetheless give the performance deeper authenticity.

In theory, Stanislavsky's Method is an amazing tool for an actor. It requires the complete submersion of the self into the body, psyche, and thoughts of another person so that an actor's performance rings of the truth.

I use the phrase "in theory" above because, in my opinion, too many actors use Stanislavsky's Method as an excuse for self-indulgence masking itself as research. Don't misunderstand—when you get a Method actor like Marlon Brando (in his prime), Paul Newman, Dustin Hoffman, Sean Penn, Meryl Streep, or Bob Hoskins (to name a small handful) who has the discipline and wherewithal to employ the Method to all its power, you can have something glorious.

But I didn't get to work with any of them. I got to work with Method actors who would spend weeks researching and writing their "inner histories," demanding that I address them only as their character (even when off stage), and never, *ever* make light of anything at any time. The prime example of how Stanislavsky's Method can be turned into rampant silliness happened when I was doing a stage production of *Sherlock Holmes* and had to do several scenes with the actor playing Dr. Watson. (I played a slimy little safecracker named Sidney Prince.) The actor playing Watson had written a seventy-five page "inner history" for Watson, researched hand-to-hand combat methods used by British troops during the Boar War, studied medical procedures practiced in London in the 1800s . . . and when the curtain rose each night, audiences were treated to his imitation of Nigel Bruce for the next two and a half hours.

But that's not the silly part. The silly part always happened off stage, right before the third scene of the second act (where Watson confronts Prince). As he and I waited for our cues, the actor playing Watson would drink a cup of vinegar. I asked him why, and this, word for word, was his reply: "Because, Mr. Prince, dealing with you leaves a bad taste in my mouth."

Time to run, not walk, to the nearest exit.

I finally came to the conclusion that for me, as an actor, Stanislavsky's Method was useless. Every Method actor I had worked with wound up giving stiff, overly-mannered, obvious performances (in that it was obvious they were "acting"). I don't know that I'll ever do theatre again, but if I do, I'll use the same "technical" approach that I always used.

While Stanislavsky's Method might have been useless to me as an actor, it was priceless to me as a writer. I still approach characterization, especially during the early stages of a story or novel, from a technical standpoint, but almost always fall back on Stanislavsky's Method when it comes time to add emotional depth and authenticity to whichever character is coming to life on the page—and I won't commit a single word to the page until said character is someone I immediately recognize as an old friend.

I start with two simple questions, questions that are going to strike you as being a bit silly on the surface, but questions that, for me, reveal so much more than what is simply seen: *How much milk does he or she use when having a bowl of cereal?* and *How does this character put on his or her coat?*

Let's say that this first character uses just enough milk to barely cover the cereal, thus ensuring that both milk and cereal will be finished at the same time with nothing left in the bowl but the spoon. That's the technical starting point, the outside. Now, let's walk over and look a little closer and ask, *Why do they do this?* They do this because they don't believe in waste; they're not the type to dump the last bit of milk down the sink after the cereal is gone. (And if there *is* any milk remaining, they either lift the bowl and drink it or set the bowl on the floor so the cat can finish it.) *Why do they not believe in waste?* Because they can't afford to be wasteful. They work long hours at a job that manages to pay the bills, the rent, and buy a set amount of groceries each week, but no excesses, no luxuries, no eating out or going to the movies or buying a new CD ... ergo, no wasting of the milk.

This also suggests that this character may not be the happiest person you've ever met; after all, if they have to be this frugal with milk, then that frugality has to extend to every other aspect of their existence, as well, and with that comes an endless string of commonplace worries that, taken individually, may not seem like much, but cumulatively drain a lot of enjoyment from life.

Looking even closer, we see this character is sitting at a kitchen table that also doubles as the dinner table, because he or she lives in a three- or four-room apartment; a nice-enough place that's affordable, if not fancy. I'm willing to bet that stashed up in one of the kitchen cupboards is a set of china cups and saucers left to them by a dead relative, cups and saucers that they only use on special occasions, like those rare instances when they have company. I'll also bet you that on this character's chest of drawers in the bedroom we'll find a jar filled two-thirds of the way with an assortment of spare change—mostly pennies, dimes, and some quarters—that this character is planning on using to buy themselves a nice little something-or-other once the jar is full, maybe treating themselves to a night out, dinner and a movie, or buying a new pair of dress shoes at Target or K-mart.

I could keep going but I think you've got the idea. And it doesn't matter a damn whether or not any of the information from the above paragraphs makes it into the story because I am now well on the road to *knowing* this person. The better I know them, the more authentic and believable they will be to the reader, and we will have achieved what Stanislavsky's Method demands: complete, unflinching, undistilled truth when depicting the human condition of the character in question.

All of this discovered because of a simple visual nuance.

All of this revealed from looking at bowl of cereal ... because it's all connected.

Nearly every story I have written has begun with an image of the central character doing something mundane, but it's the manner in which this mundane task is being performed that instantly tells me a great deal about the character.

Just as a creative mental exercise, try this: the next time you go out to a club, movie, party, or restaurant, over the course of the evening choose five people at random and watch how they both remove and put on their coats. Does this person treat their coat with care, removing it slowly, one arm at a time, and then draping it carefully over the back of their chair (making sure that the lower part doesn't touch the floor), or do they just all but let it drop off of them, and then thoughtlessly sling it over the back of a chair without a second glance, even though a full one-third of it is now spread out on the floor?

As far as putting the coat back on, watch this as well. Do they exercise care when they do this—again, one arm at a time, slowly, taking time to smooth it out a bit once it's on their body, or do they make a bit of a show out of it, swirling it around their shoulders like Zorro's cape and then jamming their arms into the sleeves with such wide flourish there's a good chance they could take out someone's eye should that other person be standing too close?

This can tell you a lot about your character, albeit in broad strokes, but that's where characterization starts. The character who takes care of their coat, who is careful to remove it and hang it off the back of the chair so no part of it touches the floor (and who also exercises quiet care when putting it back on) reveals several things through these visual clues: this coat is something that has meaning for them—it may have been a gift from a family member who is no longer alive (it may even have belonged to that family member; it's your call). It may have been something for which they had to save money every month in order to purchase because they don't have a lot of disposable income (hmm—could this person also be our frugal eater of cereal?). It may be that this coat is one of the few things they feel they look good in, or it may be that this is the only coat they own. The possibilities are endless.

But here is the one thing that you'll know immediately: this is, in all probability, a shy person, one who wishes to blend in as much as possible so as not to draw attention to themselves. This is a person who will be all too happy to join in the conversation, but will rarely begin one of their own volition. The other person—the one who just tosses the coat down without a second thought and then makes a bit of a show when putting it back on—this person is not only an extrovert, but also quite probably someone who has never really known what it's like to work in order to possess the basics (like said coat). The coat may have been a gift from a parent (who is still probably alive, and thus able to provide them with a new coat when this one becomes trashed by having half of it draped across the floor so many times). It may be just one of several coats they own, so what the hell do they care? Or, it may be that—like our other person—this is the only coat they own, but because they need to foster this devil-may-care persona among their friends, they treat it with indifference . . . until, of course, it's time to leave, and putting it back on allows them to be showy, thus making sure they remain the center of attention.

Like I said, these are broad-stroke examples, but it's a way to begin. Other factors must be called into consideration to enrich this scenario: the age and sex of the character in question; the kind of coat he or she is wearing. Is it something expensive or off the rack at Target or Walpurgis-Mart? Was it tailored specifically for them? And what are the specific circumstances under which they are wearing the coat? (I imagine that our first character would exercise the same kind of deliberate care with their coat whether they were with a group of people or eating alone—and wouldn't it be interesting if our second character, when alone, treated their coat with the same care and *didn't* make a show of putting it back on? It's fun how this works, isn't it?)

Now peel back another layer from the surface: imagine what's in the pockets of each character's coat. Going with the original conceit that our first character is a shy person who, for the sake or argument, was given the coat as a gift by a deceased parent (perhaps the last gift this person ever received from said parent), they're not likely to stick a used candy bar wrapper in one of the pockets because they couldn't immediately find a trash can after polishing off . . . what? (Ask yourself that: what kind of a candy bar would this person prefer, or would they like candy at all?) I imagine that our shy person would keep a pair of gloves in the pockets (for when the outside temperature gets cold) and perhaps their car keys, but little else. Simple and uncluttered.

By contrast, our second character would have receipts, loose change, car keys, two or three wadded one-dollar bills they've forgotten are even in there, half a dozen phone numbers scribbled on slips of paper, and a partially-eaten candy bar from six months ago that is growing a fungus that is starting to breathe and develop a rudimentary language.

Okay, so now you've got a character, one who captures the reader's attention (and hopefully sympathy, as well) through a simple visual nuance, whether it be with the cereal or the coat. Questions are forming in the readers' minds because they want to know more about this character than what the writer has implied or what they as the readers have inferred, and the best way to further peel away the deeper layers of this character's emotional landscape is to have them interact with another character. This is where the real fire starts burning, because this is where we begin to draw the correlations and further reveal how everything is linked.

We begin connecting the DOTS—the Definition of the Self that every characters carries with them, that hangs about their necks like either pearls or chains and determines how they will interact with everyone else populating the microcosm of the story.

In my workshops that focus upon dialogue and the DOTS, I offer up several examples of the Definition of the Self as done by myself and other writers, but hands-down the one that I use the most comes from *The Twilight Zone* episode "The Changing of the Guard," written by Rod Serling, the first writer whose words moved me in a profound way.

In this beautifully-written episode the late Donald Pleasance (in a luminous performance) portrays Professor Ellis Fowler, an aged teacher at an all-boys boarding school. As the school begins closing for Christmas vacation, Fowler is informed by the school's headmaster that after fifty-one years of teaching, he is being forcibly retired. The news devastates Fowler, who's known nothing but the halls of the school and teaching for his entire adult life.

Back home, his housekeeper later discovers him in his study, looking though old yearbooks and reminiscing about students he's taught over the years. In the midst of this nostalgia he suddenly stops, removes his glasses, and delivers to his housekeeper the following Definition of the Self:

> "They all come and go like ghosts. Faces, names, smiles, the funny things they said or the sad things, or the poignant ones.

> I gave them nothing, I gave them nothing at all. Poetry that left their minds the minute they themselves left. Aged slogans that were out of date when I taught them. Quotations dear to me that were meaningless to them. I was a failure, Miss Landers, an abject, miserable failure. I walked from class to class an old relic, teaching by rote to unhearing ears, unwilling heads. I was an abject, dismal failure—I moved nobody. I motivated nobody. I left no imprint on anybody. Now, where do you suppose I ever got the idea that I was accomplishing anything?"

In reality, you'd have to practically strap someone to a chair and threaten to start pulling teeth in order to get them to express themselves so directly and eloquently; that is why your characters give you the priceless gift of rejecting that kind of reality and replacing it with your own; in the fictional world, your characters *can* define themselves to themselves and to others this directly, this poetically, this un-self-consciously. And when you know each character's Definition of the Self, you will begin to sense how those individual DOTS will connect to one another when they meet in the story.

I should also note here that a Definition of the Self can be a brutally direct one (as in the quoted *TZ* excerpt above), or it can be an indirect definition, one that is hidden within their words when they speak of someone or something other than themselves.

Connecting the DOTS gives depth to relationships (or the lack thereof); it establishes and escalates conflict; it peels back the layers of your characters' psyches because of what they reveal or struggle *not* to reveal to the others; and—perhaps most importantly—it will establish the emotional core and tone of your story. It doesn't matter if you use everything you know about the character; simply by *knowing* all that you do about them, so much will come across through a simple gesture, a small visual nuance, the way they smile . . . or treat their coat and eat a bowl of cereal. And once that emotional connection is made, readers will follow your characters through anything and always remain by their side; even if the character in question does something less than noble or kind. The readers will care about your character, they will sympathize—even empathize—and they will understand what motivates and drives that character. In short, you will have brought about a communion of sorts between reader and character—perhaps the greatest reward a story can give.

So, a quick review: establish character through visual nuance, then through Definition of the Self, then through interactions with other characters and *their* DOTS (be it a direct or an indirect definition) so relationships and conflicts can arise naturally and give birth to that elusive beast called "plot."

Now let's see how well I practice what I preach. Below is an excerpt from my short story "Union Dues," (a story I'll be referencing again a bit later) which originally appeared in *Borderlands 4*. The scene in question comes about one-quarter of the way into the story, and it's a scene (as I mentioned earlier) that numerous readers have singled out as one of their favorites. My wife thinks it's the one sequence that best illustrates what all my work is ultimately concerned with. I am just amazed that after fifteen years, this is one of the few scenes that I've never had a desire to go back and "fix." It still holds up, I think.

As we go through the scene, I'm going to insert some bold-face comments pointing out visual nuances, where the DOTS are established, where they collide to illustrate conflict and establish relationships, and how connecting the DOTS compels the shifting dynamics within those relationships.

In the scene, Sheriff Ted Jackson (a recurrent character in my Cedar Hill stories) has come to the house of Darlene Kaylor on the same evening that a massive riot between striking factory workers and scab laborers has left several people dead—including Darlene's husband, Herb, with whom Jackson was close friends. Jackson was also the person who helplessly watched Herb Kaylor die in a manner that defied logic, reason, or explanation. Jackson has come over to pay his respects and see if there is anything he can do for Darlene and her son, Will, but he also needs to have a few questions answered. Darlene invites him into the kitchen, where she fixes them each a cup of coffee. We come into the scene when Jackson asks the first of his several questions:

"Darlene," he said softly, staring down into his coffee cup, **[Visual nuance: he can't look her straight in the eyes because he still feels at this point in the story that he should have been able to do something**

to save Herb, so the nagging guilt and shock of what he witnessed makes it impossible for him to look Darlene—or anyone else—in the eyes for the first two-thirds of the story.] "I hate to ask you about this but I gotta know. Why was Herb working the picket today? He wasn't supposed to be there again until Friday."

"I swear to you I don't know. I asked him this morning right before he left. He just kind of laughed—you know how he always does when he don't want to bother you with a problem? Then he kissed me and said he was sorry he'd got Will into this and he was gonna try to fix things."

"What'd he mean?"

"He got Will on at the plant. Was even gonna train him." She shook her head and sipped at her coffee. [**Visual nuance—Darlene shaking her head. There is a sad resignation in her that something like this was bound to happen, and now that it has, it seems nearly absurd to her—especially considering what she's about to tell Jackson.**] "You know Herb's father did the same for him? Got him a job workin' the same shift in the same cell. I guess a lot of workers get in that way. Didn't your father work there, too?"

Jackson looked away [**Visual nuance; same reason as before.**] and whispered, "Yeah."

"Place is like a fuckin' family heirloom." Will stood up in the doorway.

Jackson turned to look at him as Darlene said, "What did I tell you about using that kind of language in the house? Your Daddy—"

"—was stupid! Admit it. It was stupid of him to go down there today."

Darlene stared at him with barely-contained fury worsened by weariness and grief. "I won't have you bad-mouthing you father, Will. He ain't—" her voice cracked "—here to defend himself. He worked hard for his family and deserved a hell of a lot more respect and thanks than he ever got." [**Indirect Definition of the Self; by characterizing her late husband as a hard worker, she reveals a little of her deep admiration for Herb.**]

"*Thanks?*" shouted Will. "For what? For reminding me that he put his obligations over his own happiness, or for getting me on at the plant so I could become another goddamm factory stooge like him? Which wonderful gift should I have thanked him for?" [**Another**

Indirect Definition of the Self: by characterizing his father as a "factory stooge" and then contemptuously asking which gift he should be thankful for, Will reveals his anger at—if not contempt for—his father.]

"You sure couldn't find a decent job on your own. Somebody had to do something."

"Listen," said Jackson, "maybe I should come back—"

"When was I supposed to look for another job? Between running errands for you and helping with the housework and cleaning up after Dad when he got drunk—" [**Wandering off the highway for just a moment, can you see here how dialogue, when used in tandem with the DOTS, gives you the opportunity to slip in necessary background information that, had it been presented any other way, would have come off as forced or awkward?**]

"I think you'd better go to your room."

"No," said Will, storming into the kitchen and slamming down his coffee cup. "I'm eighteen years old and not once have I ever been allowed to disagree with anything you or Dad wanted. You weren't the one who had to sit down here and listen to him ramble on at three in the morning after he got tanked. To hear him tell it, working the plant was just short of Hell, yet he was more than happy to hand my ass over—" [**The first part of Will's direct DOTS.**]

"He was only trying to help you get some money so you could finally get your own place, get on your own two feet. He was a very giving, great man."

"A *great* man? How the hell can you say that? You're wearing clothes that are ten years old and sitting at a table we bought for nine dollars at Goodwill! Maybe Dad had some great notions, but *he* wasn't great. He was a bitter, used-up little bit of a man who could only go to sleep after work if he downed enough booze, and I'll be damned if I'm gonna end up like—" [**The second part of Will's DOTS.**]

Darlene shot up from her chair and slapped Will across the face with such force he fell against the counter. [**The exchange between Will and Darlene that preceded this unexpected act of violence on Darlene's part illustrated the shifting dynamics in their relationship—the balance of power, of who was in control of the situation and conversation, kept going back and forth, and Will's direct DOTS collided with Darlene's indirect definition to create and**

heighten conflict, all of it leading to this inevitable desperate act on Darlene's part to silence her son's contemptuous words about her dead husband.] When he regained his balance and turned back to face her, a thin trickle of blood oozed slowly from the comer of his mouth. His eyes widened in fear, shock, and countless levels of confusion and pain.

"You listen to me," said Darlene. "I was married to your father for almost thirty years, and in that time I saw him do things you aren't half man enough to do. I've seen him run into the middle of worse riots than the one today and pull old men out of trouble. I've seen him give his last dime to friends who didn't have enough for groceries and then borrow money from your uncle to pay our own bills. I've seen him be more gentle than you can ever imagine and I've been there when he's felt low because he thought you were embarrassed by him. Maybe he was just a factory worker, but he was a damn decent man who gave me love and a good home. You never saw it, maybe you didn't want to, but your father was a great man who did great things. Maybe they weren't huge things, things that get written about in the paper, but that shouldn't matter. It's not his fault that you never saw any of his greatness, that you only saw him when he was tired and used up. And maybe he did drink, but, goddammit, for almost thirty years he never once thought about just giving up. I loved that . . . that *factory stooge* more than any man in my life—and I could've had plenty. He was the best of them all." [**The first part of Darlene's Direct DOTS.**]

"Mom, please, I—"

"You never did nothing except make him feel like a failure because he couldn't buy you all the things your friends have. *I* wasn't down here listening to him ramble at three in the morning? *You* weren't there on those nights before we had kids, listening to him whisper how scared he was he wouldn't be able to give us a decent life. You weren't there to hold him and kiss him and feel so much tenderness between your bodies that it was like you were one person. And almost thirty years of that, of loving a man like your father, that gives you something no one can ruin or take away, and I won't listen to you talk against him! He was my husband and your father and he's dead and it hurts so damned much I want to scream." [**The second half of her Direct DOTS.**]

Will's eyes filled with tears. "Oh god, Mom, I miss him. I'm so . . . sorry I said those things. I was just so angry." His chest began to hitch with the abrupt force of his sorrow. "I know that I . . . I hurt his feelings, that I made him feel like everything he did was for nothing. Can't I be mad that I'll never get the chance to make it up to him? Can't I?" [**The final part of Will's Direct DOTS, and the moment where his Definition of the Self merges with that of Darlene's.**] He leaned into his mother's arms. "He always said that you gotta . . . gotta look out for your obligations before you can start thinking about your own happiness. I know that now. And I'll . . . I'll try to . . . oh, Christ, Mom. I want the chance to make it all up to him . . ."

Darlene held him and stroked the back of his head, whispering, "It's all right, go on . . . go on . . . he knows now, he always did, you have to believe that . . ." [**And here, where the DOTS connect, the core tone of the story is revealed; one of resigned sadness and regret, where individual sins of omission overpower even the strength of immediate grief.**]

If you've not read "Union Dues," this excerpt should give you some idea that it's perhaps not the happiest story ever written, but I like to think that the emotions at the core of the piece give it the ring of truth, of authenticity, of a story that grapples with honest feeling instead of trying to manipulate the reader.

And you can employ Stanislavsky's Method here and turn it on yourself: how many of you reading this have been lost in depression, or sadness, or lingering grief, or loneliness, or doubt, or any of the thousands of shadowed corners in the human heart where even the blackest darkness would look like a star going nova, and found some moment of comfort in a book or short story that you've read?

This is why you, as a writer, have to present your characters' emotional cores as truthfully and naturally as possible. If you are willing to access your own feelings—especially those you have difficulty expressing to others—and gift them to your characters, then your characters will take those honest emotions and, with you as their guide, adapt them to their own situations within the microcosm of the tale in which they have been cast. Because just as everything that happens within that story is connected to what came before and what will follow, every aspect of the story is connected to you, the writer. If you're not willing to express honest emotions to yourself, your characters aren't going to do it for you, and your readers will faced with a piece of work that—while it may be technically dazzling—has only a cold hollowness where its heart should be.

So connect the DOTS and let the honest emotions be expressed by the imaginary people and things in your story—even if those imaginary things live in dark corners and aren't sometimes particularly pleasant or uplifting.

And here's the thing I promised, the point of reconciliation between John Gardner's earlier directive and the holy chore of writing the best kind of horror fiction: as long as there is fear of the darkness, there will be hope.

Keeping in mind what's been examined here, allow me to present you with someone:

Female. Mid-thirties. Her coat is wool, with a removable lining. It's tan. It's in very good condition and, in fact, might be thought brand-new until you get close enough to see that it's at least ten years out of style. She removes it carefully after entering the restaurant (she's alone) and instead of draping it over the back of her own chair, places it lengthwise across the other chair at the table so that the collar is just hanging a little over the back of the chair and the bottom of the coat hangs a little ways past the seat, nowhere near touching the floor. She's wearing a wedding ring, but it's on the ring finger of her *right* hand. She takes her cloth napkin and spreads it across her lap, then smoothes it out. She picks up the menu, takes a small sip from her water glass, and begins reading. If you watch closely, you can see that her hands are trembling slightly.

What's her story? You sense it, don't you? Maybe you already *know* her story.

So . . . ?

Third Intermission:
"Oh, My God, What *Died* in Here?"

In an introduction I once wrote for a collection of Elizabeth Massie's short stories (*Shadow Dreams*), I made the following comments concerning the often flippant and careless use of the word "Art":

> There is, in my opinion, not one writer, actor, painter, sculptor, dancer, director, musician, what-have-you living today who has the right to call him- or herself an artist. To loudly declare, "I'm creating a piece of art!" is to invite pretension and arrogant high-mindedness; it is to proclaim to anyone who cares to listen that you're so cocksure your work will have a profound impact on everyone who encounters it that they should feel privileged to encounter it. Art is not something that can be consciously created; it has to *occur*. Usually, it's a happy accident. Timing, luck, happenstance, a person's mood at the time, all of these come into play—and the creator's underlying intent is always secondary. *Always.* No exceptions. Period. It's more than just 'liking' a piece of work, it's experiencing a complete, pure, and total communion with the work; for one

> second—maybe longer if you're blessed—you are submerged in the emotions summoned up by the piece and the world is reduced to only your burning core and what this work does to it, gives to it, asking for nothing in return, and what, finally, this communion means to the rest of your life. You come away from the work more than you were before. Art lingers, a ghost of emotional resonance, and from that moment on *you*, not the creator, have the right to call this something a "work of art."

Looking at it now, perhaps that mini-rant is a bit high-minded and hoity-toity its own self (especially considering the context in which it's about to be applied, which I warn you is in questionable taste), but at its center it remains something I fervently believe: art cannot be created, it has to *occur*. So the next time you hear someone defending the context of their work while brandishing the "because I am an artist" shield, do me a favor and smack the living shit out of them.

Moving on.

A few years ago, a very dear friend of mine—one of those rare friends you have from childhood who remains close to you throughout the rest of your life, even if you lose contact for years at a time—passed away suddenly. It was a tremendous shock and a heartbreaking blow to anyone who knew him, because he was one of the most gracious, good-natured, and outright kindest people I have ever known. Some of my fondest memories of childhood and early teen-aged years (like there's really a difference when you get right down to it) feature him in a major role. (Those of you who've read the original edition of *Fear in a Handful of Dust: Horror as a Way of Life* will know that the word "fondest" is not used lightly by me . . . childhood (for me), was not a great time; not a lot of laughs; not a lot of material that's gonna make my highlight reel anytime soon. Once again, moving on . . .)

For the moment, we are back in early 1973: *The Sonny and Cher Comedy Hour* and *The Partridge Family* are at the top of the TV ratings, *Bananafish, Rolling Stone, Creem, National Lampoon* and *Melody Maker* are the only magazines the Utterly Groovy read, *The Joy of Sex* is topping the bestseller list, *Shaft* and *Superfly* (both films featuring incredible, award-winning scores by, respectively, the late, great Isaac Hayes and the late, great Curtis Mayfield) have ushered in the era of the so-called "Blaxploitation" flick, and *The Sting* is fast becoming one of the greatest Hollywood blockbuster movies of all time and has everyone refusing to tell their friends about the surprise ending.

A small group of friends—five guys, myself included—are continually spending our weekends hanging out in someone's basement room because the Girls We Were Madly in Love With have yet to realize how Utterly Groovy we were. Sometimes we read comic books; sometimes we work on Aurora monster models; sometimes we flip through *Famous Monsters of Filmland* magazine (or *Creepy, Eerie* or *Vampirella* because most of our parents think they are wicked and evil and will warp us for life—in my case, they did, but my folks were Fairly Hip, if not Utterly Groovy, and had no problems with my monster magazine collection, knowing that monster were my bag, man), but mostly we hang out in various of our basements because that's where the central and most important piece of our kid hardware is located: the holy record player.

Yup—mostly we listened to records, always accompanying the best songs with our various air instruments (except for the air bass—ever notice how no one ever plays air bass? Seriously—when was the last time someone in an air band said, "Hey, man, I wanna play the bass because the bass player gets all the girls"? There may be a lesson here. Think on it and get back to me). And, of course, being twelve years old, we'd decided that we were all going to form the World's Greatest Rock Band and be big, big stars, so that the Girls We Were Madly In Love With would come to our concerts and see us in all our rock glory, realize how foolish they'd been in refusing our affection, and throw themselves at our feet, begging for our eternal love.

Ahem.

If you were around back then—that is, if you're now staring down the barrel of middle age as I am—then you'll recall that *the* album that every Utterly Groovy person had in their collection and on their turntable was Deep Purple's *Machine Head*; none of us were any exception. (A bit of trivia here: when "Smoke on the Water" was originally released as a single from *MH*, it all but tanked here in the states; it wasn't until the live version from *Made in Japan* was released as a single that it became the monster hit we all know and claim to loathe. Remember this the next time you play Trivial Pursuit.)

In truth, none of us had any idea what the hell we were going to do with our lives, so rock stardom seemed the most obvious choice—

forget that, between the five of us, not a one could play any instrument worth a damn, unless you count the armpit as a musical instrument, in which case we could have formed the world's first and greatest armpit orchestra. (*There's* an image for you . . .)

But it was Johnny, my now-late friend (miss you, buddy; miss you every damn day) who one night, in the basement of his house, provided what was for me one of the earliest examples of what can happen to a person when art occurs.

Understand that Johnny, like me, did not come from a well-to-do family; his folks worked factory jobs just like mine. There wasn't a lot of money for allowances, so you had to save for weeks—if not months—if you wanted to buy a model kit or a record album (which cost you a whopping three or four bucks back then). He wore old clothes that were not in fashion; he wasn't particularly articulate (we were twelve—*all* of us sounded like idiots when we talked for more than four minutes at a time); and—and this was the killer for his social life at the time—he was a bit too tall and bit too fat for his age. (That fat later turned to muscle and made him unstoppable on the football field; I remember with great joy the sight of many a fullback deciding to plow into Johnny's mid-section head-first, freezing in their tracks once they'd slammed into his gut, and then dropping to the ground like a bird that's just flown into a window.)

On this particular night in 1973, we'd exhausted all our usual time-killers and were just sort of sitting around wondering whether or not if the Girls We Were Madly in Love With were going to magically come knocking at the door to keep us company (they didn't), when Johnny made the announcement: "Hey, I wanna show you guys something."

Now, we'd all pooled our money that night and bought a couple of pizzas and an eight-pack of bottled Coca-Cola, then Johnny's mom had insisted on making popcorn for us. Despite being stuffed the to eyeballs, some of us ate a little of the popcorn (Johnny consumed most of it). We were all stuffed and sleepy, so whatever in the hell it was he had to show us had better be pretty Utterly Groovy. Johnny opened—I kid you not—a can of cold beans and ate precisely one-third of it, then finished off the last of his bottle of Coke and crossed the room to his Chair.

I use upper-case for Chair because no one—*no one*—but Johnny was ever allowed to sit in this thing; you weren't even allowed to park your ass on one of its arms, lest Johnny come barreling across the room like some freight train from Hell and push you into a wall (for which he'd later apologize, and then give you one of his comic books so you wouldn't stay mad at him).

I *have* to tell you about this Chair.

In all the history of chairs, there has never been an uglier, sadder, more rickety, patched-together, malevolent, taped-up, uncomfortable-looking, and potentially dangerous monstrosity than this *thing* that lived in Johnny's basement; I mean, this was the kind of chair that would cause every other chair in the world to cross the street were they to see it heading in their direction. Had such a thing as chair Most Wanted posters existed, this Chair would have been Public Enemy Number One. It was the Captain Ahab of chairs, the Frankenstein's Monster of chairs; it was the Chair that other chairs warned their children against at night so they would behave.

Not an attractive piece of furniture, is what I'm saying. Covered in what we used to call "banana-skin" (now referred to as "pleather"), it had countless springs sticking out from the seat that were covered in duct tape; stuffing spilled out of its back like the innards from some victim in a Romero zombie flick; one leg was held together with chicken wire; the left arm was covered in red banana-skin (the rest of it was an ungodly shade of green); and—perhaps its most horrifying characteristic—the seat appeared to sometimes *breathe* of its own accord after Johnny rose from it: for several minutes on end, the seat would expand and then contract, making low but nonetheless terrifying hissing sounds, bubbling and undulating like some evil experimental fluid in a mad scientist's laboratory. Many of us were convinced the thing was alive, *possessed* even. It attacked us in our nightmares. Came after our family members. Made us eat our vegetables. Forced us to sit in it and watch *Hee-Haw* or *The Lawrence Welk Show*.

This was the terror that Johnny began to approach on the night in question.

One more aside, and then I'll reveal the remarkable thing that occurred a minute after Johnny sat down in the Chair from Hell.

Johnny had an unfortunate biological quirk during childhood that he often could not control; he had a tendency to suffer

AGIOs—Audible Gastro-Intestinal Occurrences, popularly know by the layperson as *farts*. And Johnny's farts were, well, *loud*. And sometimes frightening. Think Godzilla's roar in a lower register and you'll have some idea of how these things sounded. I've heard foghorns that sound like a newborn chick's peeps compared to these things.

We're back in the basement now, and Johnny is approaching the Chair. He sits. Looks at us and smiles. Shifts his weight around a little, moves one of his legs a little to the side, and then puts a finger to his mouth to tell the rest of us to be quiet, please.

"I've been practicing this for a couple of weeks," he said.

Then he closed his eyes, shifted the position of his behind a fraction to the left, took a deep breath, and did one of the most remarkable things I have ever witnessed.

He *farted* the opening riff of "Smoke on the Water," all thirteen notes, on-key.

It was not only miraculous to hear, but to see, as well. He reddened with effort and concentration; a small vein bulged in the center of his forehead; his face, neck, and arms became almost instantaneously lacquered in perspiration; he would partially raise one cheek while shifting a leg, then lower that cheek as he raised the other, sometimes using one of his hands to press in on a certain area of his abdomen. He twisted his features with each note, biting down on his lip, closing one eye, flaring his nostrils. A sick walrus in the midst of an agonizing breach birth would have been more appealing to look at.

But none of us cared. We were witness to something extraordinary in the annals of kid mythology. No human being had ever done anything like this before. Perhaps no human being would ever do this again in the remainder of world history. I wondered if perhaps we should kneel and make the sign of the cross to acknowledge the sanctity of the moment. And pray that he wouldn't accidentally shit his pants. (Soiled underwear has a way of taking some the *oomph* out of a miracle.)

Still, Johnny continued with the second bar of the opening:

Bwap-bwap-*bworf*, bwap-bwap-bworf-*BWOOOORF*, bwap-bwap-*bworf*, bwap-bworf . . .

When it was over, we all stood there, nailed to the spot in a kind of twisted awe.

And, yes, the odor was enormous, which explained the tears in our eyes. But the loss of air in our lungs was a small price to pay.

When the moment of awe and near-suffocation passed, we broke into loud cheers and applause, crowding around Johnny, slapping him on the back, wiping his brow, rubbing his shoulders, and basically acting like a bunch of trainers at ringside after a championship fight. So loud were the accolades we were bestowing on Johnny that his sister came down to see what the hubbub was all about. No sooner had she hit the bottom step and taken in a breath than she cowered back, exclaiming, "Oh, my God—what *died* in here?"

There was no way to make her understand the inexplicable, astounding, epoch-marking event that had just occurred; mere words could not do it justice. All we were capable of was staring at her little brother in open-mouthed (and pinched-nosed) wonder. He had done something no human being in our experience had ever done before.

(I feel it only appropriate to add this bit of trivia for your further edification: there was a man who had, in fact done this before. *Le Petomane* was the stage name of the French professional farter and entertainer Joseph Pujol [June 1, 1857 to 1945]. He was famous for his remarkable control of the abdominal muscles, which enabled him to break wind at will. His stage name combines the French verb *peter*, "to fart," with the -mane, "maniac" suffix, found in words like *toxicomane*. In English, a translation might yield "the fart maniac." His profession can also be referred to as a "flatulist" or a "fartiste.") (By the way, I lifted that bit of information, word-for-word, from the *Wikipedia* entry about him; after all, why try to improve upon perfection?)

That night became legend very quickly, and within a few weeks, we would have parties where Johnny and his unique, amazing talent would be the high point of the festivities. Even the Girls We Were Madly in Love With began to attend these gatherings, and Johnny never failed to deliver the anticipated finale.

But he always had to be in the Chair, the one and only Chair, which we carried to and from the various parties with the greatest of care and reverence, as if it were a Van Gogh painting, or a Da Vinci sculpture, or Raquel Welch's breasts.

And Johnny always prepared for the big event the same way: pizza, Coke, popcorn, and one-third of a can of cold beans, consumed in that order, in precise quantities, at pre-determined times so that it would all settle into him in the same way before each performance. He always moved the same way, always lifted this cheek or that at the right moment, clenched and unclenched so as to maintain the right pitch . . . it was Utterly Groovy, ya dig?

Johnny's gone now, dead of a heart attack at age 45, and not a day goes by that I don't miss him, or recall how, every time we saw each other, one of us would bring up the Chair Concerts, as they came to be called. He died watching a football game, sitting in the Chair, eating pizza, after a too-short but rich and happy life wherein he met and married a wonderful and beautiful woman, made dozens—if not hundreds—of friends, worked at a job he loved, and always had a kind word for you, a smile on his face, a joke to tell, or a great-big, rib-bruising bear hug at the ready should you need one to brighten your day.

The Chair, by the way, is still in his family, and no one sits in it. It is proudly displayed, and even children—nieces, nephews, cousins—who never met Johnny know the story about the Chair Concerts, how Uncle Johnny could fart "Smoke on the Water" perfectly every time . . . providing he could properly prepare. It is a story that will be passed on from generation to generation, and there will always be, eternally, the Chair as proof.

So how does this apply to the subject of art? (And, yes, it has crossed my mind more than once that "fart" and "art" rhyme, which I find oddly appropriate.)

This story applies to the subject because, whether we're willing to admit it or not, every person we know possesses some gift that they bestow upon the world; a skilled auto mechanic, a detail-oriented brick-layer, an expert toolmaker, even the proficient janitor—all contribute something of the aesthetic to everyday life, something that impacts you and adds to or enhances your existence. Okay, maybe a well-tuned engine isn't exactly on the same level as Kurosawa's greatest films, but that doesn't mean that it doesn't have deep and abiding value. Doctor or doorman, composer or custodian, sculptor or sales clerk, *everyone* possesses some skill or talent that makes them unique among the carbon-based life-forms we pass every day. What they do on an everyday basis may not obviously be an occurrence of art as I described it at the start of this column, but bear in mind that the definition was more than a bit insular: occurrences of art are all around us, we just have to be willing to see them for what they are, regardless of how mundane or trivial they may appear on the surface.

Have you ever seen the film *Babette's Feast*? It's not about a woman who prepares a meal for a bunch of people; it's about the creation of a moment of art that can never be repeated, but makes such an impact on those who experience it that it will live on in their hearts and memories forever.

Kind of like Johnny's farts.

As crude as it may seem. I know in my heart that long after I am gone, people will still be talking about Johnny's farts while my books and stories will be, if I'm lucky, a minor footnote in some genre textbook gathering dust on a dim shelf somewhere.

But you know what? That's okay. Because for the rest of my life, I will have readers who appreciate what I do, and I am thankful for that. I am thankful that I knew Johnny, that I knew my parents, that I knew my uncles, that I knew the too-numerous amounts of people who are no longer part of this world.

If this sounds like something of a pep-talk, that's because it is; not just for you, but for myself. It's too easy to give in to grief and sadness and despair—believe it or not, as dark and depressing as my work gets, that is one of the core points I try to get across with it.

So next time, when you're sitting with your family and friends and (hopefully) enjoying one another's companionship, be grateful that you have people in your life who care about you and respect what you do and are pleased to be in your company. (I say this as someone who remains constantly baffled and humbled that *anyone* is glad to see him.)

Enjoy your family, your friends, your meal, and your memories.

Just—and trust me on this—don't try to entertain everyone afterward by belching the opening of Beethoven's Fifth Symphony, or everyone might be put off that pumpkin pie for dessert.

1

Fear; “But That’s the Way it Really Happened!”; and Staying the Hell Out of Your Own Way, for Chrissakes

If horror is indeed the literature of fear, then everything is arguably a horror story. From the intense terror of films such as *Alien* and *The Ring* to lighter fare such as *E.T.* and *Stir Crazy*, novels from *The Shining, Ghost Story, Interview with the Vampire* to books like *What Color Is Your Parachute, Who Moved My Cheese?* and *Nickel and Dimed*—hell, even the most lame of thin romance novels—fear lies at the core of everything we do. We work in order to make money and pay bills because we’re afraid if we don’t, our families will wind up on the streets; we do what we can for those who love us because, on some level, we’re afraid that if we don’t, we will lose them; we keep up on workplace practices because we’re afraid of losing our jobs or being passed over for promotion; we take vitamins and go to the doctor and work out three times a week because we want to stay healthy and look good because we’re afraid of growing (and looking) old, which leads us back to ye olde fear of death—the ending to every story, fictional or otherwise—that we want to stave off for as long as possible.

But let’s keep this in the context of fiction. Choose any novel or short story from any genre, remove from it the element of fear, and see how much of a story you have left. Odds are, not much.

It is my fervent belief that, like it or not, it is ultimately fear that lies at the core of all our actions. Since horror writers deal primarily in the exploration of this fear, that exploration has to include the reshaping of things from the writer's own life experience.

For the record, any writer who claims that their fiction is not based on or drawn from some aspect of their own lives—be it past, present, or worries about the future—is one of two things: a liar or unpublished.

I know fear, and I know regret; I know sadness, and I know anger; I know the fragile nature of joy, and I know the ethereal state of hope; I know integrity, and I know duplicity; I know the wonder of finding a true friend, and I know the pain of how it feels to lose one. I also know that the more I learn, the less I know, and that no discussion of the craft of writing can be restricted to just the nuts-and-bolts aspects lest it read like some dry, outdated textbook on the subject.

For this penultimate section I'm going to discuss writing a bit more. Since the only thing more tedious than listening to a writer talk about writing is having to *read* one talking about writing, I am going to try to make this as direct and clear as possible, with a minimum of technical jargon, and will dissect for your glee a pair of my own stories.

I have been, over the years, fairly up-front about the influence my life has had not only on what I choose to write but how I choose to write it, so be warned that no discussion of my work can come without equal discussion of those events and people and sensibilities that led to the writing of a particular story or novel.

Have you ever been present at a writer's workshop where, after hearing their story critiqued by the other members, a writer will point to a certain event depicted in the story—an event the others have dubbed hard to swallow or unbelievable—and say, "But that's the way it really happened"? Well, I've been at these meetings, and I've said there what I'm about to say here: fiction doesn't give a Sumatran rat's ass about how something really happened; it has no use for your real-life experiences if you are hell-bent to depict them as they actually occurred. The story doesn't care about your trivial little self-exorcisms, it cares only that you tell it as well as possible and that you care enough to be quiet and stay the hell out of its way.

One of my most popular stories, "Union Dues" (which originally appeared in *Borderlands 4*, edited by Tom and Elizabeth Monteleone), was almost crippled beyond repair early on because of my bull-headed insistence on portraying an event as it "really happened." As a result, "Union Dues" remains only one of three stories that I had to rewrite four times before I got it right. (I can usually get it in two passes, three if there's a serious glitch; I almost never have to go that desperate, ulcer-inducing, sleep-depriving fourth pass. I tend to have everything thought out well before I apply ass to chair and hands to keyboard.)

Here's a section from the scene in question:

Sheriff Ted Jackson held a handkerchief over his nose and mouth as he surveyed the wreckage of the riot.

A cloud of tear gas was dissipating at neck level in the parking lot of the factory, reflecting lights from the two dozen police cars encircling the area. Newspaper reporters and television news crews were assembling outside the barricades along with people from the neighborhood and relatives of the workers involved. Silhouetted against the rapidly-setting cold November sun, the crowd looked like one massive duster of cells; a shadow on a lung x-ray—sorry, bud, this looks bad.

Men lay scattered, some on their sides, others on their backs, still more squatting and coughing and vomiting, all wiping blood from their faces and hands.

A half-foot of old, crusty snow had covered the ground since the first week of the month, followed by days and nights of dry cold, so that the snow had merely aged and turned the color of damp ash, mottled by candy wrappers, empty cigarette packs, losing lottery tickets, beer cans, and now bodies. The layer of snow whispering from the sky was a fresh coat of paint; a whitewash that hid the ugliness and despair of the tainted world underneath.

A pain-filled voice called out from somewhere.

Fire blew out the windshield of an overturned semi; it jerked sideways, slammed into a guardrail, and puked glass.

The crowd pushed forward, knocking over several of the barriers. Officers in full riot gear held everyone back.

The snow grew dense as more sirens approached.

The searchlight from a police helicopter swept the area.

A woman in the crowd began weeping loudly.

You couldn't have asked for an uglier mess.

Jackson pulled the handkerchief away and took an icy breath; the wind was trying to move the gas away but the snow held it against the ground. He turned up the collar of his jacket and pulled a twenty-gauge pump-action shotgun from the cruiser's rack.

"Sheriff?"

Dan Robinson, one of his deputies, offered him a gas mask.

"Little late for that."

"I know, but the fire department brought along extras and I thought—"

"Piss on that." Jackson stared through the snow at the crowd of shadows. The strobing visibar lights perpetually changed the shape of the pack; red-*blink*—a smoke crowd; blue-*blink*—a snow-ash crowd; white-*blink*—a shadow crowd.

"You okay, Sheriff?"

"Let's go see if they cleared everyone away from the east side."

The two men trudged through the heaps of snow, working their way around the broken glass, twisted metal, blood, grease, and bodies. Paramedics scurried in all directions; gurneys were collapsed, loaded, then lifted into place and rolled toward waiting ambulances. Volunteers from the local Red Cross were administering aid to those with less serious wounds.

"Any idea how this started, sir?"

"The scabs came out for food. Strikers cut off all deliveries three days ago."

"Terrible thing."

"You got that right."

They rounded the comer and took several deep breaths to clear their lungs.

Jackson remembered the afternoon he'd had to come down and assist with bringing in the scabs—the strikers behind barricades on one side of the parking lot while the scabs rode in on flatbed trucks like livestock to an auction. Until that afternoon he'd never believed that rage was something that could live outside the physical confines of a man's own heart, but as those scabs climbed down and began walking toward the main production floor entrance he'd felt the presence of cumulative anger becoming something more fierce, something hulking and twisted and hideous. To this day he couldn't say how or why, but he could swear that the atmosphere between the strikers and scabs had rippled and even torn in places. It still gave him the willies.

He blinked against the falling snow and felt his heart skip a beat.

Twenty yards away, near a smoldering overturned flatbed at the edge of the east parking lot, a man lay on the ground, his limbs twisted at impossible angles. A long, thick smear of hot machine oil pooled behind him, hissing in the snow.

Maneuvering through the snowdrifts, Jackson raced over, slid to a halt, chambered a shell, and dropped to one knee, gesturing for Robinson to do the same.

Jackson looked down at the body and felt something lodge in his throat. "Damn. Herb Kaylor."

"You know him?"

Jackson tried to swallow but couldn't. The image of the man's face blurred; he wiped his eyes and realized that he was crying. "Yeah. Him and me served together in Vietnam. I just played cards with him and his wife a couple nights ago. *Goddammit*!" He clenched his teeth. "He wasn't supposed to be workin' the picket line today. Christ! Poor Herb . . .

The stumbling block came with that "smoldering overturned flatbed at the edge of the east parking lot." There was, in the first three drafts, a little boy hiding inside that truck.

Here's what *really* happened (which I should have remembered fiction doesn't give a shit about):

When I was seven years old, the workers at the Roper manufacturing plant where my dad was employed went on strike. This strike, occurring as the war in Vietnam was gearing up for its final, protracted, bloody hurrah, went on for nearly six weeks. The men who walked the picket line did so 24/7. A group of wives, my mother included, arranged to take turns providing the picketers with food; each of them would, on their assigned day, make sandwiches, potato salad, cold chicken, whatever they could afford (the strike fund ran out very quickly, so most of this food was paid for with money no one could afford to be spending) and deliver it to the workers.

My parents did not own a car; we couldn't afford one. Since the plant was only a fifteen to twenty minute walk from our front door, it was decided that seven-year-old Gary would do his part for the American worker and be the one to deliver the food on Wednesdays, Mom's assigned day. I had no problems with this; I'd load up the sacks of sandwiches and chips into my trusty old Radio Flyer wagon and trundle on down to the picket line. (Mom would always sneak in a couple of twelve-packs of Blatz beer, donated by other wives or neighbors, and tell me, "Make sure you keep this covered so that no one can see it. We don't want anybody getting into trouble." Yeah, I could have been technically charged with bootlegging at age seven; ain't life cool?)

On this particular Wednesday I was running a little late. I was supposed to be there no later than 2:00 PM. because Dad wanted to make sure I was out of there by two-thirty; neither he nor Mom would tell me why. That bugged me, because usually on Wednesdays I got to hang around, carry a picket sign, and talk with the guys. It made me feel all accepted and liked and grown-up. But today wasn't going to go like that, and I resented it, as well as not being told why I couldn't hang around. So I piddle-farted around (Mom's term) longer than necessary and didn't get out the door until five minutes until two. I arrived at the picket line somewhere between two-ten and two-fifteen.

I knew as soon as I got there that something wasn't right.

Aside from the dozens of workers manning the picket line, there were three large flatbed trucks with a bunch of other guys riding in them. The workers were standing in front of the trucks, and the guys riding in the backs looked really scared—I figured that must be the case, since not one of them was making a move to get out.

I didn't know or understand about scab labor in 1968, so I had no way of knowing that the guys standing in the backs of these flatbeds were considered to be the lowest of the low on the totem pole of blue-collar workers. And I sure as hell didn't know that the strikers had gotten wind of the company's bringing in scab labor and so had gathered *en masse* and armed themselves to prevent the scabs from getting inside the plant.

A little pause here to make something clear about so-called scab laborers: until I hit my late twenties I was a feverish—almost rabid—

pro-union guy; in truth, I still think labor unions are, *in theory*, a great thing, because God knows the blue-collar worker in this country doesn't have anything else in his or her corner, but I saw the union eventually turn its back on both my parents when they desperately needed the support. I saw the look on Mom's face when she and I had to go downtown to the welfare offices twice a month to stand in these ungodly long lines waiting for our free allotment of bread, cheese, food stamps, and milk coupons (when these last were available, which wasn't often). I saw the shame on Dad's face when he had to accept charity from neighbors who were employed and wanted to help us out. I saw the way people in the grocery store lines would wrinkle their noses and shake their heads in disgust when Mom pulled out food stamps instead of cash. And I saw the way the cashiers would roll their eyes, *tsk* none-too-quietly, and make a show-stopping production number out of having to re-enter numbers when Mom discovered that we didn't have enough to cover everything and so had to choose what items to put back. To this day I want to roundhouse-punch both cashiers and other people in line who act like someone having to put an item back because they don't have enough money is somehow an insult, embarrassment, and inconvenience to *them*. After all, who *cares* about how the person putting the items back must feel; they're the ones holding up the line. They're the ones who should have done their math, who should have kept their jobs or had fewer children or borrowed from family members so they'd have enough money to pay for their groceries and not fuck up everyone else's day. I lost count of how many times Mom walked out of a grocery store in tears because she'd been humiliated by cashiers, managers, and other customers in line behind her.

What does this have to do with scab laborers?

Simple: when you consider what my parents—who were supposedly under the protection of their unions—went through while toeing the line and sticking to the rules, can you imagine how desperate, how at the end of their ropes, a worker would have to be in order to work scab? These are the people who, for whatever reasons, can not get hired on at plants or anywhere else, and so are reduced to hanging out in front of the unemployment office every morning like beggars at the entrance to a bus station in the hopes that someone is going to drive up in a flatbed truck and say they need able bodies to work, payment in cash at the end of the job. These workers go into a situation like this knowing that they're going to be threatened, spit on, and probably physically assaulted, all so they can hole up inside a factory where they'll have to remain, day and night, until the outside situation has been resolved. Only then can they collect their pay, which, odds favor, will be about one-third to half of what a regular union worker gets for the same job. So the next time you read about a factory that is bringing in scabs to work the line while the other workers are on strike, bear in mind that neither the workers nor the scabs are to blame; both are desperate and doing what they think is best for themselves and their families.

Grey areas.

I deal with those a lot in my fiction.

And sometimes it's a grey area from real life that I try to graft onto a story because I make the mistake of putting my ego and not the story's own good first.

Let's get back to seven-year-old Gary with his Radio Flyer full of sandwiches and beer.

The first thing I think when I see these guys in the trucks and the workers on the picket line is: *I don't think there's enough sandwiches for everybody.* Still, I figured, if some of the guys were willing to split their sandwiches (bologna and cheese, pimento loaf and cheese, ham and cheese) with the other guys, we might be able to make it stretch (which is actually what Jesus said right before the whole loaves-and-fishes thing: "I can make this stretch").

So I trundle on down right toward the middle of it and I'm about ten, twenty yards away when a gun goes off and the guys in the trucks jump down and the picketers surge forward and then there's nothing but clubs and fists and things smashing and people falling all around me and police cars and sirens and visibar lights and fire trucks and then tear gas and I wet myself and I was so frightened because I couldn't find Dad and then a couple of guys fell over my wagon and knocked the sandwiches and bottles all over the parking lot, and I screamed and started running away but I tripped and fell face-first onto the asphalt and skidded a few feet, tearing up the side of my face and my arms and knees and it hurt like nobody's business, and I couldn't get up to run so I sort of crawled over to where this truck had been knocked over on its side and I hid underneath its bed and just lay there, shaking and holding my ears because of all the noise. In the midst of all this I saw two guys fighting their way over toward the truck; one of them kicked the other's feet out from under him, and when the second guy was on his back, the first guy dropped down on him like a curse from heaven and started hammering at his skull with an unopened beer bottle—one of the Blatzes that had been in my wagon—and there was blood and screaming, and then the bottle shattered and the guy who'd been getting pummeled by it wrenched the remainder of it from the first guy's hand and slashed it right across his face. The second guy fell backward, clutching at the blood on his face, and scrambled around until he found something on the ground, then he came back up and he had this mother of a crowbar that must have fallen from the truck I was hiding underneath, and he struck the second guy in the head once, twice, three times. Once the second guy went down the first guy still didn't stop; he hit him a couple of more times, hard, then took off—and me, I was lying there underneath the truck and the second guy, he was lying a few feet away with blood all over his face and body, and he was shuddering and jerking and the whole time he was looking right at me.

And I watched him die.

Beaten to death in part by a bottle of beer that had fallen from my wagon, which, if I'd been on time, if I hadn't piddle-farted around, would have been drunk and disposed of well before the trouble started and maybe wouldn't have been used to make this guy horizontal in the middle of a riot.

So I watched him die, his eyes never closing, but growing dimmer nonetheless.

I found out what his name was later, which helped a little because it gave me something to put with that face, and I did eventually realize that it was the beating with the crowbar and not the beer bottle that killed him, but still ... no snowflake in an avalanche ever feels responsible.

When it came time to write "Union Dues" I was determined to have a little boy (standing in for me) hiding either inside or underneath that "smoldering overturned flatbed at the edge of the east parking lot" because, goddammit, *that's the way it really happened.*

Little son-of-a-bitch kept getting in the way. The whole time I was writing and rewriting this story, this whiny little useless literary construct (a person or thing in a story that serves no other purpose than to be a convenient symbol or plot device) kept calling out from that truck and causing Sheriff Jackson and Deputy Robinson to drop everything (forward momentum and internal logic of the story included) and run over there to drag his pointless ass out of the wreckage. I kept struggling with his presence, and finally managed to work out a logical way for the kid to be there and contribute something to the scene (he was initially the one who recognized the dead man), but then another problem arose: once I had dragged his butt from the wreckage and used him to identify the dead man, I had no effing idea what to do with him. He was in the sheriff's way, he was in the deputy's way, he was in the story's way—a story in which he now served no further purpose—and he was in my way, but I was going to keep him there because, goddammit, *that's the way it really happened*, sniff-sniff, wah-wah-wah, boo-hoo, stamping foot on the floor.

I was—to paraphrase Megan's Law—suddenly all will, all purpose and design. Note that last word, because once design enters into the storytelling equation, you're dead in the water. You're not following an outline or sticking to the plot or expanding on the theme; you're grafting onto the narrative something that probably has no business being anywhere near the story, let alone in it.

So, reluctantly (and after a major chewing out from Tom Monteleone, who informed me in no uncertain terms that I should with all haste slip my sphenoid bone and everything attached to it from the protective covering of my sigmoid flexure and remove it hence through the sacro-iliac symphysis—"Get your fuckin' head out of your ass, Braunbeck!" is I think the way he actually phrased it), I cut The Little Boy Who Couldn't out of the story—

—and every last problem that I'd been having with "Union Dues" vanished completely, resulting in what is, if I do say so myself, one of the best short stories I've yet written, and one that serves as a loving and respectful testament to my dad's memory.

All because I finally realized that in order to give a story its due, you have to care enough to be quiet and keep yourself out of it.

Because fiction doesn't care about how something "really happened."

It's a rare occurrence when a writer is able to lift something wholecloth from his or her own life, portray it as it actually happened, and have it positively serve the story. It's even more rare for that positive service to include enriching the story in simple terms of narrative flow and structure.

Of the two hundred or so short stories I've published, only four times have I lifted an event whole-cloth from my past and been able to use it with no embellishment to the advantage of the narrative. I don't know that I'll ever do it again, especially after the fourth and most recent occurrence, which I will discuss near the close of this book. But before getting in to those examples, we need to look at some of basics of the craft so you will understand what, in my opinion, constitutes good storytelling. Non-writers always hear writers going on (and on . . . and on . . .) about "knowing the rules," about "following structure," about "maintaining a consistent tone," and dozens of other seemingly secret code catch-phrases that soon puts a tired gleam in the eyes of everyone within hearing distance as they surreptitiously start looking for the nearest exit.

The next section is not at all meant to be patronizing, condescending, or—God forbid—instructional; it is simply meant, for the non-writers among you, to shed a little light on this not-at-all-mysterious process we call writing.

2

Brought to You by the Law Firm of Beguile, Intrigue, and Assault

OPENING LINES.

I have grown to hate them.

One of the unpleasant realities we have to face as writers today is that we have, on average, about 500 words in which to grab and hold a reader's interest when writing a short story, twenty-five to fifty pages if it's a novel. I, for one, think this unfair, but I also voted for Dukakis, so what the hell do I know? Yes, it would be nice, be wonderful, be just oh-so-*peachy* if we lived in a world where readers had the patience and the time to be eased into a narrative, to be seduced by the ebb and flow of the language, the musical composition of sentences, the overall rhythm and atmosphere filtered by writers through their own sensibilities and re-interpreted for you here on the printed page as a magnificent feast of words.

I also voted for Al Gore and John Kerry.

Back from Oz now, the harsh reality is and will remain that you absolutely *have* to hook and hold a reader's attention with your opening lines; if they get to the second or third page of your story and are still not interested in what's going on, they'll turn to the next story in the anthology. So your opening lines have to be intensely immediate, somehow grabbing the reader's attention while simultaneously establishing time, place, situation, character, and conflict.

Here is what remains the greatest opening line I've ever read, from Dan Simmons' short story "Metastasis":

> On the day Louis Steig received a call from his sister saying that their mother had collapsed and been admitted to a Denver hospital with a diagnosis of cancer, he promptly jumped into his Camaro, headed for Denver at high speed, hit a patch of black ice on the Boulder Turnpike, flipped his car seven times, and ended up in a coma with a fractured skull and a severe concussion.

It's really too bad that Simmons meanders around the action like he does, being all wishy-washy and passive and—

—oh, wait, hang on a second; I was reading an opening line from one of my old stories. Never mind.

In one powerful sweep, Simmons not only grabs your attention and holds it, but establishes everything that a good short story needs to establish as soon as possible. Whenever someone asks me for a good example of the opening line, "Metastasis" is always the story to which I refer them.

Take note of Simmons' expert control of cadence while you're at it, as well as the sly manner in which he keeps punching that cadence with carefully-chosen verbs: Steig *jumps* into his Camaro; he *hits* a patch of black ice; he *flips* his car—words that have definite associations for the readers, summoning up specific impressions in their minds, which they then use as points of personal reference to draw them deeper into the narrative and make themselves a part of the story.

I have, through the experiences of my own reading and writing, come to the conclusion that there are three and *only* three types of opening lines, which can best be summed up by the following words: Beguile, Intrigue, Assault.

The opening line of "Metastasis" is one of the more obvious examples of the Assault brand of opening line. It machineguns so much information at you so rapidly and so skillfully that it might as well grow a leg and kick you in the teeth. No, it's not heavy-handed or consciously forceful; its power emerges naturally from the rhythm of the words and the situations those words are being used to convey. I say it's one of the more obvious examples because you'd have to be asleep or clinically brain-dead not to discern Simmons' intent; you know this is going to be a story that deals with high stakes in a head-on manner.

Don't let me mislead you: an Assault brand of opening line doesn't *have* to be jam-packed with details and action; it can achieve its desired effect with only a few words, such as this expert stab from Dennis Etchison's "The Dead Call," one of the most famous opening lines in modern horror:

> Today I rubbed ground glass in my wife's eyes.

Or this, from Harlan Ellison's "In The Fourth Year Of The War":

> In the fourth year of the war with the despicable personage that had come to live in my brain, the utterly vile tenant who called himself Jerry Olander, I was ordered to kill for the first time.

Or this modest example, from my own short story "Saviour":

> I laid out the rifles, loaded the shotguns, and stacked up the cartridges along the wall.

Or this, from, William F. Nolan's "Fyodor's Law":

> They were at nearly every street corner in Greater Los Angeles, standing or sitting cross-legged in their ragged, dirt-stiffened clothing, their faces stubble-bearded, eyes slack and defeated, clutching crude, hand-lettered cardboard signs:
>
> HOMELESS!
> HUNGRY!
> WILL WORK FOR FOOD
> PLEASE HELP???
> GOD BLESS YOU!!!

And, as a final example of the more obvious Assault opening, try this, from another story of mine, "The Projectionist":

> It was an old movie theater full of winos and thugs and snoring bums and it stank horribly and was overcrowded and overheated and usually showed lousy movies, but the projectionist didn't mind; it was better than the two-room shit-hole he called his "place" and gave him something to look forward to, especially on those days when the movies changed because then he got to splice the reels together, and that made him feel like he was creating something, like he was part of the movie; it gave him the only taste of real power he'd ever known.

Working backward on the list, next we have the Intrigue brand of opening line. While not as immediately overpowering to the reader, the Intrigue opening is nonetheless just as effective—and in some cases, more so—than the Assault approach. The idea here is to tap the reader on the shoulder and whisper something interesting in their ear—not too much; just enough to make them turn your story's way and see what they can make of this. The Intrigue opening can be a bit mysterious, off-putting, even whimsical, and while it doesn't offer as easy an opportunity to establish all the setup information right away, if you do it correctly, the reader will go along with you for a little while before they start asking who-what-when-where-why-how. The Intrigue opening can be just as subtle as you'd like, or as hard as a slap across the face.

From the first chapter of Joe R. Lansdale's *Cold In July:*

> That night, Ann heard the noise first.

From Tom Piccirilli's "Inside The Works":

> Art, sex, and madness crawled and spun side by side down deep inside the Works; the walls dripped with drama, floors covered in genius, soul, and a phalanx of talent.

Peter Crowther checks in next, with this beauty from his short story "Cleaning Up":

> Mostly it was only in his room when Chris woke up or as he waited for sleep, but just now and again, particularly on dry nights when he wasn't dodging puddles, he would think of Susie when he went out to the park for his evening toiletries.

To throw more of my own work on the fire, here's the first line of my story "All Over, All Gone, Bye-Bye":

> There should have been more left once the children were gone, more than just empty bedrooms, broken toys discovered in the backs of closets, the occasional pair of gym socks or pantyhose found hiding under the furniture, collecting dust like the little ones used to collect dolls or model cars.

From Gene Wolfe's "Black Shoes" (a personal favorite of mine):

> I heard this story from an old college acquaintance, a man I hadn't spoken to for twenty years; I do not vouch for its veracity, but I do—I will—vouch for his: he believed every word of it.

And, from Rod Serling's novella "The Escape Route":

> He lay on sweat-logged, soggy sheets—his ice-cube-blue eyes, set deep in a bald, bullet head, staring up at the cracked ceiling; his aching, middle-aged body pleading for sleep, but his mind a runaway dynamo, racing back and forth across the bombed-out landscape of his life.

In each case, if the writer has done their job correctly and the Intrigue opening has been accomplished, the reader's first reaction should always be this: *Well? What happens next? Go on.*

Which brings us to the last and infinitely most difficult type of first line, the Beguile opening. (Almost sounds like the name of Robert Ludlam novel, doesn't it?) This type of opening combines the elements of Assault and Intrigue while adding a heavy serving of the enigmatic to the recipe.

Take, for instance, this opening volley from Shirley Jackson's "I Know Who I Love":

> Catherine Vincent began her life in a two-room apartment in New York; she was born in a minister's home in Buffalo; the shift from one to the other might be called her tragedy.

From John O'Hara's magnificent story "Afternoon Waltz":

> In many American towns it often happened that on the main residential street there would be one or two blocks that for one reason or another gave the impression of retiring.

The opening of Jack Cady's heart-wrenching "The Burning" goes like this:

> Sunlight gleamed as Singleton and I walked down the hill to the charred wreckage of what had been a truck.

Compare that to the opening line of Karl Edward Wagner's "More Sinned Against":

> Theirs was a story so commonplace that it balanced uneasily between the maudlin and the sordid—a cliché dipped in filth.

And I'll throw yet another one from me into the mix and offer the first line of my story "She So Loved Her Garden":

> After the death of her husband the old woman spent countless hours alone in the house for the purpose of making it emptier; it was a game to her, like the one she'd played as a child, walking on the stone wall of the garden, pretending it was a mountain ledge, not daring to look down for sight of the rocks below, knowing certain death awaited her should she slip, a terrible fall that would crush her to bits, walking

> along until her steps faltered and she toppled backward, always thinking in that moment before her tiny body hit the ground: *So that's when I died.*

And the finest example of the Beguile opening comes to us courtesy of *Last Call* and *Earthquake Weather* author Tim Powers, from one of his rare short stories, "Night Moves":

> When a warm midnight wind sails in over the mountains from the desert and puffs window shades inward, and then hesitates for a second so that the shades flap back and knock against the window frames, Southern Californians wake up and know that the Santa Ana wind has come, and that tomorrow their potted plants will be strewn up and down the alleys and sidewalks: but it promises blue skies and clean air, and they prop themselves up in bed for a few moments and listen to the palm fronds rattling and creaking out in the darkness.

I readily admit that I may be stuffed full of wild blueberry muffins when I say there are only three types of opening lines, but remember: nothing I've said thus far is meant to be taken as an absolute. Some opening lines can arguably fit in categories other than those I've assigned them here, but in my experience, I find that most memorable opening lines are usually brought to you by the law firm of Beguile, Intrigue, and Assault.

Now for a little exercise, just for fun.

Below you will find an assortment of opening lines, all culled from my own stories; see if you can figure out which of the three types of openings each line is. There are no right or wrong answers, nor will any answers be offered in footnotes or appendices—mostly because this book ain't got none.

Here are the lines. Have fun.

> Lucinda turned her wheelchair away from the painting, adjusted her belly-bag, and decided that sadness was the color of rain.
>
> –"At Eternity's Gate"

A weary remnant of the young woman she once was, Fran McLachlan stood in the center of the midway holding her five-year-old son's hand and trying not to think about the way her life had gone wrong.

–"In a Hand or Face"

The ghosts of New Orleans are restless tonight

–"Down in Darkest Dixie
Where the Dead Don't Dance"

Sarah Hempel glimpsed her reflection in the protective glass of a vending machine in the nursing home's tiny lounge, looked into her bloodshot eyes, and thought: *The question is, can she do it?*

–"Rights of Memory"

Blood from the wound on my neck matted the fur on the left side of my chest and piercing agony throbbed somewhere in my center as I reeled shrieking to the side, my heart triphammering.

–"Some Touch of Pity"

The customers in the truck stop restaurant paid no attention to the man in the parka until he started shooting.

–"Haceldama"

Jeremiah Culpepper screamed over the boom of cannon and crack of gunfire as he saw his son Joshua take the full force of a Yankee musket ball directly in the center of his chest, stagger backward, crumple against the trunk of a pine tree, then slump to the gore-muddied ground where he curled into a ball like a little child, his face turning white as blood seeped through his heavy wool uniform.

–"News From the Long Mountains"
(co-written with Lucy A. Snyder)

The baby rolled over inside the trash dumpster and coughed as blood trickled from its mouth.

–"Drowning With Others"

> He lowered the towel, unveiling the rest of his face, and looked into the reflection, past his eyes, past the skull underneath his skin, past the veins and blood and grey matter until it seemed he was staring into the ancient heart of some holy mystery whose answer had been, until this moment, out of his reach.
>
> –"Geoff #1: Dreams and Permanence"

> The thing which most bothered Levon about the other members of the grief support group—besides their voices seeming too loud because he was starting to get one of his corkscrew headaches—was not so much that they looked like prisoners awaiting the hour of their execution, but that every last one of them had the air of a *falsely-accused* prisoner, one who'd resigned him- or herself to dying for a crime they knew they did not commit—*'Tis a far, far better thing I do now than I have ever done before* and other such urp-inducing romantic fal-de-ral.
>
> –"One Brown Mouse"

> When Quasimodo awoke he found that sometime during the night he'd turned back into Simon Kaiser and the woman who was his Esmeralda had broken into particles of dust that drifted before his eyes like so many unobtained goals.
>
> –"For Want Of A Smile"

By now you've undoubtedly notice the preference I show toward writing that has a solid grasp of cadence. Not to hammer this into the ground, but as a writer I strive toward giving my prose a certain musical quality; if it reads smoothly aloud (and I at some point read everything of mine aloud), then it's going to read twice as smoothly when it's just the story and the reader.

Why does he have such a thing about cadence?

The first time I was ware of art "happening" to me was when I was a little boy and was watching a first-run *Night Gallery* episode with my mom. The episode was "The Messiah on Mott Street," starring Edward G. Robinson, Tony Roberts, and Yaphet Kotto, about a dying Jewish man on Christmas Eve whose grandson—oh, for chrissakes, I don't have to actually *tell* you about this episode, do I? Didn't think so.

(Yes, I remember when each episode of *Night Gallery* was brand new and never-before-seen. Thus endeth the Old Fart moment.)

I realized about two-thirds of the way through that there was this little lump in my throat, and by the time the episode reached its unapologetically sentimental conclusion, I was bawling like a baby. So was my mom. Until the day she died, "The Messiah On Mott Street" remained her favorite Christmas episode of any television show. We had both been moved by Serling's simple tale of redemption and miracles among the tenements, and as Mom was pouring herself and me some hot chocolate afterward, she wiped her eyes and said, "Oh, I swear, that Rod Serling can sure write good stories."

That's when art happened for me. It wasn't until Mom said those words that I came back to reality long enough to realize that Rod Serling (who I knew from *The Twilight Zone*) had *written* the words that those people had said, and that his story had made both me and Mom cry (in that good but embarrassing way you never want to tell anyone about later), and that meant that words and stories could *affect* people.

Not a major unveiling as far as art exhibits go, but it did the trick for me. Watching that episode, knowing my reaction to it, Mom's reaction to it, and then her reaction *about* her reaction, brought it full circle and I started crying again (silly, sentimental boy), and when Mom put her arm around my shoulder and told me it was all right, it was okay, it was just a television show, just a story, all I could manage to say was, "No, it wasn't," before I started in with the spluttering again.

I hadn't the experience or the brains to fully realize what was happening to me, so how in hell was I supposed to articulate it? It seemed to me then that, if this were a fair world and just universe, everyone would be able to articulate their thoughts and feelings as well as the people on *Night Gallery* had, and then maybe people wouldn't find themselves standing around with snot running down their face and tears in their eyes, frustrated because they couldn't find the words to express all they needed to convey.

So I began seeking out Rod Serling everywhere I could. I found collections of his short stories at the local library (Serling was a much-underrated prose writer) and read them all cover to cover, then started in again. Anytime a movie written by Serling came on television, Mom or dad would call me down to watch it. I became a *TZ* rerun junkie (still am), and you can bet *your* ass that *mine* was there in front of that television set every Wednesday night at 9:00 PM tuned to NBC for the next new episode of *Night Gallery* (I have every episode, uncut, on videotape). As I grew older and sought out more information and programs and books and stories about Serling, I also studied the work of other writers from the days of live television drama—Paddy Chayefsky, Reginald Rose, Robert Alan Arthur, Ernest Kinoy, Ronald Ribman, Horton Foote, J.P. Miller, and many others. I began to detect a certain recurring element in all of their scripts: the cadence of their dialogue.

Their dialogue had to have that musical quality to it; after all, movies were still their biggest competition, and their dramas were being watched mostly by a generation home from World War II or on its way to Korea, a generation whose only two outlets for entertainment had been either the movies or the radio, so there were both the visual and audio aspects to compete with. Given the financial and physical constraints of live television, the only hope these dramas had was for the scripts to be overflowing with magnificent, musical dialogue that the actors could sink their teeth into and make the audience forget about the radio or the latest big Hollywood movie.

And their cadences were—and remain—a wonder to behold.

Not that all of them wrote in the same meter or consciously attempted to emulate each other's style. No, far from it. Each writer's cadences were very much their own, but thing is, these definite, crackling, brittle cadences were *always* present in every line of their dialogue. It sounded like music when read aloud by me or spoken by the actors, but somehow reading it silently to myself was even better; what was restricted to one reader's or actor's interpretation when acted or read aloud, inside my head produced concertos, symphonies, *operas* with only the spoken word. It stunned, amazed, and mystified me that anyone could sit down at a typewriter and create something as glorious as this using mere language. The work of Serling and the other television dramatists led me to the work of Charles Beaumont, Jerry Sohl, William F. Nolan, George Clayton Johnson, Theodore Sturgeon, James Blish, and Harlan Ellison; Ellison led me to the work of Dan Simmons, Kobo Abe, Borges, Pushkin, Schiller, José Ortega y

Gasset, and numerous others, who led me to the work of other writers I had never read before, on and on and on, this incredible chain of storytellers and thinkers creating concertos upon symphonies upon operas in my head as their words poured off the pages and ricocheted around inside my brain, forcing me to think outside the boundaries of my everyday world and consider things such as imagination and meanings and possibilities that never, ever end, and, above all, most importantly, first and foremost, what a puny little kid from Newark, Ohio might one day know a taste of if he dedicated himself to the sole purpose of making sure that each time he sat down to write something he strove to make his words one-tenth as skilled, polished, and honest as those that lay between the covers of the books lining his shelves.

Craft.

But all of it always comes back to that moment I stood there in the kitchen with Mom after watching *Night Gallery* and realized the power that words could have, which means it always comes back to the one man whose work had the first and most profound effect on me: Rod Serling, to whom I'd like to stop and pay tribute before we move to the next section.

I never knew Rod Serling; I never had a chance to meet the man, never had the opportunity to shake his hand and thank him for all that his work has given to me as both a writer and a human being, never had the chance to express my appreciation for all he taught me.

And Rod Serling *did* teach me.

He taught me that it's okay for characters to express their humanity with words—and not the introverted running monologue that underscores the action in a novel or short-story narrative. I mean *solely through what they say*:

> "I've been living at a dead run, Dad. I was so tired. And then . . . one day . . . I knew I had to come back. I had to come back to get on a merry-go-round and listen to a band concert and eat cotton candy. I had to stop and breathe and close my eyes and smell and listen."
>
> –"Walking Distance"

> "Something's happening to me. I keep getting beckoned to by ghosts. Every now and then it's 1945. And if you think that

> sounds nuts, then try this one—I wish to God those ghosts would stick around. They're the best friends I've got. I feel a whole helluva lot more comfortable with them than I do with all those warm, living, flesh-and-blood bodies I ride up and down the elevators with! I rate something better than what I've got. Honest to God, I do. Where does it say that every morning of a man's life he's got to Indian-wrestle with every young contender off the sidewalk who's got an itch to climb up a rung? I've put in my time. Understand? I've paid my dues. I shouldn't have to get hustled to death in the daytime and then die of loneliness every night. That's not the dream. That's not what it's all about."
>
> –"They're Tearing Down Tim Riley's Bar"

He taught me that the natural human predilection for repetition in everyday speech was not a liability to the writer, not something that has to fall shrill and tuneless on the ear; it was, rather, a grace note:

> "Odd? It's not odd. Odd is when you go thirty days on the line and not lose a man. That's odd. Odd is when you walk twenty-five miles and don't get a blister. Now you're talking odd. This isn't odd, Captain. This is . . . this is nightmare. This is a lousy dog-face line officer who can see death on peoples' faces. A lousy dog-face officer who'd like to give back the power to whoever gave it to him."
>
> –"The Purple Testament"

He taught me that a character's helplessness and rage can be expressed not through the lazy tool of violence, but through a simple, eloquent sadness whose clarity hits as hard as any fist:

> "I would prefer, though never asked before, a job—any job at all where I could be myself! Where I wouldn't have to climb on a stage and go through a masquerade very morning at nine and mouth all the dialogue and play the executive and make believe I'm the bright young man on his way up. Because I'm not that person, Janie. You've tried

> to *make me* that person, but that isn't me. That isn't me at all. I'm . . . I'm a not very young, soon to be old, very uncompetitive, rather dull, quite uninspired, average type of guy . . ."
>
> –"A Stop At Willoughby"

He taught me that even the shabbiest, most downtrodden, cheerless, and inelegant of characters, when filled with enough need, can express themselves with a simple, dark poetry:

> "Listen, boy, I been wishin' all my life. You understand, Henry? I got a gut ache from wishin' and all I got to show for it is a face full of scars and a head full of memories of all the hurt and all the misery I've had to eat with and sleep with all my miserable life."
>
> –"The Big, Tall Wish"

He taught me that anguish has a language all its own and, when it is given the proper voice, can move even the most hardened of hearts:

> "All I know is that I'm an aging, purposeless relic of another time and I live in a dirty rooming house on a street that's filled with hungry kids and shabby people, where the only thing that comes down the chimney on Christmas Eve is more poverty . . . I wish, Mr. Dundee . . . on just one Christmas . . . only one . . . that I could see some of . . . the hopeless ones and dreamless ones . . . just one Christmas I'd like to see the meek inherit the earth!"
>
> –"The Night Of The Meek"

He taught me that when a character offers a moment of self-revelation, a whisper always rings louder than any scream:

> "Because I'm sad. Because I'm nothin'. Because I'll live and die in a crummy one-roomer with dirty walls and cracked pipes. I'll never have a girl because I'm an ugly little gnome. I'll never be anybody because half of me is in that horn. I can't

> even talk to people . . . not without the horn. That's half of my language."
>
> –"A Passage For Trumpet"

Rod Serling was the best teacher I never knew I had.

I would have no career if it hadn't been for the effect his words had—and still have—on me. He taught me the importance of cadence, the necessity of compassion, and the impact of narrative control; he taught me the difference between style and substance; and, above all, he taught me that the direct and simple expression of human emotion is perhaps the single most powerful tool at the writer's disposal.

And so, to the teacher who never knew he had me for a student, to the man whose stories sparked the desire in a young boy from Newark, Ohio to try his hand at writing, to the man from *Night Gallery* whom my mom thought wrote such good stories, to the tourguide with the clipped speech who every week took us into a dimension beyond that known to man, I offer, at last, four simple words of gratitude, expressed about thirty years too late, but whose sentiment is, I hope, timeless and sincere:

Thank you, Mr. Serling.

Whenever someone tells me that my dialogue reminds them of yours, I feel like I might be on the path to finally getting it right.

3

Opinions, and the One Who Offers Them

Near the beginning of this book I stated: "It's not enough for someone to simply say, 'I liked it' or 'I really hated it'; those are not opinions in and of themselves, they are prefaces to opinions. To qualify as actual opinions, they must be followed by reasons why, and in order for you to understand the reasons *why*, you have to understand something about the person giving the opinion."

Since you've stuck with me this far, I think it safe to assume that you know more about me now than you did before, so the next won't come as much of a surprise.

I've written numerous introductions and afterwords for others' novels and short story collections over the years, and any writer who does this more than a few times will quickly realize there's no way to keep part of him- or herself from creeping into the proceedings. Can't be done, I don't care how much you try to put some emotional distance between yourself and the material you're introducing or discussing after the fact; intros and afterwords depend solely on the writer's emotional reactions to the material and how those reactions are used to inform the readers of why they should be reading this.

I want to share a series of introductions and afterwords that I have written for other writers' books over the years. None of them are terribly long, and two of them never saw print because the publisher decided at the last minute they weren't needed. It happens.

What I hope you'll come away with from this section is a better understanding of how rich, literate, emotionally challenging (and rewarding) horror fiction at its best (i.e., when it has the guts to move away from the traditional expected elements) can be.

I'm not going to preface any of these pieces; I think they speak pretty well for themselves. I will, however, give you a quick list here of the books, in order:

**Cursed Be the Child* by Mort Castle (intro)
The Snowman's Children by Glen Hirshberg (afterword)
Mama's Boy and Other Stories by Fran Friel (intro)
A Whisper of Southern Lights by Time Lebbon (intro)
Eyes Everywhere by Matthew Warner (afterword)
Laughing Boy's Shadow by Steve Saville (intro)
Thundershowers at Dusk by Christopher Conlon (intro)
*'*Nids and Other Stories* by Ray Garton (intro)

*never before published

I sincerely hope you enjoy these and that they shed a little more light not only on the opinions, but also he who offers them.

The Castle Tshatsimo

Before discussing some specifics of *Cursed Be The Child*—re-released by Overlook Connection press in this spiffy new edition you hold in your hands—we need to chat about Mort Castle, the writer.

Like a lot of you, I'm guessing, my first exposure to Mort's work occurred in the early 1980s, with the appearance of his story, "Altenmoor, Where The Dogs Dance" in *Twilight Zone Magazine* (it can also be found in *Moon on the Water*, so go out and buy a copy now). "Altenmoor" is a tale reminiscent of the best of Ray Bradbury or Rod Serling. I say "reminiscent" because—though it may wear its influences on its sleeve—it is very much its own story; assured of voice, rich in characterization, and surprisingly epic in scope, considering that it's less than ten pages long and takes place in only three rooms of a single house. A young boy's dog dies, you see. But his grandfather, now living with the boy and his family, tells him otherwise. Grandpa, now blind, once wrote books about this fantastic land called "Altenmoor." He tells his grandson that his dog isn't dead, he's gone to Altenmoor to dance with the other dogs, because Altenmoor is a wonderful place, and . . . and you'll have to track it down and read it for yourself; I won't spoil it for you. What sounds like a three-layer treacle cake (thanks to the inadequacy of my description) is a very literate, gentle (but never sentimental), honestly haunting piece that has yet to achieve the status of "classic" it deserves. There are moments in the story where Castle expertly hits you with something unexpected—a moment of anger, a moment of hopelessness, a moment of remorse—and as a result, gives the story a slightly darker edge than it would have had in the hands of a Serling or Bradbury.

The key words in the above paragraph, by the way, are "literate" and "unexpected"—none could better describe Castle's work in general, and this novel in specific. Castle writes from a very literate standpoint; he knows it's just as important—if not more so—to read outside the horror field as within it; after all, how can a writer hope to bring a unique sensibility to their work if that sensibility is not informed by exposure to all styles and fields of fiction? Though a devout student of Hemingway, Castle's own work never stoops to imitation of the renowned Ernest's intensely clipped style; instead, Castle has mastered (and, in my opinion, even refined) Hemingway's gift for effective understatement: he knows that a well-turned phrase can replace ten pages worth of description, and how the precise, exact, meticulously-placed word can completely change the rhythm or tone of a scene. Castle's sentences have the deceptively easy flow that comes only after hours of backbreaking revision—and I chose that word—"deceptively"—with a great deal of care; like all of our best writers, Castle makes it *look* easy. Trust me, it isn't. A smoothness of prose like his or that of Ed Gorman, Dean Koontz, or Jack Cady is achieved over years of constant refinement and unwavering practice . . . and an undying respect for the craft.

I think that, of all the things I admire about Castle's writing, it is that last that I admire the most: his reverence for what Harlan Ellison called "the holy chore" of writing. You cannot write a novel or short story without being deadly serious about it, and that, Castle is. He takes his work *very* seriously (it's himself that he tends to make fun of, which is very entertaining after he's had a few drinks and picks up his banjo, but we're not here to discuss his dreadful personality problems).

But as serious a writer as he is, Castle never forgets that one of his primary duties as a storyteller is to *entertain* his readers—and do not take that word to represent only the light and fluffy and unchallenging; need I remind you that when *Othello* originally premiered at The Old Vic it was billed as "Wm. Shakespeare's Latest Entertainment"?

And entertain he does; with his slightly skewed vision of the world in which we live; with his unflinching eye for the nuances in human behavior that make for the fully-realized character; and with his compassion for even the lowliest of people who populate his stories—and this is somewhere Castle really excels: it's easy, even expected and acceptable, for writers of horror fiction to have villains who come up just short of a moustache-twirling Snidely Whiplash or faceless homicidal maniac; it keeps everything in black and white terms, makes it easy to tell the good guys from the bad and all that lovely, predictable, tiresome rot. Castle isn't interested in pointing out the black and white to you—those are always obvious—no; his fascination lies within the moral and spiritual grey areas that all people grapple with but few are willing to talk about. In Castle's world, his characters talk about these quandaries, they confront their moral dilemmas, they deal with the consequences of compromise; fairly commonplace stuff if you read Russell Banks or Michael Chabon or Alice Walker . . . but in *horror?* Who're we kidding here?

You're about to confront a novel that tackles many dark subjects—murder, rape, child molestation, adultery, alcoholism, ethnic and inter-racial prejudice—in a balanced, subtle, and thoughtful way, and it's that very subtlety and thoughtfulness that gives *Cursed Be the Child* its lasting resonance; this is much more than just another book about a possessed child and the disintegration of another traditional nuclear family; this is a book that deals with issues of personal integrity, self-redemption, and the lengths to which people will go to protect the ones they love. It's also—mostly, most probably—about loneliness and the fear that can arise, unbidden and unreasonable, from it.

Is it scary? Yes. But unlike many of the novels being published around the time of its initial appearance in 1990, the scare factor of *Cursed Be the Child* is not built upon a foundation of violence, cheap shocks, terror, and gore; it is built, rather, on the foundation of something that is still in danger of being left by the wayside if the next generation of horror writers aren't careful: *dread*. Simple, powerful, irreplaceable dread. The threat of the horror you cannot see; the implications of what *might* be happening; the unconfirmed suspicion, the sudden silence from a child's room, the aching fear that you might be losing control of parts of your character that you'd rather not think about.

Dread.

This novel is full of dread, and as a result, is one of the most genuinely suspenseful horror novels I've read in years. Without giving anything away, I will tell you that about mid-way through this novel, there is a sequence where Warren Barringer, one of the major characters in this book, goes out by himself to shop at a mall. In and of itself, doesn't sound like much, but by the time you reach this sequence you are *not* going to want to accompany him on this little trip, and why?

Because you dread what might happen.

This novel is filled with dread, yes, but it's also filled with some pleasant surprises; for once, we have a television evangelist in a horror novel who is not a hypocritical, self-righteous caricature—he is, in fact, a man of great humility and integrity; we have an "avenging spirit" who is uncomfortably sympathetic; we have a refreshingly low body count—only one person dies in the first 340 pages; we have a husband and wife who are trying to repair their marriage after the wife's affair, and for once this painful and ugly process of healing is not presented in easy shorthand so the reader can pretend that such pain doesn't exist—it's depicted with all the anger, regret, and sorrow of the best of Raymond Carver's work, and shares Carver's tough sensibilities about how people react when confronting the reality of betrayal.

And there is an absolutely stunning sleight-of-hand that occurs about two-thirds of the way through, wherein we are jolted from the flow of the narrative and suddenly transported back to Auschwitz in the company of a young Polish Jew named Stefan Grinzspan, a man who has never been mentioned anywhere before and whose story—as compelling and exquisitely written as it is—seems to have nothing to do with what has been happening up to this point. Emphasis on the "seems."

It is with these three chapters dealing with Stefan that Castle's sure literary hand flexes some serious muscle, because it becomes evident as Stefan's story unfolds that his fate is strongly tied into that of another character with whom we have spent time and *think* we have come to know. I won't say any more, lest the revelations be spoiled, but I will say this much: the effect Castle achieves with this detour, and how he does it, is something that should be studied and taught in creative writing classes; it's that good.

As is the entire novel. Oh, some people will quibble about the last few chapters, I've no doubt—put any five readers of this book in the same room and even money says that all of them will have strongly divided opinions about the controversial narrative choices Castle makes toward the end—but even those who don't agree with the ending won't be able to argue that Castle didn't set it up like an expert (hint: pay close attention to the Romany fables scattered throughout the book and you'll realize, as I did on a second reading, that the ending Castle chose was inevitable); others might object to the way the novel is structured—though it's the most linear of his books, in my opinion, *Cursed Be The Child*'s patchwork design may be a little off-putting to readers who expect horror novels to unfold with all the complexity of R.L. Stine; still others, weaned on novels inspired by splatter movies rather than challenging ideas, might complain about how much time he spends on characterization; but for me, this book was and remains everything that most horror novels in the 80s were not: literate, intelligent, well-crafted, and thought-provoking—no small feat when you consider its subject matter.

Some are saying now that Mort Castle has arrived, which makes me laugh quietly to myself; I knew he was here, all along. As you will by the time you reach the final page. This novel reveals *tshatsimo*; it tells the truth.

You'll understand that soon enough.

Let Me Into the Darkness Again: An Afterword to *The Snowman's Children*

There is a poem from Stephen Crane's *The Black Riders and Other Lines* that reads:

> I was in the darkness;
> I could not see my words
> Nor the wishes of my heart.
> Then suddenly there was a great light—
>
> "Let me into the darkness again."

I have always believed that this poem—which in five succinct lines holds as much subtle fear as Dickens at his most atmospheric and ghostly—should be held up as the model for *how* one should thematically structure a modern horror story. I qualify this with the word "modern" because there is a penchant among current writers in the field to wrap everything up in too neat a package so as to be more palatable for readers; after all, one turns to fiction for *escape*, does one not? And in escapist entertainment, we want everything to be neat, tidy, satisfactory, with happy endings where the main characters emerge slightly worse for wear but wiser and, of course, triumphant.

Horror fiction, more so than any other genre, should eschew tidy endings at all costs—after all, when one is dealing with subject matter that explores the darkest corners of the human psyche, easy resolutions are the coward's way out, the written equivalent of the television sitcom where everything is fixed in twenty-three minutes, plus commercials.

The Snowman's Children is, in my opinion, one of the few horror novels written in the past three decades that perfectly follows the thematic pattern set down in Crane's poem—whether this was a conscious effort on Glen's part or not (I suspect not) doesn't matter; what does matter is that he has produced a novel of rare and terrifying beauty, populated by some of the most richly-drawn and unromanticized characters the genre has ever met.

Some of you might think my characterizing of *The Snowman's Children* as a "horror novel" is a bit unfair; after all, it's not gory, most of the violence is kept off-stage, and it grapples, intensely, with hard spiritual and moral issues—what Faulkner so beautifully characterized as "the human heart in conflict with itself."

That's what the best horror fiction is *supposed* to do. And make no mistake here; *The Snowman's Children* is most *definitely* a horror story: remove the central horrific event—the Snowman and his hideous actions—and there would be no story to tell. But instead of focusing on the horrors inflicted by the Snowman, Glen chooses to focus on his victims, as well as the friends and families of those victims. The Snowman never makes an appearance, but his presence hangs over every scene.

Unlike other writers whose penchant for downplaying the horrific elements in their fiction comes off as apologist, Glen's deft handling of his themes seems to me wholly natural and effectively quiet—like the best of M.R. James or Charles Grant, though I cannot help but get the feeling there may be a bit of John Cheever and Thomas Wolfe lurking in his shadows.

I don't recall when I've read a better fictional exploration of loneliness and unearned guilt—and that Glen both begins and ends the novel with Mattie surrounded by whistling wind and swirling snow, alone and anxious, is a true stroke of inspiration; to bookend a story with the exact same image suggests on the surface a definite resolution, a redemption, a coming full circle to end where we began but with renewed strength and purpose

Not exactly; life isn't that neat, and neither should be fiction.

Sure, at novel's end Mattie's answered many of the questions he started out with, only those answers have not brought him the closure he was hoping for (though he never once admits to himself that closure is what he was after); in fact, one can easily imagine Mattie whispering the final line of Crane's poem to himself as he drives away into the snowy night: *Let me into the darkness again.*

Revelation has not brought with it *resolution*; Mattie may now know the answers he sought, but he is by no means redeemed for having found them; if anything, his lifelong guilt, once unearned, is now fully deserved in his own eyes. But he will continue, because life goes on, and continuation is sometimes the only triumph left us.

To my mind, there are three major set pieces in the novel, and Glen knocked me for a loop by placing two of them back-to-back: Mr. Fox's "assault" on the basement window, followed by Mattie finally finding Spencer in the church, left me stunned. The description of the service at the church is magnificent—it's a rare thing to be able to make readers *hear* music and sound with mere words. Brilliant sequences, as is the entire section wherein Mattie and Spencer fake Spencer's abduction, only to have Theresa disappear.

And what a tragic, heartbreaking character he has created in Theresa. So many writers still function under the misguided idea that genuine schizophrenia is multiple personality disorder (it's *neater* that way); and if they *do* know the difference, they feel compelled to have some talking head come into the story and *explain* what it is; here, Glen simply presents it (with frightening accuracy, by the way) as it is in Theresa's everyday existence, no explanations; after all, it's a day-to-day struggle with her, her friends, her dad, something that would take on qualities of the commonplace, so why not present it as such? To present it in so unsentimentalized a manner was a courageous choice on Glen's part, because it would have been too easy and too neat to present it otherwise: *She'll be fine, there's hope, she's getting better every day.*

No, no, and no.

Theresa only continues, and that is triumph enough, because *it has to be*. The darkness has covered all, the light has been turned on . . . and all are left with realization that the darkness was a blessing of sorts, after all.

Not neat and tidy, but richly human, candid, haunting, and so very moving, making *The Snowman's Children* not only one of the best thematic illustrations of Crane's verse, but one of the most heartfelt and honest horror novels I've ever read or am likely to read.

This is a brilliant novel, and I hope that you will return to its snowy streets again and again, as I have and will continue to do.

What Are We Witnessing?
An Introduction to *Mama's Boy and Other Stories*

"We enter, we find our way through. Maybe something we experience changes the way we look at the world."
—Robert Freeman Wexler, *In Springdale Town*

I blame Peter Straub.

(I was going to blame Hemingway, but since he's been dead for as long as I've been alive, it hardly seems fair since he's not here to defend himself. The last thing I want is for Hemingway's ghost to come back from the Otherwhere and kick my ass, so the blame goes to Straub—who can also easily kick my ass, but I digress.)

Why blame Straub?

For the same reason that a lot of comics in the 50s and 60s blamed Lenny Bruce.

To whit: in the 50s and 60s, the club stages in Vegas and New York and Los Angeles were filled with comedians who'd cut their teeth in burlesque and on the radio, many of whom—like the late, great Myron Cohen (Google him)—came out onto the stage, said "Good evening," to the audience, and then, for the next forty-five to sixty minutes, proceeded to *simply tell jokes*. The same kind of jokes we tell one another, those of the classic two-line setup, followed by the punchline: "A man walks into a doctor's office with a duck on his head. The doctor looks at the man and says, "Can I help you?" And the duck says, "Yeah—is there any way you can get this guy off my ass?" (Insert rimshot.)

Audiences loved it; a comic tells jokes for an hour, everybody laughs and tips their waitresses, a win/win situation all around.

And then came some Jewish punk named Lenny Bruce . . . and nothing was ever the same again. Bruce was not only one of the first comedians to use profanity in his act, but he did so much more than just tell jokes. His routines would go on for ten, fifteen, even twenty minutes; he used different voices for characters; his routines often had *actual storylines*; he wasn't afraid to address the hot-button issues of the day or satirize the political and Hollywood icons of the time in these one-man multi-voiced mini-plays. Once audiences got over their initial shock, Bruce became, for a little while, the hottest comedian around.

And the old-school comics *hated* him for it. In what seemed less time than it took for a joke to bomb, the traditional two-line setup/ punchline gags were antiquated. If they wanted to stay in the business, the old-schoolers had to adapt or step aside. Some hoped that Bruce's style of comedy was just a flash in the pan. But by the time of Bruce's tragic death in 1966 at the age of 40, his influence had spread; young comedians like Bill Cosby, Richard Prior, and George Carlin had picked up on Bruce's complex, multi-voiced story routines and were running with it. Some worked "blue," some didn't, but all were moving forward on the basis of Bruce's legacy.

What does any of this have to do with *Mama's Boy and Other Dark Tales*, and for what, precisely, am I blaming Peter Straub?

Easy: until the 1990 release of Straub's remarkable collection *Houses without Doors*, the genre writer was content to release his or her short story collection with either A) just a dozen or so stories between the covers, or, B) with newly-written introductions before each story, discussing some aspect of the piece that was to follow (something Harlan Ellison has turned into an art form). On the surface, *Houses without Doors* comprises three novellas, three short stories, and seven briefer short-shorts and what is now called flash fiction. But—like Hemingway's *In Our Time* (hence my almost blaming him) or Russell Banks' *Trailerpark*—it was much more tightly focused and unified in theme than readers were accustomed to seeing in a genre collection. The "Interlude" pieces between the stories did not really stand on their own, but seemed more like smaller pieces of a bigger puzzle (which they were). And the stories themselves read as if they all sprang from a single core obsession, one that initially seemed to have little in common with the briefer pieces surrounding them. But as the reader delved further into the heart of the collection, the connections began to reveal themselves like fog-shrouded figures walking slowly into the glow of a streetlight. The effect was (and still is) stunning. For all intents and purposes, Straub *had* reinvented the wheel of how a writer of dark fiction could go about presenting his or her stories in a collection. The template set down in *Houses without Doors* remains unequaled. (I say this as one who attempted to adapt that template for my first collection, *Things Left Behind*. Looking at that collection now, I think I was about 75 to 80 percent successful, though lacking Straub's profound subtlety.)

Which brings us to Fran Friel and her debut collection that you now hold in your hands.

Whether it was her intention or not (and part of me suspects it was), Fran, instead of endeavoring to echo exactly Straub's template (as I tried to do), has used it as a jumping-off point, and as a result made it her own, including not only stories and novellas, but short-shorts, flash pieces, and some truly exquisite poetry along the way. The end result is dazzling—and a little mystifying. Dazzling because she writes with the confidence of a seasoned author; mystifying because you can't help but wonder how such a vibrant, funny, compassionate, and lovely human being could create some of the *nastiness* that's between these covers. (If you doubt this book gets nasty, read "Close Shave" and see if you don't wince. In *fifty-five words* she manages to hit harder than some writers can in five thousand.)

That's the thing, if you ever have the chance to meet Fran—she is one of the most *radiant* people I've ever encountered. Seriously. Her face actually glows with her love of life, her love of reading, of writing, her love for her friends, a good meal, a good film, a certain passage from a piece of music. She's got a laugh that rings like fine crystal . . . there ought to be a law against a person being *this* happy.

But it is, I think, this happiness, this total, passionate, almost evangelical joy for existence, that fuels her fire; it is this very thing that makes her strong enough to access its darker and unsettling counterparts. Fran is a big believer that speculative fiction, in all of its forms, is the supreme mythic literature of our time, and that belief is on full display in *Mama's Boy and Other Dark Tales.*

But seeing—or in this case, reading—is believing, so I offer you what is to my mind the core image of this collection, taken from "Beach of Dreams," a brilliant, hallucinatory, mesmerizing dark fantasy that could, methinks, hold its own in the company of an Ellison tale. The central character of "Beach," Simon Rodan, an anthropologist living among the natives of an unidentified island, is taking pictures of mysterious giant figures whose bodies have washed up on the beach:

> Fumbling inside his vest, Simon tried to protect his camera from the rain with a baggie. He ran up and down the spaces

> between the lifeless giants, snapping pictures, desperate to document the incredible images. He felt a strange split in his mind—focusing on the task at hand and an eerie concern for what he was witnessing. *What was he witnessing?*

Indeed that last line—*What was he witnessing?*—could very well be the reader's mantra as he or she moves through the singular, unified experience of this collection. Like the flashes revealed to Simon in the brief burst of camera light, each small glimpse hints at the majesty of the unseen whole, and (as if to echo the quote from R.F. Wexler at the beginning of this introduction) they have no choice but to find their way through. Along the way, perhaps, something in or of their worldview will be changed.

Pieces of a larger whole.

Now, I called the above-quoted passage the central *image* of the collection, not the central obsession that in the end unifies everything. *That* would be the pain (physical, emotional, psychological, and spiritual) that is part and parcel of familial obligation, be it the family one is born into or the family one assembles for oneself throughout life.

And in the middle of all of this is "Mama's Boy," the tour-de-force novella that earned Fran a Bram Stoker Award nomination for Outstanding Achievement in Long Fiction. It is the thematic centerpiece of this collection, in which virtually all of the themes grappled with in the other fictions and poems are touched upon. I'm not going to spoil it for you by talking about any of its plot—aside from saying, "Frank's back!"—but I will say this much: upon second reading, it remains a work of terrible insight (and I mean that as a compliment) and unnerving power. A shattering study of unearned guilt and what happens when one takes familial obligation to an unspeakable extreme, it is simultaneously horrifying and heartbreaking . . . and surprisingly funny in a few places. (Lest you start to think that all contained herein is Doom and Gloom, Doom and Gloom, check out "Under the Dryer" for a beautiful example of Fran's humor; you'll laugh, but you're going to feel so *dirty* about it.)

Then there are pieces like "Special Prayers" wherein Fran displays her deft touch at the surreal, opening with yet another image that is arguably iconic to this collection:

> Babies fell from the skies over Eastville. They bounced, they bled, but none cried. Their silence was eerie—their tiny bodies splatted and split open as they hit the rooftops, the road, and the sidewalks of our little street. For miles and miles, the sky was full of falling babies, dark blots against the blue.

And there is heartbreak, also; "Orange and Golden" is a brief story, but its lingering effect still haunts me, weeks after having first read it.

With this collection, Fran Friel accomplishes what all serious writers of dark fiction strive for: she entertains, she instills honest emotion by filtering her own sensibilities through those of her characters, and she leaves the reader with more than a little food for thought afterward. We may not be able to put into words an exact explanation of what we have witnessed, but we emerge richer for the experience, perhaps even with our worldview slightly altered.

What are we witnessing?

The beginning of a long and grand writing career.

I have kept you long enough, so it's time to do what I was asked to do.

Ladies and gentlemen, it is my very great pleasure to introduce you to Fran Friel.

Introduction to *A Whisper of Southern Lights*

> A day after arriving at the jail, they sent us out to cremate bodies.
>
> Singapore was full of them. Thousands dead, maybe tens of thousands, and the Japanese wanted someone else to clean up the mess they had made. So they chose us, of course. The prisoners, the defeated and dishonoured. They gave us matches and paper and told us to break up furniture and fences, pile bodies, and burn the evidence of slaughter.

The above are the words of one Jack Sykes, a POW of the Japanese during WWII, whose first-person accounts in this superb novella form the core of this story—which, not surprisingly, is structured somewhat like a Japanese puzzle box; you have no idea how to open it, except through determination and trial and error. Because Tim

Lebbon has chosen to tell this third installment in the *Assassin* series in both first and third person, you're going to find yourself in the same position as someone who is actually holding a puzzle box: *I know this element is part of the solution, but why does it do* this?

And like the elation one experiences when the puzzle box is at last solved, the epiphany reached when you near the end of this story is like emerging from the depths of the ocean to pull in that holy life-giving gasp of air.

Allow me (not unlike Temple and Gabriel) to backtrack in time a little bit to the first time that the Twin was introduced to us: 1997's *Mesmer*.

I was, I'm embarrassed to say, a little late in discovering the work of Tim Lebbon; oh, I'd read a few short stories here and there and enjoyed *The Nature of Balance* (which I borrowed from the library) to no end, but it wasn't until I decided to take a chance and purchase *White and Other Tales of Ruin* in 2003 that I became an immediate Lebbon addict and set out on a period of binge reading the likes of which I hadn't experienced in years, maybe even decades. I bought and read *everything* of his I could lay hands on, and it was an autumn of great story feasting for me. My God, to this day, I still finish the novella "Hell" and have to have a day to recuperate; never have I encountered a story so filled-to-bursting with such Fusellian nightmarish imagery that also has such a strong, humane, compassionate heart.

So I was midway through this binge reading period when the copy of *Mesmer* that I'd ordered showed up in my mailbox, and I immediately tore into it.

I'm going to tell you a professional secret: sometimes, for whatever reasons he or she might have—*Oh, this is a terrific idea, I have to get this down on paper* right now; *This idea intrigues me; My God, the rent's due in three weeks and I've got to SELL SOMETHING!*—we writers will write a story before it's ready to be written, and what emerges, while still very much worthwhile, might seem to us later a bit rushed, a tad looser in structure than it needed to be, or just downright sloppy. (I have published a few not-yet-ready-to-be-written tales myself, so I speak from experience.)

Mesmser—like the first book in Stephen King's *Gunslinger* series—struck me as something that was produced before it was ready to be written down. This is not to say that I disliked it; far from it. It's got all the pacing, imagery, and ingenious ideas that I've come to expect from a Tim Lebbon work—but something at its core seemed to me to not yet be completely formed, that I was watching a writer trying to force a concept into existence.

But still, there was that central conceit, there was the Twin, there was Temple; so galvanizing a character was he, so frightening a bastard, so unapologetically hateful, that he dominated the somewhat cluttered storyline. *Mesmer*, for me, read like something that was trying to be a polished mosaic but emerged—despite the obvious talent and skill of the writer—as a patchwork quilt with a few of the seams still showing.

But that's what discovering a great writer is all about, isn't it? Being able to read their work and trace the arc of their ongoing evolution as a storyteller. That is what gives *Mesmer* its lasting value (lest you think I am dismissing it altogether): it's where Temple first showed his vindictive, destructive face.

And things haven't been quite the same since.

Which brings us back to *A Whisper of Southern Lights*, the third—and in my opinion, the best yet—installment of the *Assassin* series.

I mentioned at the beginning of this introduction that Lebbon employs a very difficult—and in the eyes of some, unacceptable—structure here: that of shifting between third person and first. Either POV on its own is difficult enough; to combine them in the same narrative without offering a linking device or an explanation as to *why* these shifts are made is damn near impossible to pull off, but Lebbon does, and beautifully. In a world where Gabriel and Temple are constantly battling and chasing one another through a quantum game of cat-and-mouse, reality is an at-best subjective notion, if not an outright liquid concept. Employing both the first and third persons to tell this stunning fable (and make no mistake, a fable it very much is), Lebbon is able to put the reader right smack in the middle of the pliable multiverse and the two beings waging their own war throughout its history. And because reality is such a malleable conceit, the shifting—even clashing—POVs make the overriding sense of less-than-benign corporeal changeability a fierce and immediate threat—not only to the characters, but to the reader, as well. It's a beautiful and (especially in its closing sequences) brilliant balancing act, handled here by the hands of a master.

And what about the writing itself? Over the past five years, Lebbon's prose has been honed to something so sharp and deadly he ought to be required to register it as a lethal weapon. Consider this passage from *A Whisper of Southern Lights*:

> The road was a scene of chaos and pain. One of the hospital trucks had caught fire, though everyone in its open back already appeared to be dead. It had tipped nose-first into the roadside ditch. Some bodies had fallen into the dust, and those still on the truck were adding fuel to the flames.

It's the very definition of clarity; to be able to evoke such nightmare in four deceptively simple sentences is one of Lebbon's many redoubtable gifts as a writer. The grubby, tiring, soul-weary sense of fear and hopelessness that is war permeates every page of this story. I cannot help but think that Arthur Machen and Graham Greene would heartily approve of Lebbon's depiction of the soldier in wartime.

So here you are, the puzzle box in your hands, its secret daring you to discover it.

I am a huge admirer of Tim Lebbon's work and was honored to have been asked to write this introduction.

Temple is back.

Make sure to watch yours.

"And it Starts When You're Always Afraid"
An Afterword to *Eyes Everywhere*

The title above is taken—as I'm sure a lot of you knew instantly—from the famous Buffalo Springfield song, "For What It's Worth." Now, while Stephen Stills, Neil Young, and company were couching the line in political terms to suit the unrest of the times, the line (which refers to paranoia) nonetheless remains timeless as well as timely—two words that I think will be applicable to the novel you've just read in the years to come.

But before getting to the novel itself, I want to start with Mike Bohatch's elegant and deceptively simple cover. When Matt first sent me an electronic file of the cover, I looked at it and thought, "*Very* nice." And it is; I like the color balance, I like the visual composition, I like the eyes staring out at you. But at the same time, something about the central image—that of the man sitting with his head held in his hands—struck me as awfully familiar. I initially shrugged it off, but something about the image stayed with me (bugged the hell out of me, in truth), and I eventually realized what, and why.

It is almost a direct inversion of a sketch done by Vincent Van Gogh entitled "Worn Out: At Eternity's Gate." In that particular sketch (done near the end of Van Gogh's life on the advice of the physician, Dr. Gachet, who was treating him at the time), we are shown an old man sitting in a chair beside an open window, and despite there being what appears to be a wonderfully sunny day outside, the old man sits with his face buried in his hands. There is an air of utter despair and helplessness about the scene, which remains (for me) one of Van Gogh's most startling studies in visual contrast: the beautiful day outside, the anguish inside, made all the more internal by the man covering his face so that his eyes cannot see what is just immediately outside the window.

In a letter to his brother Theo—dated May 1890, a mere two months before he took his own life—Van Gogh described that particular sketch like this: "I look at it and realize I need not try and go out of my way to try to express the sadness, confusion, and extreme of loneliness that too often darkens my daily life here. He [Gachet] had simply asked of me to offer him a visual image of how I feel—how *it* feels. During the attacks I feel a coward before the pain, fear, and suffering, like an old man cowering in the disintegrating shell of his own flesh . . . altogether now I am trying to recover like a man who has meant to commit suicide and, finding the water too cold, tries to regain the bank."

We now know that Van Gogh suffered not only from epilepsy and depression, but from what is now recognized as schizophrenia. The sketch in question was his visual representation of how it felt to be schizophrenic, so it was an arguably ingenious move by Bohatch to invert this image and use it as the focal point of the cover. (Some might look at this image and think it clichéd, but I would be inclined to disagree; sure, it seems that a lot of artistic representations of mental illness involve figures sitting in this position, or positions similar to it, but both Van Gogh's sketch and Edvard Munch's "The Scream" (or "The Cry")—the latter being the more famous piece—have both been reproduced in psychology textbooks in those sections that deal with schizophrenia.)

As to the disease itself, I have found no single explanation that is fully satisfying—and the ones that come closest are so filled with technical jargon as to be nearly incomprehensible—so permit two brief asides.

I once knew a woman who was being treated for schizophrenia (an affliction that I did not understand at the time), and I once asked her, during one of her more lucid periods (read: when the meds were still working), to tell me what it was like. While I can't quote her word for word (nor can I ask her—she took her own life at the ripe old age of twenty-five), what she told me was something like this: "It's like there are two layers of reality in the everyday world—the surface layer, all the traffic, ringing phones, passing conversations, radios playing music, all of that, and most people can filter it out. I can't. It's like my brain is plugged into everything around me and there's no shutting it off. But it doesn't stop there. You feel like there's this second level underneath the surface where all the power grids are functioning, where all the electricity is jumping around. I feel like my brain is plugged into *that*, too, and can't shut any of it out, and sometimes the two of them, they kind of come together to create a third, different reality that only I can see and hear and smell and taste."

A decade or so later, I heard a psychiatrist describe schizophrenia in these almost-laughable sentimental terms: "When someone's life becomes so empty and sad and unsatisfactory that they can't deal with it, they will invent an alternate reality wherein they *are* happy, wherein everything they do brings them a feeling of great accomplishment and self-worth . . . but the more they retreat into this world to find comfort and peace, the stronger the likelihood that they will begin to confuse this invented world with the real one, and perhaps even find that the two are overlapping during everyday existence to the extent that they will no longer *wish* to differentiate."

For all my reading on the subject, I have come to the conclusion that the truth lies somewhere in the middle of these two extreme explanations. I wouldn't be surprised if I found out that Matt Warner shares that opinion.

I read an early draft of *Eyes Everywhere* about a year ago when Matt was just beginning to shop it around, and was damned impressed by it (hence my blurb that's been used to publicize this novel). Reading this version, which has been tweaked a bit so as to make certain minor details add up more efficiently, my opinion of this novel hasn't changed; I think it's an important book, not only because it's a solid example of Matt's evolution as a writer (compare this to his previous novel, *The Organ Donor*, and it's hard to believe they were written by the same person), but because it does something that you almost never see in the horror and suspense fields these days: it never talks down to the reader—and by that I mean it assumes a certain level of intelligence on the part of those who choose to visit this unnerving microcosm of ones man's emotional and psychological disintegration. At no point in this story do we have a talking head literary construct come onstage to explain to us in exact terminology what is happening to Charlie. It would have been easy to have a psychologist forced into the narrative to talk about the function of, oh, say the hypothalamus, and how if it doesn't produce enough of a certain chemical the brain can go wonky in a hurry. It's not hard to imagine some run-on monologue like this: "The hypothalamus is a region of the brain located below the thalamus, forming the major portion of the ventral region of the diencephalon and functioning to regulate certain metabolic processes and other autonomic activities. The hypothalamus links the nervous system to the endocrine system by synthesizing and secreting neurohormones that function by stimulating the secretion of hormones from the anterior pituitary gland—among them, gonadotropin-releasing hormone (GnRH). The neurons that secrete GnRH are linked to the limbic system, which is very involved in the control of emotions, and it would appear that in Charlie's case . . ."

Zzzzzzzzzz—huh? What? Were you just saying something?

Or Matt could have brought in some equally dull explanation about how lack of sleep screws up the function of the pineal gland, prohibiting it from flensing melatonin from the brain (whenever in-depth study of human behavioral disorders is conducted, one of the standard results is almost always an unusually high level of melatonin in the system, such as those found in people who suffer from chronic insomnia or night workers who have to sleep during the day in places where light cannot be filtered out).

Zzzzzzzzzz—huh? Oh, sorry, I must have dozed off again.

Each of the above have been linked to both paranoid and schizophrenic behavior. Though a myriad of other symptoms and causes must be present to really kick things into the danger zone (depending on whose diagnosis you follow), there are dozens—if not hundreds—of theoretical explanations for what causes paranoid schizophrenia. And you know what? Not a damned one of them would have been welcomed in this novel, because it's the *why* of it that absolutely *must never* be explained for the sake narrative cohesiveness. No; what matters here is the *how* of it, nothing more. I've no doubt that more than a few readers—those used to being spoon-fed a detailed, neat explanation for everything that occurs over the course of a novel—are going to come away from *Eyes Everywhere* feeling more than a bit frustrated, because they are never told why these events happened and so may fail to understand why they spiral out of control so quickly and tragically.

But one thing that became clear to me before I reached the halfway point of this novel is that Matt did his research—*oh, man,* did he do his research, because anyone who has made a serious study of paranoid schizophrenia will recognize all the symptoms and behaviors displayed by Charlie (and, for the record, if you do any research into the symptoms after reading this novel, you'll find that Charlie displays them in almost the exact order that many psychiatrists say they *will* be displayed, though these same psychiatrists admit that the order does vary from person to person, depending on the severity of the affliction). But unlike other novelists who fall victim to the temptation to flaunt their research, Matt never reverts to a talking head scenario; he never explains, he *illustrates*; in writers' terms, he never tells, he *shows*.

And that, my friends, take a lot of nerve. (I, for one, applaud Matt for taking this approach, even though I suspect it's going to come at the price of more than few pissy and pissed-off reviews.)

There have been, to my mind, two superior novels about paranoid behavior published in the horror and suspense fields; one is Roland Topor's underrated masterpiece, *The Tenant*, and the other is Tim Lebbon's recent *Desolation*. Now, while Lebbon's novel does ultimately offer a supernatural explanation for what is happening to his central character (though not in easy, clear, or condescending terms), what it shares in common with Topor's novel (and this one) is that it painstakingly depicts the rapid disintegration of its central character's psyche without ever stopping to catch its breath.

I now gladly add *Eyes Everywhere* to that small list of superior novels about paranoia.

And like the line from "For What It's Worth," the paranoia starts when Charlie Fields is afraid.

Go back and re-read the first two chapters to see just how deftly—almost undetectably—Matt starts introducing the elements that propel this novel to its tragic finish. Starting with the very first paragraph, Matt establishes an atmosphere of anxiety and paranoia—after all, Charlie works in post-9/11 Washington DC, a city where everyone's nerves have been on edge for years. Charlie is dealing with several high-stress factors in his life, not the least of which is the ever-present threat of losing his job. A casual remark during a meeting is misinterpreted as a racist comment, thus earning him not only a "chat" with one of his bosses, but an actual black mark next to his name on a list.

Consider, if you will, the headache-inducing thought process behind the following passage, a checklist of workplace anxieties that come nagging when Charlie considers asking his boss if he can leave work early in order to go home and help take care of his sick children:

> Sue was probably sitting there with her steno pad tally of demerits, just waiting for a call like this. If it wasn't her steno pad, then it was some sophisticated HR computer program that cross-referenced performance reviews, individual paid-time-off balances, company profit reports, workload summaries, and ratios of personal-versus-professional e-mails sent from his computer.

Anyone who's worked in a corporate environment will tell you that such considerations are not just a daily but often *hourly* concern. (In fact, Charlie's anxieties here probably seem mild in comparison.)

So we have Charlie Fields, who's already on edge, who's working in an environment where—whether they intend it to or not—the people in charge are fostering an atmosphere of paranoia.

Now re-read the sequence where Charlie travels home the day after the meeting that leaves a black mark next to his name.

The black security guard gives him "a dirty look" as he leaves the building, and Charlie's defenses are put on High Alert. Perhaps word of his supposed racial remark had spread—after all, one of the men in the meeting, Dwight Mason, was black.

Outside, he spots another man—possibly black—talking on a cell phone. Seeing Charlie, the man seems to hide. Charlie wonders if he's being followed.

Before going on, trace this trail of logic in reverse and you can see how subtly and matter-of-factly Matt has set up this chain of events.

Charlie spots the man several times more, and each time his impression of the man changes ever-so-quietly; at first the man is simply "following" him; then the man is "chasing" him; then the man becomes his "pursuer"—and by the time Charlie is convinced that the man is Dwight's son, sent to follow him in order to gather personal information to use against him in Dwight's or Sue's next performance review, the dominoes have already started falling, the chain reaction has begun, and there's no stopping what follows. Charlie disembarks his train one stop early in order to lose his pursuer, grabs a local bus, and finds that the man has followed him onto the bus, as well. But is it *really* the same man, or is it Charlie's fear-tainted perception?

Therein lies the core enigma of this novel, for even though Matt chooses to tell Charlie's story in third person—a narrative voice that would allow him (and in the eyes of some readers, *require* him) to include multiple viewpoints—he monomaniacally filters *everything* solely through Charlie's sensibilities; we see, hear, sense, taste, touch, and, most importantly of all, *perceive* everything as Charlie does. Yet, because the story unfolds in third person, we as readers are constantly nagged by this sense that there is a sheet of glass separating us from Charlie, keeping us at arm's length, forbidding a deeper communion, perhaps even manipulating our perception by showing us only reflections of Charlie's increasingly warped view of reality—a metaphor that is made horrifyingly literal in the powerful closing scene.

I imagine most of you who read this wonderful novel will have your own choices for favorite moments, so I thought I'd close with a handful of my own choices:

The opening three chapters, of course, wherein Charlie's paranoia starts off small and begins to build, and build, and build, plugging him into that "second layer" of reality that will all too soon merge with the first layer to create a third and terrible level of perception.

The scene where he rents the apartment after deciding to run and hide. This is, if you read it carefully, the very definition of subtle black comedy; Charlie has gone to such unbelievable and exasperating lengths to cover his tracks that the whole thing is almost—*almost*—outright funny, yet the palpable air of desperation underneath makes it seem impolite to laugh.

The heart-wrenching scene wherein Charlie, convinced his wife has turned against him, wields a gun in front of her and their children. This is an expertly-executed sequence for a variety of reasons, not the least of which is it's a textbook example of the cardinal rule of characterization: if you have reader sympathy on your character's side, they will stay on his or her side regardless of what he or she does. This particular scene is a real tightrope walk all the way through, because while your heart is breaking for Charlie, it's also breaking for his wife and children; you don't know who to believe at this point in the story, and Matt uses that uncertainty to great advantage.

And there is, at last, the amazing final scene between Charlie and Lisa, the two of them separated by a sheet of glass (the literal realization of Charlie's final detachment from reality), where by now even Charlie is convinced he's crazy . . . right until the lights snap off and he sees the reflection of the true (?) image, leaving both him and the reader in almost the same place where we began: doubting the validity of the reality we *think* we are perceiving.

Eyes Everywhere is an important piece of work, one whose true value, I think, will not be immediately apparent, but will nonetheless be proven over the course of time. It is a personal triumph for Matt and should leave all of us waiting impatiently for his next novel.

And if there is a moral to this story, it's to be found in this old joke:

Just because you're paranoid, that doesn't mean they *aren't* out to get you.

Remember that the next time you're riding the bus or train and think you feel someone's eyes watching you.

The Search For Greater Meaning: An Introduction to *Laughing Boy's Shadow*

> "The whole conviction of my life now rests upon the belief that loneliness, far from being a rare and curious phenomenon, is the central and inevitable fact of human existence."
> –Thomas Wolfe, "God's Lonely Man."

> "Loneliness cries deep from my soul
> Keeps trying to tell me about the world growing so cold"
> –Grand Funk Railroad, "Loneliness"

This time around, you get two introductions for the price of one; the short and sweet one, and the longer, more analytical one.

The short one:

Laughing Boy's Shadow is a mesmerizing, disturbing, compelling novel of modern-day horror and alienation that might possibly change you once you've finished reading it. It is a novel that perfectly fits my own personal definition of what constitutes the best kind of horror fiction, and reading it was nothing short of a genuine experience (in the dictionary sense of the word) for me.

This novel will hit you hard in the mind and heart, as well as scare the bejeezus out of you more than a few times.

There. Now if you want to read the more analytical version that follows, do me a favor and *wait*; jump ahead, read the book, and then come back to read the rest of this. You can thank me later.

Whenever I sit on a panel at a convention, the question of "What is horror?" inevitably comes up. I almost always point out that the question—a pertinent one, no argument—is nonetheless incomplete; nine times out of ten, what the person actually means to ask is either, "Why do people read horror?" or "What purpose is served by horror fiction?"

Not to dismiss the first question, but debating the nature of what constitutes horror is tantamount to trying to offer a universal definition of Art; it exists solely in the eye of the beholder. Yes, it's easy enough to point to stories in the news about war, famine, natural disasters, child abuse, or any of the endless nightmares that afflict humankind, but in all those instances (most of the time) there is a certain, safe *distance* involved; it's happening to someone else, somewhere else, and while we may very well be horrified at the events, each lacks (again, most of the time) the element of *personal terror* that makes horror a very intimate, personal experience.

And nowhere is this personal experience more delicate and intimate than in horror fiction. What terrifies you may be nothing at all to the next person; what moves you at the core of your being may very well be thought silly or inconsequential by someone else.

But there is, I believe, one universal element that unites all horror fiction at its core, be it fiction about vampires, or zombies, or ghosts, or child abuse, psychological disintegration, the collapse of society, nuclear war, etc., and it's this universal element that I always offer up at conventions when asked about the purpose of horror.

The best horror fiction concerns itself with exploring the connections between violence, grief, loneliness, and suffering, and how we as a species reconcile these things with the concept of a just universe watched over by a supposedly loving Supreme Being wherein even the most mundane and trivial of our everyday tasks carry *some* kind of greater meaning.

Even if you're an agnostic or atheist and remove the Supreme Being element from the above equation, the central concern of horror fiction remains unchanged. To offer a concrete example of what I'm talking about, ask yourself this question: what purpose is served by my doing the goddamned *laundry* when there are children being murdered by their parents every day?

Woody Allen had a fairly funny line in *Annie Hall* that touched upon this concept: "If one guy is starving, it puts a crimp in my evening."

You get the idea.

Being a stubborn subscriber to string theory (what used to be known as the grand unification theory), I fervently believe that on a quantum level, *everything* is connected; every thought, belief, action, event, philosophy, object, and sentient being.

It would not surprise me one bit were I to discover that Steve Saville feels the same way, for *Laughing Boy's Shadow* is that rarest of horror novels: one that grapples with sociological, theological, philosophical, and—*gulp!*—metaphysical issues, yet never once becomes didactic or ponderous. Saville never has any of his characters climb up on a soapbox and shout through a bullhorn that *I Have An Important Message, Dammit!* He *illustrates*, he *shows*; and considering the core of his subject matter, it would have been oh-so-easy for him to preach, but he never does. In fact, his first-person narrator, Declan Shea, describes many of the events with the semi-detached, unsentimental eye of a documentary filmmaker; he presents things as they are and leaves it up to the reader to decide how much emotional investment he or she cares to give to the scene or event in question. As a result, much of what Declan encounters is powerfully heartbreaking and often terrifying on a deep, organic level.

Take, for instance, Declan's encounter with a homeless man named Matthew early in the book. Declan and his girlfriend, Aimee, meet Matthew in the wee hours. Matthew is a denizen of the streets and has accepted his fate. (I'll leave you to discover the reasons behind Matthew's circumstances for yourself.) It would have been tempting—perhaps *too* tempting—for a writer to sentimentalize Matthew's plight, to present him as an object of pity, but thanks to Saville's restraint and Declan's world view, the sequence never even *flirts* with sentimentality, and is all the more affecting for it.

It is Declan's encounter with Matthew, however, that serves as the main catalyst for Declan's entering the "Underground"—the world from which Matthew has come, populated by other denizens of the streets. (And Declan's voyage into the Underground is arguably horror's equivalent to Dave Bowman's entering the Monolith in *2001: A Space Odyssey*: surreal, poetic, terrifying, lyrical, and mind-bending.)

And once Declan enters the Underground, reality becomes twisted and warped beyond (sometimes) his ability to adequately describe it. Think Neil Gaiman's *Neverwhere* by way of Lovecraft and Jean-Paul Sartre. It is here that Declan learns more about the connections between the Haves and the Have-Nots, as well as the purpose behind suffering, loneliness, violence, and grief, and why these darker elements of existence must be perpetuated.

The Underground sequence comprises the bulk of this novel, and accomplishes what all great fiction strives to do; it transports you into another world, one so far removed from your daily existence that you'll rarely recognize the elements waiting there.

It is also in the Underground sequences that Saville turns *Laughing Boy's Shadow* into the type of horror novel that is so infrequently seen these days it's in danger of making the Endangered Species list: a study in genuine alienation.

Now, before you shrug off that term, consider the psych textbook definition of that word: a psychological condition in which an individual comes to feel divorced from the objective world or parts of his or her own personality or feel that he or she is nonexistent.

Alienation goes well beyond mere loneliness—in fact, it would take *the light* from loneliness a few thousand years to reach alienation. It is the complete and total subtraction of the Self from not only the world but from one's self, as well. There is no purpose, no meaning, no psychological, spiritual, physical, or even *imagined* connection to anyone or anything. You cease to be, even to yourself. It is misery personified, and damn few writers have dared to grapple with the concept the way Saville does here. Camus' *The Stranger* is arguably the prototype for this kind of story, followed by Kobo Abe's existential masterpiece *The Box Man*; I can think of only a small handful of modern-day horror writers who have attempted to explore the subject of alienation with an unflinching eye: Tim Waggoner's *Like Death*, Tim Lebbon's unjustifiably overlooked and underrated *Desolation*, and Matthew Warner's *Eyes Everywhere*. (Humility and common sense prevent me from adding my own *The Indifference of Heaven* (a.k.a. *In Silent Graves*) to the list because, in the end, the central character's alienation is nullified, whereas in the other novels mentioned it is only intensified.)

But in the end, Declan emerges from the Underground, and I can say in all honesty that the final thirty pages of *Laughing Boy's Shadow* achieve a level of stunning, chilling lyricism that left me shaking; Declan's final statement to the world, contained in the last four pages, is simply amazing; the passages are so luminous that the words threaten to shimmer right off the page.

What makes this book all the more remarkable is that it was Saville's first novel; for 95 percent of its unfolding, it doesn't read like a first novel; it's polished, beautifully-paced, and written with the sure craft of a writer who knows precisely where the story is going and who's refined his narrative voice to razor-sharpness.

Sure, there are some bumps along the way; the prologue (herein called the intro) strikes me as a bit superfluous; there are a few too many instances where one character "hisses" a line at another, only the words they "hiss" contain no sibilants; and a couple of the events described seem surreal and nebulous for the sake of being surreal and nebulous.

But in the end, these are *minor* quibbles that in no way detract from the feverish power of this novel; think of them as being scratches on fine, hand-tooled leather: proof of the authenticity of the product.

And just to reiterate: this novel will scare the hell out of you more than a few times. It will also move you, sometimes deeply so.

It is, as I said before, a novel that fits perfectly my own personal definition of what constitutes the best horror fiction.

So, if you've picked up *Laughing Boy's Shadow* thinking you're going to find a novel filled with the traditional tropes of horror (zombies, werewolves, vampires, etc.), then you're holding the wrong book; if you think you're going to find a tale jam-packed with the usual ooga-boogas, bloodletting, and big-budget set pieces, put this down; and—most especially—if you think for one second that you're going to be spoon-fed everything in crystal-clear terms that even a sixth-grader could understand so you needn't tax your brain dealing with the implications of everything that happens in this story, if you think you're going to come out of this unscathed, all safe and sound in the warm embrace of a happy ending wherein the hero overcomes all obstacles and life returns to normal, then close this book right now, start the car, and drive to your nearest Walpurgis-Mart to pick up a copy of this month's newest horror paperback release featuring zombies, werewolves, vampires, or an ominous-looking house on its cover.

But I hope you won't; I hope you'll dive into this redoubtable achievement and indulge in the dark feast Saville has set out for you.

Laughing Boy's Shadow has garnered something of a legendary reputation here in the states due to its lack of availability; as a result, those who have read it have hyped it to high Heaven, leaving more than a few readers to ask, "Can it possibly live up to its reputation?"

The answer is a resounding *yes*.

This novel will knock you onto the floor and remain with you for years to come.

In the event that you didn't take my advice at the beginning and start the book right away, then you've no choice but to do so now, because I have kept you from it long enough.

Meet Declan, who hates cities, and follow him to the Underground. Bring all the courage you can.

You're going to need it.

Awaiting the Swimmer:
An Introduction from the Safety of the Shore

I see her loosed hair straining.
She is trying to come to me, here.
I cannot swim, and she knows it . . .

I can stand only where I am standing.
Shall she fail, and go down to the sea?
Shall she call, as she changes to water?

She swims to overcome fear

–James Dickey, from *Into the Stone*

In the fall of 2000 a collection of five novellas, entitled *Saying Secrets*, was released by the author of the book you now hold in your hands. It featured a simple but elegant cover illustration (badly reproduced by the printer, unfortunately), accompanying commentaries by science fiction and fantasy stalwarts William F. Nolan and George Clayton Johnson, and some of the most powerful and restrained writing I have encountered in years. Despite the impression one might have upon noting the participation of Nolan and Johnson, none of the pieces in *Saying Secrets* were genre tales; all but one had been previously published in the excellent literary journal *The Long Story*, a publication whose commitment to—and demand for—quality writing has always been, to put it mildly, intimidating. However, for whatever bizarre and unfathomable reasons, no major mass-market publishing house would take it, and so Christopher Conlon did something that was still uncommon at that time: he went to iUniverse and published it himself. While this did get the book into print, because it was self-published, it had virtually no chance of finding a place on the shelves of major bookstore chains. Which is why you've never read it, and the loss is yours, because had *Saying Secrets* been published by St. Martin's, Carroll & Graf, Dutton, or another highly visible publishing house, it would have been widely recognized not only as one of the best collections of the year, but Conlon would have seen it contents compared to the stories of Salinger, Cheever, and Carver—among whose works his stories can stand as equals—and this particular introduction would be unnecessary, because you'd already know who Christopher Conlon is.

I can guarantee that you'll know who he is by the time you reach the final page of this, his second collection of stories.

As a poet, Conlon has been nominated for the prestigious Pushcart Prize (for a portion of his poetry chapbook *What There Is*) and to date published two full-length collections, the most recent of which, *The Weeping Time*, contains some of the darkest yet most eerily beautiful verse you're likely to encounter this side of James Dickey (of whose work Conlon's often reminds me).

The excerpt from Dickey quoted at the beginning seems to me wholly appropriate, considering the underlying themes and recurring motifs of the stories collected here; there is a loneliness, a longing, and a quiet, sad, desperate form of anger lurking beneath the surface of these tales; and—like the excerpt—each story ends mid-breath, as if both the storyteller and his characters were pulling in a lungful of air before releasing a final, soul-piercing cry that is, at the last moment, held in, leaving you standing helpless on the shore, awaiting the unseen swimmer's call to echo back over the whispering waves and assure you that they're all right, after all. But the call doesn't come, the swimmer remains unseen, and the breath remains held.

But before that final cry that is never released, you are going to find some remarkable passages, each of which displays not only the poet's skill at reducing language to its most necessary and vital elements, but does so in a manner that is often spellbinding.

Take this passage, from the title novella, an almost agonizing depiction of the slow death of the American Dream:

> ...he saw his life as a burst hourglass, saw the sand gripped frantically in his palm but still seeping away, dropping grain by grain out of his reach forever and that in the end there would be nothing left, absolutely nothing, that he would have lived and died and done it all wrong, all wrong. That his entire life was a mistake.

Or this deceptively simple passage from "Ghost in Autumn" that, taken in context, reveals a depth of regret that most writers could not convey in five times as many words:

> I watched her eat but was unsure whether she did it the same way or not. I don't recall ever noticing how my mother ate.

Or, finally, this passage from "Darkness, and She Was Alone," wherein a horribly abused young girl swims toward a place of salvation, a passage that to my mind serves as the central metaphor for not only the story, but the entire collection (and note with envy Conlon's use of repetition and subtle alliteration to create a hypnotic cadence):

> She swims down underneath the waves, the water flowing around her and turning the world miraculous tints of green and blue and gold. The light from the lighthouse breaks up, reflects, refracts, shines through the water in dark rainbows

> and she begins to see, not far away, things approaching her, beautiful graceful things like porpoises, but as they draw near she realizes they are not porpoises but children, dozens of them, hundreds, all naked and swimming toward her. Some have missing limbs, some have big holes in their heads or chests, some have flesh blackened by fire, some have terrible red stripes on their bodies. But all swim toward her with perfect grace, their faces happy, their injuries and violations seemingly painless and forgotten in this wonderful world under the water.

That this particular passage appears in the middle of the collection's middle story is no coincidence. That single, startling image of a child in pain swimming toward other children who have suffered equal or even greater pain creates metaphoric and thematic ripples that, like actual ripples in a pond, vibrate outward in all directions—in this case, echoing themes of the stories that have come before and foreshadowing those of the stories that follow. Though each story creates its own individual thematic ripples that move outward in different directions, all of them have the same two elements at their core: children and water, and how the pain suffered by the former can be either soothed or intensified by the latter; witness the subtle sadness of "Bathing the Bones" for perhaps the most overt example of this. (Conlon wisely avoids any ham-fisted baptismal symbolism while employing these elements; what water is meant to symbolize in each story—or if it's meant to symbolize anything at all [sometimes it's just water]—is left up to the interpretation of we readers standing on the safety of the shore, calling for the unseen swimmer.)

Conlon's characters—like the undetected subject of Dickey's poem—swim to overcome fear; but bear in mind that those two words, "to overcome," have more than one meaning, as does the word "gothic," but for the sake of continuity, here's the one I've chosen to focus on:

> **Goth·ic** (Goth·ic or goth·ic) *adj.*
> Belonging to a genre of fiction characterized by gloom and darkness, often with a grotesque or supernatural plot unfolding in an eerie or lonely location such as a ruined castle.

Conlon's motivation for subtitling this collection *Gothic Stories* may have something to do with that particular definition (I somehow cannot imagine him dressing all in black and going to a Goth club to stand swaying to the music of Faith and the Muse or Love Spirals Downward), but I think it's more an attempt to evoke a preconception in readers' minds than an actual outright statement of the type of story they'll find here; yes, the atmosphere is often gloomy, and the locations just as often secluded (spiritually, if not physically), and some of the plots are arguably grotesque, but these are ultimately exterior elements, scrims masking the real conflict, the surface of a pond into which a pebble must be dropped so that what lies beneath can be revealed by the ripples.

In less lofty terms, a smokescreen. By evoking the word "gothic," Conlon knows that you're going to enter this collection with memories of Manderley, Dracula's Castle, and Hill House whispering in the back of your mind; perhaps you'll even find yourself drawing parallels between certain characters and Miss Havisham, Edward Rochester, or Bertha Mason, Rochester's tragic wife who in her insanity must be kept bound and isolated in her attic chamber. While these parallels might be justified in a peripheral sense, they bear little relevance to Conlon's actual achievements in these pages—the most impressive of which is his ability to use these preconceived notions of what constitutes "gothic" literature against your expectations while simultaneously adhering to their traditional storytelling functions; that Manderley has arguably evolved here into a corner market ("Thundershowers at Dusk") or Bertha Mason replaced by an aborted fetus in a jar (the brilliant "Unfinished Music," hands-down the finest novella I've read in any genre in the last few years) doesn't matter nearly as much as the way their presence and function affects both the characters and the reader. That all of these stories feature crucial scenes that take place in rain or darkness (often both) might seem on the surface an affectation, a self-conscious nod toward the traditional and expected gothic elements; but on closer examination, one realizes that Conlon's intensely intimate world view as a storyteller necessitated that these "traditional gothic" elements be transported into the modern world because it is the *sensibility behind* those elements that one should carry away from the stories, not the special effects. The so-called "gothic" essentials are here because each story demanded their presence, not because the author was making a deliberate choice to graft gloomy atmosphere onto the proceedings.

So, *Gothic Stories* . . . in sensibility only; but an *essential* sensibility, one that descends over your mind and emotions like a hard metal hood, darkening and dampening everything you see and hear and feel (a line from the title novella that I shamelessly steal and paraphrase).

So, from my safe place on the shore, while awaiting the unseen swimmer to return my call, it is my very great pleasure to introduce you to Christopher Conlon, the finest writer you haven't read, but damned well ought to be reading.

Thundershowers at Dusk is, in my opinion, a remarkable achievement, made all the more so by the brevity of its length. It is poetic, majestic, disturbing, haunting, and—most of all, most importantly of all—deeply and genuinely *felt*, a collection that will move you, unnerve you, and remind you that, in the end, there is more than one way to swim to overcome fear.

"Don't Just Stand There — *Step* On the Damn Thing . . . Oh, Uh, Maybe Not . . ." An Introduction to Ray Garton's *'Nids and Other Stories*

See if this oldie but moldy rings any bells:

"Help me . . . help me . . . help meeeeeee!"

That's right, the justifiably famous final scene of 1958's *The Fly*, wherein Vincent Price discovers the titular insect (by now wearing David "Al" Hedison's head) trapped in a spider's web in the garden. Price leans down and we're treated to a tight close-up of Hedison gawking in horror as a gigantic (to him) eight-legged horror moves closer, closer, closer . . . and then we get an even *tighter* close-up of the spider's face as it moves in for the kill and, well, it ain't pretty. Black eyes, dripping fangs, and all that hair. *Yeech*.

I saw this movie on *Chiller Theater* when I was six years old, and I have been *terrified* of spiders ever since. I don't mean just a little nervous around, a bit wary of, a tad cagey when in the same vicinity, no; I mean jump-to-my-feet, knock-the-chair-over, break-out-in-hives, pee-my-pants, leap-up-on-the-nearest-high-surface-and-scream-like-a-*castrato*-banshee-with-flaming-hemorrhoids *terrified* of the little fuckers. "Don't just stand there—*step on* the damn thing!" (Of course, what happens when the thing is big enough to step on you? *Hmmmmmm . . .*)

A friend of mine who kept a pet tarantula once thought it would be funny to see if I really was *that* scared shitless of the little eight-legged freaks, and so one night (after I'd passed out from *way* too many drinks at a party he'd given), took Lil' Abner out of his cage and set him upon my chest, then shook me awake.

I came to and saw this thing *crawling* up toward my face and I . . . well, reacted not unlike what I described above, with the exception that I also broke my friend's nose with my knee when he was so doubled over with laughter he failed to notice that my terror and embarrassment had almost instantaneously turned to rage and focused all of its energy in the limb nearest his face at the time.

Needless to say, Lil' Abner and I were never in the same room again.

In short: spiders scare me.

Oddly enough, some of my favorite horror movies are about—get this—*giant spiders.*

Tarantula. Earth Vs. the Spider. The Giant Spider Invasion. Eight-Legged Freaks. The list goes on. (The worse the special effects, the better.) Hell, I still get the creeps from watching reruns of the *Night Gallery* episode "A Fear of Spiders," which has to feature the most hands-down laughably awful giant spider in history, but at the time of its original airing scared me so bad I had nightmares for a week (I was nine). And *Charlotte's Web*? You don't want to go there with me. Sincerely.

My guess is that if Ray Garton doesn't share my fear of spiders, he at least shares my deep and twisted affection for giant spider movies—and if you're a true *aficionado* of these types of movies, you're in for some extra treats with the title novella in this marvelous crackerjack collection of tales, because *'Nids* pays homage not only to giant spider movies, but to the whole giant insect *oeuvre* of 1950s science fiction films, the ones usually featured on drive-in screens (it's no coincidence that the finale' of *'Nids* is set in a drive-in; I think I can reveal that without ruining anything for you).

For the first two-thirds of its length, *'Nids* is careful to make sure all the giant-bug-movie clichés are firmly in place: we have the mismatched teenaged lovers (the Terribly Popular Girl and the Misunderstood Juvenile Delinquent); we have the Romantic Make-Out Spot Where the Horror First Shows Up; we have the Mysterious Scientific Lab Where a Terrible Accident Happens; we have the Noble Lawman of This Quiet Little Community Where Nothing Ever Happens... you're way ahead of me, aren't you? Well, don't make the mistake of thinking that you're also ahead of Garton, because you're not.

There is nothing quite as satisfying as reading a story wherein the writer is careful to set up your expectations—and, in fact, goes out of his or her way to reinforce those expectations—then have him or her pull the rug out from underneath you. For its first two-thirds, *'Nids* isn't really going to surprise you—it's not supposed to, and no one knows this better than Garton. He wants you to be comfortable here. He wants you to feel a certain affectionate familiarity with the characters and goings-on. He wants to entertain and scare you, which he does with a vengeance—good Lord, this thing *moves*... kind of like the giant sun spider that Quickly Wreaks Havoc on the Quiet Little Community Where Nothing Ever Happens.

Does it seem like I'm giving too much away?

I'm not.

Because by the time Garton gets to the third act of *'Nids*, he's so effortlessly lulled you into this sense of affectionate familiarity that you're actually going to be dumb enough to *think* you can predict what's going to happen before the movie... uh, *story*, ends. You've heard the phrase "Shaggy Dog Story"? Well, with *'Nids*, Ray Garton has created arguably the very first "Shaggy Spider Story."

Further, deponeth sayeth not, except maybe for this: you are going to have *one hell* of a good time with this novella. You're going to be scared, you're going to be grossed out, you're going to laugh, and more than once you're going to be blindsided with several moments of surprising poignancy.

If this book consisted solely of *'Nids*, it would be worth its price. Fortunately for all of us, Ray and Subterranean Press have managed to pack five more equally effective pieces between these covers.

"In A Fit of Jealous Rage" finds Garton once again returning to Raymond Carver territory (as he did with the excellent and underrated story "The Night Clerk" in his previous Subterranean collection, *The Girl in the Basement and Other Stories*). In "Fit," we meet a man who has just killed his wife and her lover. The question throughout the rest of the story (which is my personal favorite of the shorter pieces) is: *What now?* How Garton answers this is going to throw more than a few of you for a loop—and will, in fact, likely stir debate as to whether or not he *does* answer it. (He does, but the manner in which the answer is conveyed is not one that most horror readers are going to be comfortable with).

"Kristina" is an out-and-out black comedy, culminating in a wicked punch line, deftly and dryly delivered; "Mrs. DiMarco's Corpse," a story in the E.C. Comics vein, is the most traditional horror story of the bunch, filled with nightmarish and grotesque imagery, but it also manages to pack a solid emotional wallop (check out the exquisite paragraph that begins: "Somewhere in the complex, a baby wailed, and children laughed" for proof that you are in the hands of a storyteller who knows exactly what he's doing); the ironically-titled "Talk in the Street" will leave you with the kind of cold, hard shock that only the best storytelling can—think of Shirley Jackson's "The Lottery" and you *might* be prepared for what happens here; and for those of you who had the good sense to purchase this lettered edition, you're in for a rare treat: a non-fiction piece by Ray, "Night of the Lizard Man," which provides a rather telling glimpse not only into the storyteller's psyche, but serves as a surprising and thoughtful bookend to the title novella (you'll understand what I mean when you read this telling essay).

I've been reading Ray Garton's work for a long time; I was, in fact, reading him before my first story ever saw print. He's been a personal icon of mine in the horror field for longer than either of us would be comfortable to my admitting to—pardon the convoluted syntax there, but I am still stunned and honored to be writing this introduction.

Ray Garton is one of my storytelling heroes.

'Nids serves to remind me why.

Enough of me already. I'm going to end this by paraphrasing a line from John D. MacDonald's introduction to Stephen King's *Night Shift*: why are you still reading this when you ought to be reading the stories?

Last Intermission:
In the End, Remembered Roses

"Old man take a look at my life, I'm a lot like you."
–Neil Young

I'm afraid we're about to reach the part where my abyss will expect us to make a short visit, and in order to bring this book back to where it began (more or less) we're going to visit at least one very dark place. This is not hyperbole on my part. I just wanted to let you know where things are heading.

I want to ease into the next section as gently as possible, and there is no better way that to introduce you to a marvelous man, teacher, friend, and writer who made story-telling his life, and who was never hesitant to share his knowledge with any writer who came asking.

His name was J.N. Williamson, and he became my second father.

I knew Jerry Williamson for nearly twenty years. I first met him at a World Fantasy Convention in 1986, shortly after my first professional appearance in *Twilight Zone Magazine's* sister publication, *Night Cry*. I spent a good portion of that convention wandering around in a terrified daze because everywhere I looked, there was a writer whose work I had read and admired: Robert McCammon, Stephen King, William F. Nolan, Dennis Etchison, Charles L. Grant, Joe Lansdale, Richard Christian Matheson, Robert Bloch, Peter Straub, and, of course, J.N. Williamson (whose story "Shelter Skelter" appeared in the same issue of *Night Cry* as mine). I felt like an insignificant, microscopic speck among these writers who were, in my wide and star-struck eyes, giants.

For the first day, I spoke to almost no one. I was just a guy from Ohio (who was employed at the time as a dog groomer) who had a story that had recently appeared in a professional publication (I'd had perhaps five stories previously published in the now-defunct *Eldritch Tales*, a terrific small press magazine that paid half a cent a word and contributors' copies).

In short—and despite youthful, naive daydreams that someone would read my nametag and exclaim, "*Ohmigod! You're Gary Braunbeck? You're the guy who wrote that incredible story in the latest issue of* Night Cry?"—I was there pretty much as a fan, and one who was scared shitless to approach any of these giants and giants-to-be to either ask for an autograph or tell them how much I enjoyed their work. (And to be honest, I'm still that way. When I met Richard Matheson at last year's Stoker Weekend in Los Angeles, I stuttered like Porky Pig when I asked him to autograph a book.)

Then came a Friday night party in one of the large suites the convention organizers had reserved—I'm talking not one, not two, not three, but *four* rooms, each of which could easily hold a few dozen people and still give everyone enough room to turn around and not jam their elbow up someone else's nose.

Jerry Williamson and his then-wife Mary had taken control of an area in a far corner, spitting distance from the bar, where Jerry was holding court with a small group of fans. I wandered over and leaned against the massive television cabinet, a few feet away from Mary. She immediately said hello to me, asked if cigarette smoke bothered me, and when I said not at all, she offered me a smoke and I accepted. We leaned there, quietly smoking, while Jerry continued to entertain his audience with often hysterically funny stories of his days as a musician.

Eventually—as is wont to happen at conventions—the audience dispersed to other areas of the suite, and Mary then introduced me to Jerry with the following words: "Hon, this is Gary Braunbeck, the guy who wrote *that story*." (I hadn't said *anything* to her about either being a writer or having just seen my first professional publication.)

To which Jerry exclaimed: "Oh, my goodness, *you're* Gary Braunbeck? You wrote that wonderful story in the recent issue of *Night Cry*? I'm *so pleased* to meet you!" And vigorously shook my hand as if *he* were the fan and *I* was the Big Deal Author. He and Mary spent the next hour talking to me, neither of them once looking around the room to see if there were anyone more important or interesting to speak with or call over. By the time the weekend was over, they had officially adopted me as one of their own and insisted that I refer to them as my "spare set" of parents. Mary later became my very first agent, and Jerry was responsible for securing me an invite to an anthology entitled *Phantoms*, which became not only my best-paying sale of the 80s ($375.00), but put me on Martin H. Greenberg's radar, something that led to dozens of appearances in other Greenberg anthologies that eventually put me on the radar of several publishers.

That is why I never hesitated to tell anyone—Jerry included—that I owe my career to J.N. Williamson. Sure, I had been published in the small press before I met him, and would later be honored with a place in the ToC of *Masques III* (the first time Jerry-as-editor bought my work, but only after three revisions that remain among the most astute and detailed I've ever received), but none of that, I am convinced, would have happened had not Jerry thought enough of myself and my *Night Cry* story to suggest that Marty Greenberg consider giving this new (and then much younger) author a shot.

Jerry's reaction upon our initial meeting was typical of him. He had the enviable ability to make whomever he was speaking with feel like the most important person in the room, and he treated all writers—the established pros, the giants, the novices—with equal respect, admiration, and enthusiasm. He *loved* storytelling and storytellers.

I don't want to turn this into one of those Oh-He-Was-So-Without-Flaws memorial pieces that always disintegrate into mawkishness and revisionist history. Jerry would have hated that (and probably taken his red pen to the works, all the while grumbling, "Make *me* look like a saint? What are you, crazy? Here, give me the damn thing before you completely ruin it beyond repair!").

Jerry Neal Williamson died at 1:20 AM on December 7 in his room at the Riverwalk Village nursing home in Noblesville, Indiana. He was seventy-three.

At this point, it is traditional for one to list a series of pertinent facts about the deceased's life; where he went to high school, military service, where he was employed, the names of surviving family members, etc. That has already been done elsewhere, both on the web and in print—and besides, were I to do that, and were Jerry still here, out would come that red pen of his: "You're wasting time telling people things they already know, dear boy. Give me something different. Give me something *personal*, for instance. And if it is needed, *remember your audience*."

I remember my audience, Jerry; and since all of them knew who you were, I can get right to those personal elements that you suggested.

Ahem. Those photographs that your sister showed during your memorial service, the ones of you in your Army uniform when you served in Korea; did no one ever tell you that you bore a striking—some might say *suspicious*—resemblance to Phil Silvers as Sergeant Bilko? Was Silvers' character perhaps based on your exploits? It wouldn't surprise me one damned bit, you sly dog.

The records that were played, those recordings of you singing with the family band, The Williamson Variety Serenaders; did no one ever tell you that your wonderful singing voice arguably rivaled that of Sinatra? And why, one wonders, did they not play the one and only rock-n-roll record you ever recorded? Was it because many of those gathered to pay their respects had already suffered enough pain? (Yes, it was a hideous thing, that particular record; I still wake up drenched in sweat some nights when it creeps back into my dreams. The refrain—"*Let me rock with you on the dance floor, baby/Let me rock you until we drop*"—taunts my delicately-balanced inner peace every minute of every day. It scarred me for life. *Why* did your family not play *that* song for those gathered to honor you? Was it because you wished for only me to remember the horror, the horror, the horror? I will get you for that someday.)

I am happy to report that Jerry's memorial service was packed nearly to the rafters. The entire dining area of the Riverwalk Village nursing home had been cleared to make room for the chairs and tables. At least a dozen people had to stand on the periphery. There were infants, there were children, grandchildren, middle-aged folks, teenagers, members of the nursing staff, elderly residents in wheelchairs, on walkers, and one dear old fellow in particular had to have his entire bed rolled in because he was too weak to be moved and his oxygen equipment was too delicate to be disconnected, even for a few seconds.

There was a movie screen set up in front, and for the first thirty minutes of the service, it displayed only a single image: that of Jerry Williamson, in his mid-fifties, at the height of popularity and writing output, looking off to the right and wearing that tight, wry, sly, mischievous grin that we who knew him came to know all too well; the grin that told us, *Oh, you* bet *I'm up to something, but you're going to have to wait to find out what it is.*

Some of the people who spoke urged us to remember you as you had been, not as you were near the end. Well, Jerry, take a look at that photograph of you and me at the beginning of this piece. Is that the famous Wry Grin I still see? Damn right, it is. Even then, some scant fourteen months before your death, you were still Up To Something. I only have to look at that grin to know.

And later, less than seven months before your death, you asked Ron Horsley, Lucy, and I to make a video to be shown to all the contributors for *Masques 5*—the edition of your famous anthology that was to resurrect the series. Remember how we joked that it seemed like the book itself had taken on a life of its own? How its road to publication was so bumpy that it seemed like the book was holding us hostage? So we decided to do something a little tasteless and stage it like a traditional "hostage" video. I was covering your head with a dark hood when Ron began taping, and all of us got a good laugh from the whole thing

Even then, you were looking ahead, you were planning things, you were still Up To Something.

You'll be happy to know that your final story will be appearing in *Masques 5*, my dear friend, and that there is no doubt in my mind that it will serve as a fitting tribute to your contributions to the field of horror, the field in which you worked for nearly thirty years. (Remember how you wept when I told you that none other than Clive Barker was going to be doing the cover? Remember how you said, "I didn't think he even knew who I was"? Oh, he knew, Jerry, Clive *knew* who you were, as did Poppy, Ray, Jack, Trish, Ray, Bill, the Mathesons Sr. and Jr., all of them, all of *us*.)

And your books? I have them all. Damn, you were good, Jerry. Your short stories were great. Most of your novels are just terrific; some of them (*Ghost, The Black School, Babel's Children, Don't Take Away the Light*) are brilliant; but—since you'd kick my ass if I wasn't completely honest—a few of them were, well . . . clunkers. You admitted this yourself. Remember how, after finishing the best-forgotten *Queen of Hell* (a book that, to paraphrase your fellow editor Thomas F. Monteleone, could "suck the dimples off a golf ball through thirty yards of knotted garden hose"), I smacked you over the head with it and said, "*What the hell were you thinking?*" It would have made an excellent project for Ed Wood, had he still been around.

You might recall that trip to New York you made a couple of years ago, where you were honored, along with Stephen King, with the Horror Writers' Association Lifetime Achievement Bram Stoker Award. I know how you'll probably worry about the fate of that particular statue—it was, after all, the crowning moment of your professional career (remember how you *beamed*, even months later?); well you needn't worry, Jerry; after your memorial service, your son Eric tracked me down, and with a sad smile handed it to me with great care, even reverence. It sets on my desk as I write this: *Lifetime Achievement Award, Honoring the Talent of J.N. Williamson.* I will keep this safe for you, I will show it to everyone who comes to my home, I will keep it near me as a reminder of that golden moment in your life when your peers gathered to cheer you and all your achievements.

But I need to stop with this annoying second person shift that I made somewhere toward the middle—hell, Jerry, if you were here with your red pen, this piece would be doomed.

Enough already.

I was given the honor of delivering a eulogy for Jerry at his memorial service this past Sunday, December 11, 2005. I reprint it now for all of you who were unable to attend:

Once, briefly, Jerry and I talked about funerals—specifically our own and how we hoped they'd be handled by those we left behind. After about five minutes of this happy conversation, we both started feeling a bit, well, not jolly, not really in the mood for a night out on the dance floor. A few moments of silence passed between us, and I asked him: "How would you like your funeral to begin?"

"With a joke," he said. "Something to lighten the somber mood."

"Yeah," I agreed. "Funerals are pretty sad and depressing functions to attend."

Not missing a beat, he looked at me and said, "Imagine how much fun it is for the guest of honor."

So there. Even though he's no longer with us, Jerry provided the opening joke for his own memorial service.

There is a wonderful line from Richard Llewellyn's magnificent novel *How Green Was My Valley* that goes: "It is strange that the Mind will forget so much, and yet hold a picture of roses that have been dead for thirty years and more."

I don't need to tell anyone in this room how, in the last few years of his life, Jerry's mind forgot quite a few things: names, dates, sometimes even whom he was speaking with at the time. And while it would be easy, and perhaps even tempting, to focus on these times when his memory began to fragment before us, the one thing that we should hold close to our hearts is this: despite his deteriorating condition, Jerry Williamson remembered the roses. He remembered the kindnesses, both large and small, that were bestowed on him; he remembered the thanks and admiration from the dozens, if not hundreds, of young writers he took under his wing; he remembered moments of shared laughter, moments where he felt he had achieved whatever particular goal he had set out to meet; and, most of all, most importantly of all, he remembered the precious rose whose petals were composed of those he loved, and who loved him.

I think it's very important that we keep this near us in the days and weeks to come, whenever we look at a particular space in the world where Jerry used to be and become all too aware that this empty space now hums with his absence: in the end, Jerry Williamson remembered the roses.

Jerry was a spiritual man, but for most of the twenty years I knew him, he chose to keep that spirituality held close to his chest, like a sly card player who doesn't want to show his hand too soon. He spoke to me of his admiration and affection for the Book of Ecclesiastes, and of his love for one passage in particular, one I'm sure you'll all recognize:

> To everything there is a season
> and a time to every purpose under Heaven;
> A time to be born, and a time to die;
> A time to plant, and a time to

pluck up that which is planted;
A time to kill, and a time to heal;
A time to break down, and a time to build up;
A time to weep, and a time to laugh;
A time to mourn, and a time to dance;
A time to cast away stones, and
a time to gather stones together;
A time to embrace, and a time to
refrain from embracing;
A time to seek, and a time to lose;
A time to keep, and a time to cast away;
A time to rend, and a time to sew;
A time to keep silent, and a time to speak;
A time to love, and a time to hate;
A time for war, and a time for peace.

When I asked him why this passage so moved him, he responded: "Because of the deceptive contradictions it contains. Every verse pairs something with its direct opposite, and if you don't take the time to think about it, it can be confusing. But at its heart, it's about the cycles of physical and spiritual existence. 'A time to be born, and a time to die; a time mourn, and a time to dance.' How's a person supposed to connect, to reconcile such opposites? Because each is simply one side of the same coin. What comes at the end gives greater value to what there is at the beginning. I find it very uplifting, and if I have one regret, it is that I will never, ever be able to write anything that equals that passage for it beauty and wisdom."

Well, like most of the times when Jerry judged his own work—and I told him this on countless occasions—he was wrong. I would like to read a brief passage from one of Jerry's novels, *Ghost*, a passage that not only seems to me to be one of the most beautiful, poetic, and deeply spiritual passages he ever penned, but one wherein he—whether he knew or it not—expressed to us the nature of the legacy he hoped to leave behind.

Allow me a moment to set this up: the narrator, Zach Doyle, is a writer who has recently passed away but who—for reasons that are not yet clear to him—is not yet ready to move on to whatever awaits him in the afterlife. His spirit returns to the home he shared with his wife to discover that she is selling many of his personal possessions—among these possessions is the typewriter on which he wrote all of his books. He watches as the old black man who has been his family's garbage collector for many years walks back to his truck carrying that typewriter:

> His eyes shone with pleasure. For him, this trash pickup wasn't just another; with me, he shared the knowledge that it was an important one. He would recall it always with delight. Why, it might very well be his Find of eighty years! I watched those huge, ebony eyes glitter, I saw the way he held the typewriter with caring purposefulness, even affection; and I saw then that he was thinking about That Book. Yes, That Book, with capital letters, the one the old man had always meant to write.
>
> I stepped out of his path then, with the same respect he had for my machine.
>
> I wondered intensely, *What is it you'll create with it, old man?* In my heart, I asked him that, knowing he couldn't hear the words had I spoken them, and not wanting to deter him any longer. But I trailed in his limping path, my eyes watering, yearning to know. *What verses do you compose in your soul, old fellah? What memories have refused to leave your mind and will not rest until you write them down? . . . Will it at last illuminate the world? Will it enlighten us all?*
>
> I wiped away my tears as I followed him down the driveway to my old familiar street, and I looked back at the familiar window on the second floor of our garage. Soon, I saw, it would be empty; soon there would be no trace remaining of Zach Doyle or his work.
>
> So I said, in that strange "aloud" voice I have come to know will not be heard, standing behind the aged man as he reverently handed the typewriter to his son seated in the truck, I said: "Will you write something beautiful on my old Royal pal, sir? Something beneficial? Will you do that for me, please?"
>
> "I'll sure be trying, Mr. Doyle," he answered. His head had not turned in my direction. "Yessir, I'll surely *strive* to be as good someday as you was."

"Thank you," I said.

For me—and the other writers who were blessed enough to call Jerry both their mentor and their friend—this is the rose that I will always remember, the rose I will carry close to me at all times, the one I will be able to recall in minute detail even after all other memories have run their cycle between birth and death, between mourning and dancing: I will strive to be as good as Jerry Williamson; I will strive to make my life and my work beneficial to the world I will someday leave behind; I will do this so, when we meet again, my good and dear friend Jerry, my second father, will embrace me with joy, pat me on the back, and say: "You did all right, son. You were a good person. You were beneficial. It all mattered, and I'm happy to know that you never forgot about me. Now come on, dear boy, do what you did best: tell me a story."

I loved you dearly, Jerry Williamson, and have come here today to say good-bye; but not farewell; never farewell. Just know that I will never forget you.

Part Three: To Each Their Darkness

"I have the horror of death with the still greater horror of living."

–Oscar Wilde, Letter to Robert Ross
from Reading Goal Prison, March 10, 1896

Forty-Five Minutes at the Bar with Bill; Getting It Right; "This Is Where I Came In"; and A Prayer For The Coming Revolution

AUTHOR BILL RELLING WAS A SUICIDE AT AGE FIFTY. TO LOSE A writer of his quality is a tragedy at any age; to lose one to a death at his own hands makes the tragedy only more hurtful.

I met Bill Relling a couple of times at conventions—mostly back in the 1980s when he was riding the "horror boom" with excellent novels like *Brujo* and *Silent Moon*. He and I once spent a terrific forty-five minutes sitting in a hotel bar talking about the work of one of our mutual writing gods, William Goldman. I found him to be an upbeat, intelligent, thoughtful, instantly *likable* man who treated me like I was an old friend. That someone whose writing I so admired treated me, a newcomer, like one of his comrades-in-arms, made my day.

I'm not going to pretend that he and I were friends, because I hardly knew the man, save for our appearing together in some anthologies and, of course, his wonderful novels. But in the hours and days immediately following his death, there was much discussion on certain boards concerning the reasons why—and this of course sparked controversy, especially when other writers who *were* his friends, who *did* know him well, and who had spoken with him as little as *five days* before his suicide, chimed in to try and say a few words about their fallen comrade. These fellow writers were in a great deal of pain, and trying hard not to let too much of it come through. They, like everyone else, couldn't figure out *why* he'd done it.

Then—as more and more details about his suicide began to emerge—these questions of "Why?" raised by everyone (both those who knew him and those who didn't) started turning into "How could he?" And, finally, at a message board that I will no longer frequent (*not* the Shocklines Board), one especially sensitive person, upon finding out that Relling left behind a family, made the following statement: "Well, I sure as hell won't be reading him anytime soon. I refuse to spend my money on books written by some coward who'd do that to his wife and children."

There is so much arrogant ignorance in that statement that I won't even *bother* commenting on it, save for this: That statement was *not* the only time the "cowardice" of suicide was brought up during the days immediately following Relling's death.

We're going to wander off the main highway here for a moment, so stay close.

"How can you write this shit? I mean, doesn't it ever *bother* you to write about horror all the time?"

That question was put to me recently, and after I recovered from my surprise (I was expecting the traditional "Where do you get your ideas?"), I realized that I had no ready answer.

It *seems* like a simple enough question at first glance, but if you think about and examine it closer, you might find some disturbing implications. I know I did.

One possible answer might be, "Yeah, sure, it bothers me sometimes. I wish it were in me to write something more humorous and genteel, something like *The Wind in the Willows* or *Sense and Sensibility* or the Dortmunder novels of Donald Westlake, things that would appeal to a wider audience and not clear the room of humans every time I announce what I do for a living, but I can't; my particular point of view won't allow me."

That's one answer.

God, if only it were that easy.

Allow me to repeat, for the sake of argument, that the purpose of all good horror fiction (aside from its holy duty to entertain) is to explore the relationship between violence and grief while trying to reconcile the existence of those things with the concept of a just universe, and to do so in a manner that will disturb the reader in such a way that maybe they'll come away from the story or novel a little more able to deal with the suffering and injustice that exist in the real world.

That horror fiction deals with subjects of a dark and unpleasant nature is a given; so, too, is it a given that the writers of horror fiction spend a decent portion of their waking (and sometimes sleeping) hours thinking about and exploring these self-same dark and unpleasant things in order to strengthen and enrich their fiction. The horror writer has to accept that darkness, pessimism, anger, violence, loneliness, grief (and all the other more unpleasant aspects of life that no one else wants to talk about) will always be a part of their daily thought processes, and therefore, to an extent, their own personality. This eventually becomes something of a necessity, because any combination of those darknesses *has* to be available to them at a moment's notice when the story or novel demands they make an appearance.

The result (and I'm basing all of this on my own personal experiences) is that all of these darknesses exist a bit closer to the surface than they do with most folks. In order to make their fiction as rich as it can be, in order to ensure that the bigger-than-life events they portray on the page are still very much *in touch* with life, to some degree or another, the horror writer has to make these darknesses a permanent part of their psychological makeup.

Admittedly, that's probably an oversimplification, but I think you get the point.

That's one implication of the question "Why do you write this shit?"

Here's another: Is it possible that the horror writer can end up disturbing him/herself just as much, if not more, than the reader?

Think about it: If something gets too ugly or too intense or too *real*, the reader has the luxury of putting down the book and returning to the story at a later time, when they've had the chance to rally.

The horror writer has no such luxury. Sure, we might stop the physical act of writing for the day, but the thoughts and emotions of the work are still there, churning around inside our teeny skulls in an effort to shape themselves into something worthwhile.

That led me to the following question: Can writing horror fiction have an adverse effect on your life? Can it eventually begin to poison you?

Hell, yes.

But it can also enable you to produce powerful fiction, if it doesn't kill you.

Sometimes, it doesn't work out for the best.

I would not purport to speak for the friends and family of Bill Relling, but as a horror writer who has struggled with depression since he was in high school, and who has thrice during his forty-three years on this earth attempted to keep an appointment in Sumarra, I would like to say a few words about the so-called "cowardice" of suicide.

Take it at face value: most of you (thank God) will never know what it's like to reach a point in your life when it feels like all you're doing is breathing air and taking up space, and even *that* hurts so goddamn much it's all you can do to lift your head off the pillow in the morning. It doesn't matter if you've got a successful career, money in the bank, people who love you; it doesn't matter that, everywhere you look, there's irrefutable evidence of your life's worth—a loving wife, kids who worship and respect you, life-long friends who've seen you through thick and thin, even readers who admire your work and flock to conventions in the hopes of getting your signature—*none* of it means squat, even though you know it should mean the world, because all you know, all you feel, all you can *think* about is the gnawing, constant, insatiable *ache* that's taken up residence in the area where your heart used to be, and with every breath, every action, every thought and smile and kiss and laugh—things that *should* make this ache go away—you begin to lose even the most elementary sense of self, and the floodgates are opened wide for a torrent of memories, regrets, sadnesses, and fears that no drugs, no booze, no loving embraces or tender kisses or hands holding your own in the night can protect you from. You become the ache, and despite all your efforts to do *something* to make it better, eventually the ache circumscribes your entire universe, and it never goes away, and you feel useless, worthless, a black hole, a drain and burden on everyone and everything around you, and try as you might you can't see any way out of it except . . .

Except.

And if you're a horror writer, the darknesses that come out of these floodgates can be crippling. I know what I'm saying here; I've been there, and hope I'll never have to face down that kind of darkness again.

When you reach the point of "except," there's isn't a question of cowardice; cowardice doesn't even enter the equation. To be in *that* kind of pain, where only death offers relief, and then *choose* to end your life . . . if this offends you, I'm sorry, but *that* takes the darkest form of courage there is.

I'm not defending Bill Relling's actions; I did not know the man. I have no idea how this has affected his family or his friends. What I do know is that I have been in that place he found himself that day he closed up the garage and started the car's engine, and insomuch as I can do while respecting the feelings of his friends and family, I wish him peace from whatever darknesses followed him not-so-gently into that good night.

As to those folks out there who did not know Bill Relling and are still asking their questions, offering their theories, or scattering about moral declarations like handfuls of rice at a wedding, I've got your answer: it's none of our damned business. The man is dead and no longer has any use for our uninformed theorizing. Be thankful that we who did not know him have the wonderful books and stories he left behind for us. If ever I do some day keep one of those appointments in Sumarra, my sincere hope is that people will remember me for being a writer who tried to make his fiction both entertaining and emotionally substantial.

For those of us who didn't know him, I'll bet—or, rather, I *hope* Bill Relling feels the same way.

Rest in peace, William Relling, Jr.; you were one of the good guys, and I'm grateful for the brief time I spent with you, and for the marvelous work you leave behind.

For the rest of us . . . to each their darkness, in their own way, in their own time.

So, as I said at the beginning . . . welcome to my abyss.

The late John Gardner (*The Sunlight Dialogues, Nickel Mountain, Freddy's Book*) once said: "You should write each story as if you are trying to prevent someone from committing suicide." I completely agree with that.

But how can that be applied to, of all things, *horror* fiction?

Because it's been my experience that if someone who is about to surrender themselves to the Big Bad Dark can find something, someone, *anything* that lets them know they are not alone in how they feel, then there is always hope they will not go gentle into that not-so-good night, be it the night of depression or something worse and far more permanent and irreversible. Like a lot of people, I may not embrace it, but I have to have hope in my life, and I find that hope, more often than not, by stumbling around in the shadows.

So what follows is a crash course in how I do it, and how I try to get it right.

As I said earlier, I have only lifted experience whole-cloth from my own life for use in stories four times; the first was the "Union Dues" disaster.

The second time—and one that worked out far better—was for my short story "Iphigenia," which can found in my collection *Graveyard People: The Collected Cedar Hill Stories, Volume 1*.

The bare bones of that story are this: A teenaged boy whose younger sister was trampled to death at a rock concert is goaded into attending another concert by his girlfriend. Once in line at the stadium, the horror of his previous experience begins manifesting itself once again, resulting in several new deaths . . . and one resurrection.

Okay, "Iphigenia" came about like this:

In the winter of 1978, the state of Ohio was hit with the worst blizzard it had experienced in over one hundred years. It wasn't *supposed* to be a blizzard; no, weather reporters had been warning us for a few days in late November that a collision of fronts would be dumping three to five inches of snow on us over a forty-eight-hour-or-so period. They said it would be slow in starting but heavy and steady for a little while. It would be starting sometime late Wednesday night or early Thursday morning.

Well, ask any certified meteorologist just how exact a science it is today and odds are they'll throw out terms like Doppler and storm-track capabilities and espouse the pricelessness of satellites and digital imaging and neighborhood storm-watch centers . . .

All of which is great. Terrific. Makes them tingle.

In all honesty, meteorologists have some damn fine technology to help them with their forecasts today, and I, for one, might chuckle when I hear local stations one-upping each other with their dual-Döppler radar and what have you, but, since it enables them to track the movements of a storm with such precision they can tell you almost the exact minute it will be hitting and then leaving your area, I let them have their fun.

But in 1978, forecasts were still referred to as *predictions*—not just by the general population, but often by local weather reporters. Which is to say, there was a helluva lot more guesswork involved back then. Also, a lot of today's technology didn't exist in 1978, and what there was of it was mostly the sole domain of NASA or the National Weather Advisory.

I know, I know—enough of this stroll down Meteorological Memory Lane.

I subject you to this so you'll understand there was, for all intents and purposes, no effing way that weather reporters in Ohio in November of 1978 could have tracked the third, slow-moving, warm air low-front that came up in the middle of two already-colliding fronts and caused the whole damned party to simply stall over the middle of Ohio, which is what did, dumping not three, not five, not seven, but forty-two inches of snow and freezing rain in just over thirty-six hours. Add to that wind gusts of the five-mile-per-hour variety and, by the time it was over, most of Ohio was under martial law. There were snowdrifts twelve to fifteen feet high, several people froze to death because they couldn't get out of their homes and the power was out and the phone lines were down, people were rationing food because there was no way they could get to the stores to buy groceries, which wouldn't have made any difference since most of the shelves had been emptied late in the evening the night the blizzard first began to hit.

You get the idea.

It was a mess; in some cases, a deadly mess. It took the state months to recover from all the damage, and by the time martial law was lifted and people were able to get out and go buy food again, most of central Ohio had been trapped inside their houses for the better part of two weeks.

But for a moment, come with me now back to the days of stadium seating.

For those of you under 35 who regularly attend rock concerts, I should explain that stadium seating was a method employed by concert agencies and promoters to ensure that the groups under their wing would be guaranteed to sell at least 75 percent of their large stadium/coliseum gigs. With few variations, it worked like this: you offered assigned seating at various rates, but you also offered, at a significantly lower rate, floor seats.

Yes, they were exactly what they sound like: folding chairs set in pointless organized rows on the floor of the stadium, no assigned numbers, first-come, first-served, get in early if you want to be close enough to count the guitarist's nose hairs or catch a flying drum stick.

As would be proven not too long after the night that inspired this story, stadium seating was a disaster waiting to happen.

Just ask anyone who was at The Who's infamous Cincinnati concert.

Okay, then: a Wednesday night in November 1978. I and four of my friends were piling into a car in Newark, Ohio to head over to the Fairgrounds Coliseum in Columbus to see Emerson, Lake & Palmer (who were then on the last leg of their ill-fated *Works* tour). We'd already seen them once before on this same tour, and they had blown the roof off the arena in Cleveland, so we had no doubt that the fairground would be left in ruins, as well.

We had no idea how close to the truth that would turn out to be.

In addition to the five of us, my then-eight-year-old sister, Gayle Ann, was coming along. Gayle had learned to love ELP because they were practically the only band I listened to that year, and she was also at the tail end of her "I-Wanna-Go-With-My-Big-Brother-'Cause-I-Think-He's-Fun" phase, a time I dearly miss the older I get. (Between the ages of five and nine, Gayle Ann was almost always with me wherever I went, and even though I acted like it was a big pain, I secretly loved it because I'd never had someone look up to me before, and screw the jibes my friends threw my way.)

It began to snow much earlier than had been predicted; we were probably less than halfway to Columbus when the storm began, slowly but steadily. There was a little freezing rain, so driving was tricky in some spots, but we always made it a point to leave at least two hours before a concert was scheduled to begin, just to be safe.

We get to the fairgrounds, we park, bundle up, check to make sure everyone has their tickets, then climb out and get in line.

It's still snowing at this point, but not as much as before.

Temperature is probably around twenty-seven, twenty-eight degrees and dropping.

I'm holding Gayle's hand, even though she doesn't want me to because she says it makes her look like a little kid. I acquiesce and let go, but tell her to make damn sure she stands close to me, which she does.

The line starts getting longer and deeper.

7:15 PM arrives, and the doors haven't opened yet. The concert is supposed to start at 8.

People start grumbling.

Then word comes down that two of ELP's equipment trucks haven't arrived yet because of road conditions. (They'd played in Kentucky the previous night.)

The crowd gets a little less irritable when it hears this and, for a little while, as the snow comes down and the temperature continues to drop, the long, long, *long* line breaks up into a series of microcosmic parties. Several people make hot-chocolate-and-donut runs, so even though we're all starting to get really cold, it's kind of fun.

8:00 PM comes and goes and eventually turns into 9:30.

By now, the snow is really starting to come down, along with freezing rain, and a lot of us can't feel our feet anymore. It's too late to say the hell with it and just head back to Newark because the crowd has gotten too big and too deep and too irritable.

We were trapped.

By now, Gayle isn't quite so reluctant to let me hold her hand; she even lets me pick her up and let her sit on my shoulders. When I get tired, one of my friends holds her on his shoulders, and so on. (I should add here that Gayle, like her counterpart in "Iphigenia," was—and still is—very small and delicate for her age; she was eight at this time, yes, but looked six, maybe even five.)

9:30 turned into 10:15.

Little fights have started to break out up and down the line. Through the swirling snow—heavier now than it's yet been—we can see the whirling visibar lights of several police cars. Gayle is crying because she's so cold. She wants to go home and so do I, but the crowd is now starting to push forward. I fall at one point and someone steps on my back, but I manage to get up.

I don't know if any of you have ever had the experience of being stuck dead-center in a crowd that's going to move no matter what, but if you have then you know this mass of humanity becomes a single and terrible entity; there are physical forces at work within the mass that you absolutely cannot fight against, regardless of how strong you might be. The crowd surges forward and you either go with it or are crushed; it surges back, and you respond in kind or die. It's scary as hell and reminds you, in no uncertain terms, that there are primal circumstances where the individual doesn't matter a damn, only the whole.

This was one of those times.

The crowd surges back and forth, usually *en masse* (except for one terrible moment that's coming), fights continue to break out—these much more violent—as beer bottles are smashed and a few trash can fires (set by sympathetic Fairgrounds workers in an effort to keep us warm) are overturned, scattering flaming debris into the cold, high winds. More than once I have to cover Gayle to prevent her from being burned by a piece of flaming paper that has been whipped in our direction.

10:15 turns into 10:30. Goddamn concert's supposed to be almost over by now, we're supposed to be in there screaming for ELP's quintessential encore, "Fanfare for the Common Man," and smiling as another kick-ass concert reaches its crescendo and we look forward to raving about it at school tomorrow.

Not happening.

At this point, part of the crowd toward the front starts slamming themselves into the doors; even back where we were—some seventy-five yards away—we can hear the metal starting to buckle from the force of the bodies.

It's getting really seriously absolutely goddamn terrifying, because now we can see police decked out in riot gear assembling along the line, and more than a few of them are armed with tear gas launchers.

I pick up Gayle Ann and cradle her head against my shoulder. She's shaking and cold and crying and hungry and so scared.

It wasn't supposed to be this way. This was supposed to be fun.

Then it happens.

At 10:37 the doors are finally opened.

And the crowd turns into a human meat-grinder.

The people up front who'd been throwing their weight into the doors are in the process of surging back for one more push when the doors come open; someone toward the end of the crowd sees that the doors are opening and screams, "They're opening the doors!" and the back half of the crowd begins to surge forward.

And right smack in the middle of these two colliding human fronts stands me, my friends, and my small-for-her-age sister—whom I've just set down only a few seconds before because I've gotten the godmother of cramps in my arm; all I need is just two or three seconds, that's all, just long enough to shake the cramp out, then I'll pick her back up and carry her through this mess.

It doesn't happen.

The force of the forward-moving crowd hits the force of the backward-moving crowd in front and people—I swear to God—start to shoot up like finished Pop-Tarts from a toaster. I lurch down to grab Gayle Ann and someone kicks me in the back of the head. I lose my grip on her and, the next thing I know, I'm stumbling to my feet just in time to see my little sister's arm get sucked into the crowd like a log in quicksand. I scream and try to run for her, but there are people colliding all around me. I can no longer see any of the guys we came here with. All I can hear is the blood howling though my ears and some nearby screams of panic; all I can think of is my little sister, who I pretend is a big pain but who I love more than anything, being swept along in this mass of fucking mindless monsters. I imagine her terror. I imagine her cries. I begin to push forward, slamming my elbow into a few ribs along the way, screaming her name.

A tear gas grenade goes off (by accident, as it turns out), and an already-panicked crowd goes, as the saying goes, medieval.

I was getting body-slammed all over hell's half-acre. I might have hit a few people myself, truth be told. This was a fucking nightmare.

And then, for just a second, there is a little clearing, an eye in the storm, and I stumble into it, my shoulders hunched and my head down—

—and see one of my sister's shoes lying there.

I know it is hers because I'd bought those shoes for her two days before. It had taken us three hours to find a pair she liked.

I remember bending low and picking up that shoe. I remember noticing that one of the straps was torn.

Then I looked inside, at the pristine white lining, and saw a single smear of blood.

To this day, I can't say for sure what I said or did during the next several minutes. I know that my heart tried squirting through my ribs about a million times; I know I was hit by several panicked people; I know I helped several people up from the ground and was helped up a couple of times myself; I know I hit a few people in my rabid panic.

It took me perhaps seven minutes to get from where I'd been to the Coliseum entrance. I was numb. I still clutched Gayle's shoe in my hands. I gave some faceless person my ticket and staggered through the gate—

—and saw my sister.

One of my friends back then was a fellow named Dan Butler who was a fullback on the Newark High School football team. He'd spotted Gayle about ten seconds after I'd lost her, and had cut his thumb on her zipper jacket when he'd scooped her up (the blood on her lost shoe was his), hunkered down, and charged through the crowd like a bull elephant.

I was so relived that I broke down weeping. (It occurs to me that I cry a lot. Note to self: start watching more Adam Sandler movies. Then again . . .)

I don't know that I've ever had a sweeter hug from my sister than the one she gave me a few seconds later.

I held onto her for dear life the rest of the evening.

ELP started the concert with a snarling version of the "Peter Gunn" theme, then stopped after the applause to ask if everyone was all right. I remember the way Keith Emerson apologized for the "unpardonable delay," then said, "We're not going to go on until you take a moment and check yourselves, then ask your neighbor if they need any medical attention."

The band waited while the audience checked to make sure everyone was all right. A few people had to be sent out for medical attention but, overall, there were no genuinely serious injuries.

And so, the concert went on. ELP started playing at 11:10 and—despite protests from Fairground officials and neighbors in the area—played their entire three-hour set.

"You waited bloody long enough out there to hear us," said Greg Lake, "so you're getting the whole show. If anyone doesn't like it, then piss off!"

For all I know, ELP might have played the worst set of the tour that night, but for me, with my little sister alive and well and laughing and dancing, it was the best effing concert I'd ever heard. It took us over two hours to drive back to Newark afterward—and don't think my mother wasn't, to put it lightly, beside herself when we came through the door at four in the morning. I was grounded for two weeks—which, as luck would have it, ran concurrent with the time we were all trapped in the house during martial law.

More than once since that night I've asked myself the inevitable "What If?"

Specifically: What if Dan Butler hadn't come with us that night?

He'd decided to come along at the last minute; another friend of mine, Sam Shaw, had gotten sick that morning and couldn't make it. Dan had happened to stop by the house because he needed to pick up something that my mother had borrowed from his—a cookbook or something like that—about the same time I got off the phone with Sam. When he heard there was an extra ticket, he asked if he could come along. I said sure, why not.

I'm fully convinced that if he hadn't been there that night, I wouldn't have a sister today, nor the wonderful niece and nephew, Kylie and Eric, she's brought into this world.

More than once I had puke-inducing nightmares about What might have happened If.

So, after many, many years of getting the necessary distance in order to view it through the fiction writer's lens, I finally wrote "Iphigenia" and set that particular What-If nightmare to rest.

The two immediate problems I faced when trying to use this event in a story were, A) which parts to use and how; face it, I don't remember a lot of the details about that endless goddamn walk through the corridors to the Coliseum's entrance; mostly what I have are a bunch of aches and impressions, so there would be no whole-cloth lifting of that event; I decided to use as many of the "What-If?" scenarios my brain had dredged up over the years as I could, but to filter them through my remembered impressions and current sensibilities; which brought me to, B) exactly how to portray the riot itself and its effect on Danny. I'd learned from "Union Dues" that putting myself into the story, no matter what disguise I used to convince myself I wasn't getting in my own way, would stymie the piece before it took its first step—

—and then I suddenly had my opening. It would involve Danny being interrupted in mid-step:

> He was checking the seat numbers on the tickets when he heard Mrs. Williamson scream.
>
> "Danny! Watch out!"
>
> He looked down in time to see seven-month-old Julie crawl into his path, her body so low to the ground it would be easy to step on her fragile skull and crush it all over the sidewalk. He pulled back in mid-stride and fell back-first onto the pavement, cursing both the pain and the memory of his sister—which found him as soon as the cement knocked the air from his lungs. After a moment he managed to push himself up on his elbows to see little Julie—sitting up now—look at him and giggle, a thin trickle of saliva dribbling off her chin. She looked so cute, so safe.
>
> Safe. With someone to watch over her. Protect her. Trusting was easy when you were that young. Trusting was fun.
>
> So little Julie was giggling.

Satisfied that I'd nailed the setup and tone with this opening, I set about the task of tackling what happened once Danny and everyone arrived at the concert. I knew that some rules were going to be broken, out of necessity, because the portrayal of the riot itself would be easy—it was everything leading up to it that was giving me headaches.

What I basically had once Danny and the others arrived was this: four teenagers standing in a long and massive line that isn't moving and where nothing much is happening.

Not the stuff of great suspense, that.

Still, the core of the story's action was going to happen *before* all hell broke loose, but how to create a palpable sense of tension with almost no physical movement going on?

The most obvious solution was to employ the use of a deliberate run-on sentence (see the line reprinted from Ketchum's "Gone" in Part

Two), but the problem there was that a run-on should only be used when things are immediate, when things happen very quickly, events are piling up one on top of the other faster than a character can deal with or fully comprehend them, and when you want to create an overwhelming sense of confusion and panic. A run-on might serve the story well once the violence began, but as a lead-in to the violence, it was useless.

The next solution was to portray everything in short, staccato sentences: "They moved forward a little. Stopped. Moved a little more. Someone in the back shouted. Someone else shouted back. The narrative came to a screeching halt."

Close, but still not right. The terse, disjointed brand of sentence (of which Richard Christian Matheson remains the undisputed master), while creating definite agitation, would ultimately work against the scene because each period would be the equivalent of Danny taking a breath to steady himself, and the idea here was to create a sense of constant tension and forward momentum.

Scratch the short ones. Definitely.

Which left me with only one option, and that was to somehow strike a balance between the run-on and the staccato.

Below is a sample of my solution. See if you agree with the choice I made:

> Danny looked around him as he squeezed Laura's hand tighter, trying not to give in to panic, a panic he felt pushing its way up from his balls into his throat, but there was at least the feel of Laura's hand, a good feeling, a safe feeling, even here, even now . . . pushing against them, someone was pushing against them from behind . . . he turned to get a look, maybe say something to them, tell them not to be so impatient, everybody paid their money and they were going to get in . . . but only more faces, more bodies, more red-pin-prick-black eyes that glanced around, behind, ahead, all of them meeting his own at one pint, never staying for long, and he thought for a second . . . a *fraction* of a second, that he saw a small, fragile figure making its way through the crowd, trying to get somewhere in particular, trying to get to *someone* in particular, but in a blink and a noisy shifting of the crowd it was gone, lost in the swirling mass of voices, eyes, and flesh . . .

. . . he took some deep breaths and looked down at his feet, trying to stay calm, they hadn't been here all that long, there was no reason for him to feel so panicky, so why did he . . . his shoe, there was something wrong with his shoe . . . he bent over just a little and glared down, watching as a shadow of some kind shifted under his feet . . . no, not a shadow, it was a . . . a . . . a *leg* . . . no, not a leg, just part of a bug that he'd scraped off, only . . . wait . . . only it seemed to be moving, seemed to be trying to pull itself out from under his weight, a small, twig-like hairy leg squirming from under his shoe . . . he froze as he stared, thinking for a moment that he could hear the clatter of its hard-shell body, could see its mandibles starting to jut out from under . . .

. . . Laura leaned in and kissed him on the cheek, whispering something about later on tonight, after the concert, Mom and Dad weren't home and she was all alone did he wanna come over, soft promises of flesh and tongues and bodies . . . bodies pressing, bodies sweating, groaning, pumping steadily . . . he looked at her and smiled, kissed her, but felt nothing, only the sour liquid in his stomach churning around, churning and bubbling as the crowd shifted once again, and Danny looked around, feeling the sourness spread into his mouth, drying his saliva, gluing his tongue down, unable to speak now, almost unable to breathe, but then Laura kissed him again with her wet and wonderful tongue and he was all right, moist again, able to swallow, then he noticed that Jim and Theresa were nowhere to be seen . . .

. . . the figure again, he saw the figure again, so tiny, so frightened, and he almost moved to reach for it, but then Laura grabbed his arm and said, "You're not going anywhere without me, not in this crowd," so he pulled her along beside him, positive he'd seen . . . seen someone wandering around the crowd, a frightened gleam in their gaze, maybe tears streaming down their cheeks, but no one saw because she was so small, no one heard because her voice was too weak and they were too busy trying to push other people out of the way, trying to get as close to the doors as possible, that's what counted, getting ahead so you could get inside, get a good seat, take it up, party down, drink and chug Big Time . . .

. . . "Christ, slow down, will you," said Laura, demanding that he give her a break, just wait a minute . . . Danny slowed and stood still, his eyes darting around . . . Laura moved closer to him, putting her arms around his waist . . . he took another deep breath and put a protective arm around her shoulder and said, "Are you all right?" and she said, "I'm fine, how about you, lover?" and he laughed, laughed and held her close because she'd never called him "lover" before and he liked it, liked it very much as he stretched his arms out to relax them and went to step closer to Laura . . .

. . . someone pushed from behind and he lost his balance, fell forward, rammed his foot out to try and break his fall but in the second before his foot connected with the pavement a child crawled out in front of him, a small child, a baby crawling, and he tried to cry out but someone else pushed and he felt his foot connect with the fragile skull, felt the baby's head pop like a melon below his foot, and his stomach heaved then but nothing came up as he looked down and saw the feelers worming around, saw the baby's arms flailing out as it kicked and wriggled in its death spasms, so he pulled back and lifted his foot, not wanting to see what he'd done but having to look . . .

The use of the ellipses accomplished two things: it created a sense of forward momentum in a scene where there was not a lot of physical movement, and it enabled me to structure the entire sequence (which lasts for several pages) around the agitation of the staccato with the immediacy of the run-on.

In the years since this story first saw print, I have re-read it every now and then to assure myself that I made the right choice. I think I did—in fact, I think I made the only choice that would have worked for the story as I wrote it. If someone else had written this story, they would have found another way to tell it, I'm sure. But in the end, "Iphigenia" was me telling a particular story in the best way I could.

Which became a real challenge when it came to the next incident I lifted whole-cloth and dropped into a story: the rape scene in "Some Touch of Pity."

If you've not read it, "Pity" is about a werewolf—not someone who gets bitten by same and then becomes one, but someone who, through an act of horrible violence, outwardly changes into a wolf in reaction to the violence. As the years pile up, he finds that he can tap into this violence and change into a werewolf at will.

The central event by which he defines his life—and which he relives on an almost hourly basis—is his sexual assault at the age of eight by three drunken teenagers (friends of the family) who, in order to prove their nerve to one another before they ship out for Vietnam, gang-rape him during a camping trip.

Now, bear something in mind: everything is bigger to a child, not only physically, but perceptually and emotionally, as well; a dollar found becomes a discovered pirate's treasure; a heap of dirty clothes in the corner turns into a nasty, fanged beastie after the lights have been turned out. Everything is amplified when you're a kid. I know it was when I was eight.

Let's get this out of the way so we can move on. When I was eight years old I was sent on a camping trip with four other kids and three teenagers (friends of the family), two of whom would be shipping out to Vietnam in a week or so. After everyone crawled into their sleeping bags or tents and fell asleep, the Holy Trinity of Really Wonderful Guys got roaring drunk and began playing a game of "Dare" that got louder, more violent, and progressively more outrageous and twisted. The oldest of them, while talking about what he'd heard was going on in Vietnam, said that a guy had to be willing to do anything in order to survive. "Anything?" another one asked. What followed was a bunch of eat-this-bug or drink-a-cup-of-my-spit or stick-your-finger-up-my-ass, and then one of them came up with the bright idea of a gang-bang; stinking drunk and out of control—and with no girls around to fit the bill—they decided to end their game of "Dare" with me; after all, I was the smallest, and the weakest, and the most easily terrified into silence.

So I was pulled from my sleeping bag and dragged deeper into the woods and forced to have things stuck into my mouth and ass that I'd rather had never been put there. I spent the rest of the night lying in the rain and bleeding from several parts.

Don't dig camping to this day, oddly enough.

Anyone who's ever read "Pity" remembers the rape scene. I agonized over that thing for weeks for several reasons, not the least of which was

I didn't want any element of that scene to come off as sensationalistic or titillating—what my buddy Ray Garton called "whacking material for pedophiles." It's not just the rape scene in "Pity," but the whole open wound of the narrative that was hard to approach. But an invitation came along to write a story for Marty Greenberg's *Werewolves* anthology, I needed the money from a sale, and I was right smack in the middle of finally seeking out counseling about several unpleasant incidents from my life that I had never really dealt with.

I was about a fourth of the way into writing "Pity" when I began to face the facts about what had happened to me when I was eight. No, there was no "breakthrough" or anything so melodramatic; I had never blocked it from my mind, I remembered every detail—every last lousy, stinking, goddamned detail—but had trained myself to keep it all tucked away in a filing cabinet in the background where I wouldn't bother it and it wouldn't bother me.

Well, that method of self-therapy had just about run its course at the time I got the *Werewolves* assignment, and the events of that night were pretty much in the forefront of my mind all the time.

I was not, as they say, a happy camper.

The story kept stalling on me. My central character was coming off as more of a literary construct than a fully-dimensional human being, and every situation I put him into seemed either too convenient or too contrived; nothing was going well, I had no central conflict, only a jumble of ideas and vague notions about what I wanted to do somewhere along the line, the deadline was fast approaching, I wasn't sleeping worth shit, my mood was in the toilet, my wife (now ex-wife, all my fault), Leslie, was beside herself with concern and frustration, I wasn't getting anything done around the house like I was supposed to, and all because I'd allowed myself to buy into the pop psychology bullshit about "the healing process" and was remembering the specifics about an event I'd really rather not give a second thought to, thanks very much.

So I finally gave up. I would stop writing the story, I would write about what happened to me and how I felt about it, I'd get it the fuck out of my system, and then I could move on to something constructive.

I wrote about the assault. It was nasty, it made me mad, sick, and sad all over again, and once it was finished it didn't appear to have served any purpose because I sure as shit didn't feel any better and the story deadline wasn't any further away.

I went on auto-pilot. I started the story with the narrator, in wolf form, battling a large dog. He kills the dog. He feels bad about it. He changes back into human form. Crawls to his car. Gets inside—

—only there's this little boy sitting in the car, waiting on him; the little boy's all scraped up and cut up and bleeding and naked and crying and the first thing the narrator says to him is "Get away from me," but this kid, he won't stop crying or saying "I'm sorry, I'm sorry, please don't be mad at me" over and over and all it's doing is making the narrator more pissed off and the more pissed off he gets the more the little kid apologizes and I don't know where this shit is coming from, I got no idea who this little fucker is, I hadn't planned on any little snot-nose to be in the car, it's as big a surprise to me as it is to the narrator, who's really screaming at kid now, but the kid just keeps saying how sorry he is and I'm thinking about having the narrator wolf-out on his ass just to get him out of the story—

—but as soon as I move to do that I realize that I can't.

I can't because the kid is the ghost of the narrator as a little boy.

Which, I suddenly realize, means he's the ghost of *me* as a little boy.

Which means the narrator is me.

Which means that I am doing another "Union Dues."

Which means I. Am. Screwed.

Lots of stomping, yelling at Leslie over nothing, secret drinking, taking too many sedatives to calm myself down; a regular happy camper jamboree at the Braunbeck house.

I go back, apply ass to seat, hands to keyboard, and start again.

The dog. The fight. The feeling bad about it. Crawling back to the car. Getting inside. This time he's thinking about blowing his head off with a silver bullet he has in his gun. He closes the door. Takes out the gun, turns around—

—and fuck me with a fiddlestick, that little kid's *sitting there again*.

I started worrying about serious Bin time at that point. So I could either go with it and hope that another "Union Dues" disaster didn't happen, or I could give up writing and become a cesspool cleaner.

Until then, I'd done a fairly decent job at keeping my work separate from what I was going through, but then it occurred to me that something in this character was utterly ruined because I myself had felt for most of my life that I was nothing more than damaged goods in a flashy package . . . so I went with it. I decided there was no way in hell I'd ever be able to shape this into a saleable story, but for some reason the memories of the assault and this goddamn werewolf story kept trying to join together, so who the hell was I stop them? Luckily, my little camping excursion was not only accepted but embraced by my central character—who wasn't as much like me as I'd first thought—and as a result of his embracing of the incident, the rape scene emerged as a vital, necessary, and justified element of the story. In this case, that type of line-crossing indulgence worked out for the best; I wound up with what I think is a pretty solid story, and the power what had happened to me as a kid had less hold on me because I'd finally seen it in black and white, put it into a fictional context, and thus, in my own silly way, given it some value.

Call Oprah. Ring the happy bells. Let the healing begin. (Insert rim-shot here.)

I think don't think there *is* such a beast as "healing," ultimately; things scab over, scars can be removed, blood mopped up and wounds cauterized, but the painful memories remain; oh, sure, they eventually lose their hold over you and your life, but that doesn't help win back the friends you've lost as a result, nor does it erase the cruelties and hurts you inflict on those you love, and it sure as hell doesn't get back any of the time you've lost trying to come to grips with them. The half-assed optimist would say that you learn from such things. Well, guess what I learned from what happened? I learned A) I don't like camping; B) never dare a drunken teenager to do *anything*; C) it does you no good to whine about it; and, D) for every perceived horror that's been inflicted on you, there's half a dozen other people out there whose experiences make what you've gone through look like a carousel ride in summer. To this day, every so often—usually when I'm under a great deal of stress or am incredibly tired—my ass still bleeds from the torn tissue in there, tissue that, according to the surgeons I've consulted, can never be fully repaired; so every now and then, like some misguided form of stigmata, I'll start to leak and will have to beat a hasty retreat for a new pair of pants and underwear, and usually I'll have to bum a tampon off one of my female friends to staunch things until it stops.

So let's not talk about "the healing process." You confront it, get the upper hand, and get on with life as best you can.

The strangest thing is, of all the stories I've written, "Pity" is the one that gets the most positive reaction. Go fig. I've lost count of how many people have approached me at conventions (when I attend them) and tell me how much "Pity" meant to them, because they or someone they know have/has experienced a similar violation in their lives and, for them, that story puts into words a lot of what they themselves have felt. It's one of the angriest, darkest, most violent stories I've ever written, and there are folks out there who find a great deal of hope and comfort in it.

So I guess, in its way, this goes to illustrate how, sometimes, horror can perform the duty of which John Gardner spoke.

And that word—duty—leads me into the final example of lifting an event whole-cloth from real life and creating a worthwhile story from it. Bear with me a bit longer; I'm nearly out of your hair, promise.

A little over a year ago I had to make the decision and then give the order to take my mother—who was suffering from final-stage emphysema—off life support. It was not an easy decision to make, despite her obvious suffering. She had been going downhill steadily since my dad's death nine months previous. My sister and I were burnt beyond belief; Dad had died, then our grandmother (Mom's mother, who for a while shared the same nursing home wing with her daughter), and now Mom.

She had been in a coma for nearly a week and her doctor saw no chance of her coming out of it. Gayle and I had Mom's living will, but there was no way Gayle could bring herself to make the decision on her own, and she sure as hell didn't have it in her to give the order. Not to imply that she was weak, far from it, but she had two kids to take care of, a job to hold down, a husband, and had been the one to drive Dad back and forth to and from Columbus five times a week for his radiation treatments. She was exhausted.

I was in the middle of my divorce, and it was not friendly. I admit here that it was my fault; I betrayed Leslie. After all the love and faith and support she'd given me, I threw it back in her face. I will never forgive myself for having hurt her as I did. She remains the single finest human being it has ever been my privilege to have known, and I mourn every day for the loss of her from my life.

I wasn't as exhausted as my sister, but I could see the neighborhood. Neither one of us had had a chance to catch our breath or get our bearings since Dad's death, and now here we were, about to kill our mother.

Please don't hand me any of that soft-peddling rigmarole about how it "was the right thing to do" or how it was "for the best" or all the rest of it; yeah, I know it was the right thing to do, I know it was for the best, she was sick and was never going to get better, she'd never be able to breathe without the aid of a machine, never be able to get out bed for the rest of her life.

Well, at least she was in a coma, so we didn't have to face that.

My mother, Mary Virginia Braunbeck, spent the majority of her childhood as a ward of the county, growing up in a children's home (what used to be called an orphanage) with dozens of other children whose families could not or would not take care of them. She was abused there, both physically and emotionally. But she survived. She never made it past high school. She worked hard all her life at a variety of jobs—cashier, maid, cable-assembly worker—and, as far as I could tell, never really had a happy day in her life. Whatever mechanism it is that people possessed that enabled them to be happy had been whipped out of her long before I came along. She was second only to Dad as the saddest person I ever knew.

And after all that, after a life of hard work and little reward and being humiliated by snotty clerks in grocery stores because she used food stamps and occasionally had to put items back because she couldn't afford them, after holding her husband's hand and those of both her children through some pretty rotten times, her life boiled down to long evenings alone in a house where there was no longer a Frank for her to talk to, so she contented herself with calling me or Gayle all the time to see if we'd come over and watch *Touched By an Angel* and *Jeopardy* with her. She had the house to herself for all of six months before she took the last bad turn, went into the nursing home and then the ICU where she was hooked up to machines to help her breathe, and slipped into a coma.

Gayle and I made the decision together to remove Mom from life support. When it came time to give the order, I was the one who would give it.

Gayle and I called all our friends and family to let them know what we were going to do. I contacted the parish and asked for a priest to come and give Mom Last Rights. He arrived around 1:30 PM; Gayle and I had decided that I would give the order to take her off support at 3:30—the time when Mom usually got off work during the years she'd been working. She'd always joked that she'd probably "die right at quitting time," so we hoped she'd appreciate the humor of the scheduling.

The priest arrived around 2:00; Gayle and I said hello, shook his hand, then went back to Mom's room. The doors were closed, the curtains pulled. The priest blessed us, made the Sign of the Cross, and began giving the Last Rights—

—and that's when Mom woke up.

I'm going to spare you the details of the next three hours (for reasons that will become clear very soon); Mom died, we left her body behind as we were supposed to do, made the arrangements for her funeral, and buried her on an unseasonably windy and cold day in April, the day that would have been Leslie's and my fourteenth wedding anniversary.

I came back after the funeral and, in the middle of the night, sat up in bed, wide awake and panicked because from somewhere in the back of my mind a little voice had whispered, "I hate to bother you with this right now, but . . . don't you have a story due in a couple of days?"

Shit, shit, shit.

I climbed out of bed and went straight to the computer, opened a new file, and began typing.

I had no idea what the hell I was going to write about.

Sure, I'd had some idea for a story a couple of weeks back, before things took another bad turn, but in the ensuing days I'd lost all contact with whatever that idea was. I had a big zero, a goose egg, zilch, blank slate—*nothing.*

The thing is, I needed to work right then as badly as I'd ever needed anything. Getting some kind of story down would seem like something constructive, something life-affirming, and I needed there to be something life-affirming right there in front of my face, something that wasn't all sickness and sadness and pain and regret—I'd had a fucking bellyful of that, enough to last me a lifetime, thanks so much—and I wasn't about to rise from the chair until I had at the very least the first lines of a story.

I sat there and stared at that screen for two hours. Didn't move, didn't type a word, didn't even get online and do the meandering surfing of the brain-dead. I just sat here, looking at a bright screen and thinking about nothing.

I didn't know it at the time, but I was in the early stages of the single worst psychological and emotional meltdown I would ever experience, one that would culminate in a massive and humiliating public breakdown that would land me in the Bin, doped to the gills and under a suicide watch, Stephen King's *From a Buick 8* the only thing to remind why it was I thought I had the right to go on breathing air and taking up space.

Somewhere in the early minutes of hour three of the stare-down between me and the computer screen, I put my hands on the keys and typed these words:

"Mom woke up just as the priest was giving her Last Rights."

Uh-huh.

Another frothy, light, carefree and gay chuckle-fest from yours truly, Mr. Happy-Go-Lightly.

I deleted the line, stared at the screen a little while longer, then typed the same line again.

"Mom woke up just as the priest was giving her Last Rights."

This routine of writing that line, erasing it, staring at the screen, then writing it again would go on for a while—at least another hour—before I finally got wise and did something about it.

When that at last did happen, when it occurred to me that my repeatedly writing this was starting to feel a bit like that scene in *The Shining* where Shelley Duvall takes a gander at the book Jack Nicholson's been working on and finds that he's written "All work and no play makes Jack a dull boy" over and over and over, I admitted to myself that I had no goddamn idea, but I needed to write, so what the hell—I'd write about what happened after Mom woke up. I was fresh out of original ideas, so I'd steal something from real life and hope I'd get away with it.

As soon as I started to write the second line, the writer in me elbowed his way to the front and said, "Whoa there, slick. Are you sure first person is the way to go, all things considered?"

I admitted that maybe it wasn't the best choice.

So I tried doing it in third. Third person made it far too detached and cold. So I switched to third person present tense and that was even worse; aside from seeming too cold and detached, it now had the added bonus of sounding pretentious (I almost always find present tense self-consciously literary, as if the writer is trying to draw your attention to the writing and not the story), so I went back to regular old third person.

Not doing the trick.

I was really tired by this time but knew there was no way I'd be able to sleep (severe sleeplessness was one of the things that led to the meltdown later), so I thought, what the hell? Let's go for second person—better yet, let's go for second person present tense because God knows you can't ever be *too* pretentious or self-conscious.

I didn't care.

Except it turned out that second person present tense allowed me to somehow make the events of the story (I now thought of it as just that: the story) much more immediate while giving myself a thin but necessary scrim behind which to hide from the bald, ugly facts of what had happened; it allowed me to write the events as they had happened, but also gave me the distance to view them only in a fictional context.

I had never before written a story in either second person or present tense, let alone a combination of the two; by taking this swan dive into a narrative voice I never would have considered under normal circumstances, I was able to both write an actual (and hopefully worthwhile) story and give myself a little perspective on what had happened.

I cannot judge this story, even now. I think it's pretty okay. The editor, William Simmons, accepted it, and it appeared in a nifty anthology called *Vivisections*, and people seem to respond to it, but, still . . . I don't know.

I only know that I miss my parents, goddammit, and I miss my ex-wife's friendship and affection, and all I really have to offer this world when the day is done are these little stories that I tell; so hopefully I did my job with this one and will continue to do so with the next one and the one after and the one after that.

So, after all the brouhaha of persons first or second or third, I give you the story I wrote over the course of that night and most of the next day. I won my first Bram Stoker Award for it. Mom wouldn't have cared for it, but she wouldn't want to hurt my feelings, so she would've said she liked it. This was and is my last gift to her, my way of thanking her for all she did for, and meant to, me.

See what you think:

Duty

"There are some mistakes too monstrous for remorse."
–Edwin Arlington Robinson

Mom woke up just as the priest was giving her Last Rites.

(Is this part of the penance? you asked of the Guests. *Isn't it all?* was their reply. Smug fucks.)

For six days she'd lain unconscious in the ICU at Cedar Hill Memorial Hospital, kept alive by the ventilator that sat by her bed clicking, puffing, humming, buzzing, measuring her blood, inspiratory, and baseline pressure, waveform readouts showing the fluxes of tracheal and esophageal pressure, proximal pressure at 60 to + 140 cmH_2O, 1 cmH_2O/25 mV, output flow at 300 to 200 LPM, 1 LPM/10 mV, the whole impressive shebang running smoothly at maximum system pressure of 175 cmH_2O, the ribbed tube rammed securely down her throat into her lungs, ensuring that she continued to breathe at the acceptable rates of 250 milliseconds minimum expiratory time, 5 seconds maximum inspiratory time. Details. Specifics. Minutia. Like the Drain-Swirl of the Black Flecks. Like the title of a bad 50s horror movie, the kind you used to watch with Dad on Friday nights when you were a child and there was no sibling to compete for his attention. All of this comes to you as you stand there studying the details, the specifics, the minutia. Things to look at and memorize because you can no longer look at the pale, pinched, collapsed ruins of the face and body lying motionless on the bed. A glowing number changes, a monitor beeps softly to register the new data, the pump presses down, expanding the lungs, raising the chest, and all is right in God's techno-savvy world. Except.

(Except, say the Guests; *ah, there's the rub, as Willy S. once wrote, right, pal? 'Except.' What a word that is, so much disaster and heartache and ruination and disappointment and pain and all of it always*

follows one little two-syllable word. Very dramatic, don't you think? Yes, we thought you'd agree, so what say we get back to things and see what follows that word of all words that you seem incapable of getting past right now so, as usual, we have to do it for you. Be a Good Boy and say it with us, now.)

Except that she never should have been here in the first place. Her DNR order had ceased to be in effect at the hospital when she was transferred to the nursing home, but some stupid nurse over there panicked and called an ambulance when Mom went into respiratory arrest, so she was brought back here and immediately placed on life-support; the last thing she'd wanted was to be hooked up to some goddamn machine at the end of her life—she'd told you and your sister that often enough when her emphysema had entered the advanced stage, this a full year before the double pneumonia now snarling inside her—and the two of you had promised you wouldn't let that happen. But it has happened. You wonder if she blames you. But doesn't she realize it isn't your fault? Someone should have called you, should have made sure that the DNR order was attached to her chart at the nursing home, should have been paying attention to the fucking records when her name was entered into the computer and her information came up in the ER, but all of this is for lawyers to deal with later. Right now a duty needs to be performed. You and your sister have already tracked down Mom's doctor and told him what you want; you have shown him the living will and he has nodded his head solemnly, he has picked up the phone and called the ICU; you and your sister have shown the living will to the nurse in charge, have called various friends and family to tell them what you are about to do, and have contacted Father Bill at St. Francis. The two of you have agreed to wait until everyone is present before giving the order. That's everything so far, right? Well, no, but that's *most* of it. Even now as you stand here witnessing these events, you're already replaying their beginning in your mind, as if by doing so and focusing on the details, the specifics, the minutia, you might find a way to alter the outcome, which hasn't even been determined yet. To whit: Father Bill was the first to arrive, all soft words and sympathy—"This must be terrible for the two of you, so soon after your father's and grandmother's deaths"—as he donned the garments and uncorked the vial of holy water and found his place in his book of blessings. "In the name of the Father, the Son, and the Holy Spirit: 'O God, great and omnipotent judge of the living and the dead, we are to appear before you after this short life to render an account of our works. Give us the grace to prepare for our last hour by—' "

And that's when Mom woke up.

She blinked a few times, then looked up, saw Lisbeth, and smiled as best she could with that tube in her mouth and throat.

Father Bill continued: "—a devout and holy life, and protect us against a sudden and unprovided death.' "

(Bummer, say the Guests. *Hadn't planned on this turn of events, had you, pal?)*

Mom's eyes grew wide and she began to shake; at first you thought she was having some kind of seizure, but she tore her hand from Lisbeth's and began to shake it in the air: No. Stop this. Stop it now.

"'Let us remember our frailty and mortality,'" continued Father Bill, "'that we may always live in the ways of your commandments. Teach us to watch and pray, that when your summons comes for our departure—'"

Mom started shaking her head and making wet, querulous, awful sounds as her hand shook more violently, the index finger trying to uncurl from its arthritic brethren to point at someone or something; her head jerked to the side, then back again, her eyes staring into those of your sister.

(The Guests again: *She'll cave. She will. Sis always does wherever Mom's concerned. Next stop, Cave City. And you know it.)*

"'—from this world, we may go forth to meet you, experience a merciful judgment, and rejoice in everlasting happiness. We ask this through Christ our Lord. Amen.'"

Father Bill then placed his hand on Mom's forehead—or *tried* to, rather. She was having none of it. "It's all right, Mary," he whispered. "It's all right, Frank and your mother are waiting for you, there's no need to be scared. God's love will ease your fear and carry you home."

He whispered something to her that you couldn't understand, then with a nod to you and your sister, made his way out.

You didn't want to turn around and look back into the room because you knew what you'd see, but eventually Father Bill disappeared from view and you had no choice.

There. All up to date now, yes? Yes. The outcome was determined even as you were trying to alter it by your observation at the time. And you didn't notice until it was too late. What's wrong with this picture? Too many black flecks, dancing.

Okay, so what now?

Duty.

You turn back into the room and there's Lisbeth, looking at you with a surprised smile and a "Maybe-Everything-Will-Be-Okay" gleam in her eyes. She's holding Mom's hand and trying to look happy while all the while silently asking: Should I be happy or not? She's back with us, we didn't think that would happen but here she is. Maybe this is a sign, her coming awake when she did. Maybe. Maybe?

(Cave City—this stop, Cave City.)

You shake your head. The gleam fades from her eyes for a moment, appears again as if she's thought of an argument against this, then leaves completely. She knows what you shaking your head means.

And so does Mom.

She's looking right at you, and you know what this look means. Oh, the lids are droopier than they've ever been, and the eyes are both dull and bloodshot, but the look is a classic: How can you do something like this?

How often in your forty-one years have you seen that look from her? Or, for that matter, from everyone else in your life? *Yes, Mom, look at me. I'm no longer your son—I'm what* became *of him. Forty-one, divorced, living alone* (well, sort of, but you wouldn't understand, *no one* would understand about the Guests), *no real friends, and here I am about to kill you—because that's what you're really thinking, isn't it, Mom? "My son is going to kill me." Because you know if it were just Lisbeth, she couldn't do it. You could always talk Lisbeth out of anything, but me? I inherited your stubborn streak, and you hate that. Does that also mean you hate me right now? Or maybe you always have, who knows?*

"I'm glad to see you," Lisbeth whispers to Mom, squeezing her hand and kissing her cheek. But Mom is still shaking, still trying to point a finger, still objecting.

"There's a lot of people who want to see you," says Lisbeth. "We called everybody. You're going to be real popular today."

You pull in a breath and cross over to the bed. "Hi, Mom," you say, but it doesn't sound like your voice, does it? When did you start speaking with someone else's voice? Odd—Lisbeth and Mom seem to recognize it. "I thought you were gonna stay asleep on us."

She continues to shake her head, and you notice for the first time how wide her eyes are. *('Deer in the headlights' is the simile you're looking for*, say the Guests.) For the first time you let yourself acknowledge that she's scared. She knows what's going on and she doesn't want it to happen but one look in your eyes and she knows she's toast, that maybe she'd have a chance if it was only Lisbeth but with *you* . . . oh, yeah: toast. Browned on both sides.

Tears form in her eyes as her mouth works to form words but she can't speak, not with that tube, so what emerges is a series of squeaks and whistles and deeply wet groans, a vaudeville of language but it's all she's got, that and her shaking head and pointing finger and tears.

You reach out and grab her shaking hand, squeezing it gently. "I love you, Mom," you say, and this time the voice sounds a little more like your own; an echo, yes, distant and thin, but yours nonetheless. "I'm so sorry you've been so sick for so long. But the doctor's told us that you . . . you can't breathe on your own anymore. You have to be hooked up like this, it's the only way you can breathe, you see?"

Her eyelids twitch as a single tear slips out from the corner of her left eye and slides a slow, glistening trail down her temple into her ear. You pull a tissue from your pocket and wipe the tear away before it drips into her ear canal. That's always irritated you whenever you've been on your back and crying so it must be twice as awful for her because she can't raise that arm, what with all the IV needles decorating it like a seamstress' pin cushion. So you wipe away the tear just like a Good Boy should do for his Mom.

"Please don't cry," you say, hating the hint of desperation that's suddenly there in the echo of your voice, but Mom's wrinkling her brow and every last line in her face, the short ones, the long ones, the deep and not-so deep ones, all of them become so much more pronounced, each one looking more painful than the one next to it, or over it, or crisscrossing it: the map of a face, the topography of a life: *This is from the night when your spleen burst and we had to sit in the emergency room, your dad and me, wondering whether or not you'd make it out of surgery or if we were going to lose our little boy; this one here, under my right eye, is from all those nights I spent squinting over grocery store coupons when your dad was on strike at the plant, we had to watch every penny so the coupons were a big help but, Lord, there were so many of them, and maybe I wouldn't have this line if I'd admitted to myself that I needed glasses, but even if I had admitted it we couldn't afford them, not with the strike and all, so I squinted*... and there are no rest-stops on this particular map, are there? No, not a one that you can find.

"You'll wear yourself out," you say, squeezing her hand a little tighter. "You don't... you d-don't want to do that because everyone is coming over to see you."

Her private vaudeville of language continues, and every squeak is wrapped up in sandy, sputtering, wet rawness that makes your stomach tighten and your throat constrict. Her hand in yours is cold and leathery but she's trying to squeeze back, to let you know *Please don't do this, please don't do this, I know I'm sick and I know it's hard on you kids but I don't want to die, not yet, I don't want to die not yet not yet not yet please don't do this pleasepleaseplease.*

You let go of her hand as a nurse comes into the room and asks if she can speak to you or your sister. You nod at Lisbeth and walk out into the hall, but not before bending down and kissing Mom on the cheek; it still tastes of the tear you wiped away earlier, and the saltiness is unexpected; it tastes of flavor, of something being prepared, Christmas dinner where Mom always used just a little too much salt in her stuffing, but you loved that smell, didn't you? The way it wafted up the stairs and tickled your nose to wake you: *It's Christmas, come on down, sleepy-head, and see all the goodies Dad and me have got for you!*

"I'll be right back," you whisper to the tear's trail, hoping Mom hears it, as well.

Outside, the nurse pulls closed the glass door separating Mom's room from the rest of the ICU. "Is there anything more you'd like us to do?"

"I think she might need a sedative of some kind. She's really scared and—"

"—doctor already wrote the order for a sedative and morphine, as well. I can give it to her any time you say."

You nod your head and chew on your lower lip for a moment.

(Handling things just like the Good Boy we all know you are, say the Guests. You can't tell if they're making fun of you or not, so before

you get too caught up in this moment you tell them to fuck off and simply jump to the outcome without benefit of observation.)

"I don't want her knocked out, understand? She'll want to say g-good . . . good-bye to everyone and I want her to be conscious."

"It won't knock her out, I promise."

"Then please give it to her now."

The nurse nods her head and looks at you—she has very pretty grey eyes, doesn't she? They look just like your ex-wife's—but here you are observing the moment while it rides right on by, and have to ask the nurse to repeat what she's just said.

"Is there anything we can do for you or your sister?"

"No, thank you. I just want Mom to feel . . . I mean, she's been so sick for so long and we—Lisbeth and I, we . . ."

The nurse puts a hand on your forearm. Her fingers are soft and warm, the first time a woman's fingers have touched there in—what?—a year and a half? Two years? Who remembers?

(We do, say the Guests. *We remember everything, pal. That's why you invited us here.)*

"Is everything the way you want it?" asks this nurse of the warm soft fingers on your arm.

What you want to say is: *No, everything is not the way I want it, so if you'll pardon me, then, I think I'll just go over here and scream for lost things, throw back my head and open my mouth and just scream. For a smile I haven't seen in years, or the chime that's missing from a laugh, or the noise not made by a child now ten years in its grave, for the toys my ex-wife and I don't have to pick up; I'll scream for all the school pictures that aren't decorating a mantel, then maybe for songs no one but me remembers or cares about, songs from dead singers that make me smile or cry when I hear an echo of their choruses from a passing radio accidentally tuned in to an Oldies station, and finally I'll scream for my only living parent whom I am about to kill. Yes, that sounds good. Sounds* splendid, *in fact. So if you'll just excuse me for a moment, I'll go take care of this. Sound okay? Good. If you need me I'll be right over there. Can't miss me. I'll be the one screaming.*

That's what you want to say (as you observe in the moment that hasn't quite gotten away from you yet), but what actually comes out of your mouth is: "Yes, thank you, everything is fine . . . as fine as it can be under these circumstances, I guess."

Nurse of the warm fingers lingers for just a moment longer, maybe longer than is necessary or even professional, and the sad smile on her face is echoed by the one in her eyes.

You both release a breath at the same time. She blinks, squeezes your arm, and with a soft swish of shoes against the polished tile, heads off for the syringe.

(Were you just flirting? the Guests inquire. *Oh, pal, what stones you've got. Mom lying in there choking to death on the ruined slop of her insides and you're making time with Florence Nightingale. Show of hands: spit or swallow?)*

"Shut the fuck up!" you growl through clenched teeth. An older gentleman passing by you snaps his head in your direction, his offense at your language all over his face.

"Sorry," you mumble. "I wasn't talking to you, I was—"

But he's gone, turned into another room a few yards down.

(A flirt and *a charmer. What self-respecting nurse wouldn't want some of this action?)*

Shaking your head, you go back in to Lisbeth and Mom.

"She's *scared*," Lisbeth whispers. You wonder why she bothers. Fer chrissakes she's standing right there next to Mom, holding the woman's hand, and Mom might be hard of hearing but she isn't deaf and she may not have been the ideal parent but her life's going to be over—repeat that, turn up the volume, OVER—in less than two hours and the woman deserves to not be spoken of in Third Person.

"I know you're scared, Mom," you say, taking your place by the bed. "But this is what you wanted."

The shaking of the head again.

You reach into your pocket and remove the copy of her living will, unfold it, and hold it up for her to see. "You made us promise you that if this time ever came, we'd go through with it. Even if you said 'no,' we'd go through with it."

Lisbeth snaps your name and you give her the Glare. The Glare has served you well over the years, hasn't it? The Glare scares even the Guests sometimes. Burns right through a person, makes it damn near impossible to maintain eye contact with you. You know this, and you use it to your advantage whenever you want to be left alone, which is most of the time, so many have known the terror of the Glare.

Lisbeth looks away almost at once. You feel terrible for having looked at her this way, but dealing with that is for later.

(You got that right, pal. We'll just add that to the list, shall we?)

You grab Mom's hand away from Lisbeth and hold it tight. You look at your sister—who's still not returning your gaze—then directly into Mom's eyes. You have looked into her eyes this intensely maybe three times in your entire life. "Listen to me, Mom. You will *never* be able to function without this machine, do you understand me?"

A slow nod. Another tear.

"Even if we were to call this off right now and leave you hooked up to this thing, you're not going to last another week. You're on borrowed time, Mom. You should have been dead six days ago."

Once again Lisbeth says your name, this time spitting it out as if it's some rancid chunk of food.

"You're here with us now," you continue, "and you're awake, and you're getting the chance to do something Dad didn't get to do. You're getting a chance to say good-bye to all the people who love you. They're all coming, and they're all going to stay right here with you until you fall asleep for the last time. The nurse is going to give you a shot so you'll be comfortable, and all you have to do is just let us say good-bye and tell you that we love you and then you can rest. You're tired, Mom. You've been tired for so long—" Your voice cracks on these last two words, and you have to turn your head away for a moment to get a grip on yourself.

(Aw, say the Guests, *look at this. Widdle baby cwying faw his mommy. Little late to feel sad about this now, isn't it, pal?)*

You ignore them and turn back. "—and you need to rest. You've earned it."

Her hand squeezes yours.

"I have no idea how scary this must be for you, but we're going to be right here, however long this takes. But I'm—*we're*—going to keep our promise to you, Lisbeth and me. Because this is what you wanted. But there's something you need to do for me, Mom. You need to let me know you understand. Can you do that? Can you squeeze my hand and let me know that you understand so I don't have to go through the rest of my life feeling like I've killed you?"

She looks in your eyes.

And for some reason you remember something from twenty years ago: you were still living at home and had picked up the phone one day, just to make a call, but Mom was talking to someone so you started to hang up when you clearly heard her say the words: "I love you."

Phone in hand, staring.

Dad was raking leaves in the back yard.

You lifted the receiver to your ear and listened. Details. Specifics. Minutia. Three years this had been going on. They laughed. At your dad. At you. But not Lisbeth, not the light of everyone's lives, not her.

You hung up loudly and waited. It didn't take long. Mom at the door to your room, her eyes wide and frightened by the headlights.

"How much did you hear?"

"Enough," you said.

Her face took on many forms in a very few seconds; sadness, shame, anger, indifference, confusion and, finally, resignation. "Go ahead and tell him. I don't care." Bullshit bravado, that.

"I figured out that much from what I heard. So you really think I'm useless?"

Shock, for just a moment. Then: "Sometimes."

You nodded your head. "It would kill Dad if he knew."

"I'm not going to tell him."

"Neither am I."

She'd smiled at you, then, and for a moment you thought it was a smile of love and appreciation, but it was in her eyes, wasn't it?

You were now in it with her. If Dad ever found out, she could deflect part of his hurt and anger and anguish by saying, "Your son's known about it almost the whole time." And that *would* kill Dad.

There are times you wonder whether or not it *did* help kill him, just as much as the diabetes and high blood pressure and prostate cancer. Had he somehow found out? Then just let his heart break along with everything else so he could die alone in the toilet of his room at the nursing home? That's where they found him—dead in the crapper.

You never found out what happened to the other guy, never asked his name, never kept an eye out for a strange car or truck parked near the house.

Dad's gone. Grandma, too. Now it was Mom's turn; not because you want this, because it has to be this way.

"Please squeeze my hand," you whisper, and the begging in your voice disgusts even you.

Mom looks at you the same way she had after that phone call twenty years ago.

"*Please?*"

Mom does not blink, does not try to speak, does not shake her head.

After a moment you look at your sister. "She squeezed my hand," you say. Softly.

Lisbeth releases a breath, her shoulders slumping, then smiles and weeps at the same time. The relief she feels is palpable even from where you're standing.

(She bought it, pal. Very nice, very smooth.)

You look back down at Mom. She will not look at you.

"I love you, Mom." And you do. That's the terrible part. If she's going to hate you for this, so be it. It's what she wanted, and you promised.

(That you did, pal.)

You were her son. You were a Good Boy. And it was your duty.

The first of the friends and family begin to arrive, and you're relieved to step back from the bed and give the rest of them the chance to say good-bye.

The warm-fingered nurse comes back in, smiles at you, then gives Mom the shot. "This will help you relax, Mary. You'll feel better here in just a minute, I promise."

Mom smiles at her, a smile full of gratitude and affection. Part of you wishes she'd look at you like that, just once, just for a moment, but the rest of you

(And us, pal. Don't forget us, we'll take it personally!)

knows damn well that you've already gotten the last direct look from her that you'll ever know, and there you were in the moment, observing the event while not being a part of it so now all you've got is the impression of something that may or may not be a memory of an experience you weren't really a part of in the first place.

(Let's hear it for our fearless leader, folks! Nothing gets by him, nosiree!)

The room fills quickly; aunts, uncles, Mom's co-workers from the cable assembly plant, friends of the family you haven't seen in years, and a few people you've never seen before. You wonder if one of them is Him. You wish you could figure out which one He might be so you could follow him out to the parking lot and slit his throat with your car keys, then pull back his neck and expose the wet tissue and shit right down his throat.

(Now, now, say the Guests. *Is that any way to think at a deathbed?)*

Mom smiles at all of them, squeezes their hands, gestures for them to bend down so she can hug them and they can wipe away her tears. Warm Fingers comes back in and gives Mom a shot of morphine, then stops beside you and whispers, "I have orders for two morphine shots. The second one is much stronger. I'll be at the desk, so when you want the second shot, just let me know." She touches your arm again, and this time there's a definite intimacy to her touch. You nod your head and place your hand on top of hers. For a moment her fingers entwine with yours, then she is gone.

A few moments later two technicians come in and ask for everyone except you and Lisbeth to clear the room. They wander into the hall. The first technician—a girl no older than Lisbeth, twenty-six, twenty-seven tops—closes the glass door and then pulls the curtain across it. The room becomes grey and shadowed; Death pausing to check his schedule: Here, is it? Ah, yes, I see. Okee-dokee; back in twenty minutes.

"Are you ready?" asks the technician.

You look at Lisbeth, then at Mom, who still won't look at you, and say: "Yes."

She turns off the ventilator.

The sudden silence sings a sick-making sibilance of final things that cannot be taken back.

"Now, Mary," says the technician, "we have to take out the tube now. Are you ready?"

Mom smiles around the tube and nods her head.

You look away for only a moment, hear the terrible sound of medical tape being peeled away, then decide this is something you have to see.

Mom's already wrenching upward from the force of the tube being pulled from her, her face collapsing forward, becoming a reddening gnarl of flesh as her body locks rigid and her tears stream down and her fingers shudder (somehow that is even more terrible to you than her face, the way only her fingers and not her hands shudder) and the veins bulge in her head and temples and her eyelids spasm—

—make it stop, you think. *Oh God I didn't think it would hurt this much, it's my fault, I'm so sorry, Mom, I'm not mad at you, I understand, I never hated you, never, please make it stop, please make it stop, please make it—*

"Don't swallow, Mary," says the technician, her hands moving gracefully, one over the other, as she pulls and pulls and pulls.

It takes only ten seconds but it seems like ten minutes, and when it's done, when the tube has been pulled free, Mom slams back against the bed with such force she actually bounces a little, and when she bounces a spray of thick black-flecked spit scatters across her face and down onto her chest and even onto your own hand even though you're standing a couple of feet away. Her face is covered in sweat but it's not quite so red now, and her chest is moving up and down as she pulls in breath and you feel the tears on your own face now, goddammit, and the snot running out of your nose but you don't move to wipe away any of it because look at her, she can't wipe the muck away so you won't, either, you'll stand here covered in your own fluids to show her that you understand, that you want to feel something of what she's going through now because this is the last thing you'll ever share, the last thing, the very, very, very last thing and you want to remember it, every specific, every detail, every minutia because you're a Good Boy and that's what a Good Boy does.

(And noble, to boot. Look at all this fucking nobility. It makes you want to openly weep sensitive manly tears, it does.)

The ventilator is rolled into a corner, the tubes rolled into coils and deposited into the medical waste bin, Mom is wiped clean, and the technicians leave, opening wide the room to light and sound and the waiting throngs.

You move toward a corner and stand there, no longer trusting your legs.

Looking out of the glass, you see Warm Fingers and nod your head. She nods hers in return and runs to fetch the last syringe.

Bit by bit, Mom's eyes close—but not all the way. The light fades, the readouts become erratic, the last shot of morphine is administered . . . and then all of you wait.

No one in the room will look at you. At Lisbeth, yes, but not at you. You were the one to give the orders. You were the one who didn't get off at Cave City. You were the one with Mom's stubborn streak and the living will folded neatly in your pocket and the memory of the phone call and your ex-wife's tears when the police called about your little boy who you shouldn't have let ride his bike to the movies that day but, jeez, Dad, I'm almost ten and it's not that far and the screams in your ear of You Fucking Bastard How Many Times Have I Told You I Don't Want Him Riding That Bike Outside The Neighborhood and the fists against your face again and again and again and Dad whispering No Son of Mine Would Ever Put My Ass In A Nursing Home but you're a Good Boy, aren't you?

(Well, say the Guests, *about that . . .)*

It takes Mom two hours and seventeen minutes to die. It is slow and painful to watch, but you never once look away.

When it is over and everyone begins to leave, you are the one who closes her eyes the rest of the way.

You wait until you are alone in the room with her, then lean down and kiss her. "I will miss you every day for the rest of my life," you say. "I loved you, Mom. I'm sorry for every bad thing I ever said to you. I'm sorry for all the times I forgot to do something for you, for all the times I could have called you but didn't, for every time you felt lonely and forgotten. Is that all right? Is it all right for me to say these things to you? It's just the two of us now, so I think it must be all right." Then something small bursts inside you and you're crying again. "I'm sorry I wasn't a better son, a better man, a better husband and father. But Lisbeth and Eric, they gave you two wonderful grandchildren, didn't they? And they never let them ride their bikes too far from the house, you can count on that. They never get so busy with work that they just tell their kids it's okay, ride wherever you want, it'll be fine. They never do that. They never leave the bottle of prescription sleeping pills setting out open so that their dad can sneak them into the toilet at the nursing home. They never will. They'll never disappoint you. Never.

"I have to go now, Mom, because there's a lot to do for your funeral. But I just wanted you to know that I always had the best intentions. In my heart, I always meant well. I love you. You should rest now, you've earned it."

You make sure no one is watching from outside, and you observe the moment as it passes; you can do this now, because the outcome is given. You move to one of the corners, and you take something, and then you leave.

Warm Fingers smiles sadly at you as you walk past the desk. She looks like she might cry herself. You wish she'd touch you again. Warm Fingers would forgive you all your trespasses and mistakes. Warm Fingers would understand.

You park outside your house and see that all the lights are on. You look up at the windows and see the Guests moving around. One of them is playing the stereo. NIN. "Head Like A Hole." Too loud for this hour.

You smoke three cigarettes before going inside. The Guests don't like it when you smoke inside, and you are nothing if not a gracious host.

They're all waiting for you when you come inside. All of them have their props at the ready. None of them speak to you now. They never talk to you when you're here, only when you're gone, only when you're performing a duty like the one tonight.

One of them comes up to you, empty-handed. He's the new one. The one behind him, he arrived the day you buried Dad. His is the face you wore the night you walked out of the nursing home knowing what Dad intended to do with those pills.

Lurking in a corner near the stereo is another guest. He showed up the night your ex-wife came over after little Andrew's funeral to slap you in the face yet again. You had been brewing water for tea and after she slapped you, you pushed her away and she fell against he stove and spilled the scalding water all over her arm. This Guest is holding the boiling kettle and wears the face you wore that night. Just like all of them. Wearing the faces you happened to have on when committing your trespasses.

The new Guest is still standing there, holding out his hand. You reach into your pocket and remove the coiled ventilator tube. He takes it with a smile and points to the chair. You remove your coat and sit down.

Other guests—the one who arrived after you had that brief affair with that temp before Andrew was born, for instance—bind your wrists and ankles to the chair.

The music changes. The James Gang. "Ashes, the Rain and I." The saddest song you've ever heard. It's important that you have sad music now.

One Guest has the pills. One the boiling water. One has the dart you stuck Johnny Sawyer with when you were six and you got mad because you thought Johnny was cheating.

There are pins. And burning cigarettes. And pieces of broken glass.

You wish you didn't remember what every last one of these items means, but you do, you remember so very, very clearly.

The phone rings. No one moves to answer it.

The answering machine picks up, gives its banal greeting, then a beep. A woman says your name. Her voice is soft and warm, just like her fingers. "This is Daphne. I'm the nurse who gave your mom the shots today. Listen, we're never supposed to do this—call patients' families personally like this—but, well . . . I just wanted to make sure you were all right. You didn't look good when you left and I was . . . oh, okay, I was worried. I hope you're not angry. I just thought that maybe you, y'know . . . needed to talk to someone. So I was wondering . . ."

Joe Walsh's voice drowns out the rest of the message. You almost smile. Maybe after all of this is over—a few weeks or however long it takes for you to heal this time—maybe you'll give her a call. Warm Fingers would be sympathetic. Warm Fingers would listen. Warm Fingers would understand and squeeze your hand.

The new Guest stands in front of you, reaches out, and forces your mouth open. He has lubricated the ventilator tube with Vaseline. You remind yourself that it's important to swallow as the tube goes down. You just hope the Guest with the boiling water remembers his proper place in line.

You open wide your mouth and close your eyes. It is important for a Good Boy to remember things. Remembering, that's a duty, as well.

And you are nothing if not dutiful.

Nothing at all.

There's actually a funny part to all of this.

Well, okay, maybe not fall-off-your-chair-guffawing funny, but kind of humorous; maybe not humorous so much as odd; maybe not so much odd as weird; and maybe not so much weird as it is, well . . . noteworthy.

Anyway . . .

The day I was released from the Bin I came back to the apartment where I was living and sat down on the couch in front of the television. After a few minutes of getting acclimated to being part of the real world again, I noticed that the VCR had been left on. I remembered that I'd been watching some movie before the crackup occurred, but I couldn't remember which one; so I turned on the television, grabbed the VCR remote, and fired up the movie.

I feel comfortable telling you this next part because it really happened, so it doesn't matter if you believe it or not.

The movie I'd been watching before trying to catch the oblivion express was John Frankenheimer's *Seconds*. I'd stopped watching it just before the final sequence where (spoiler ahead) Rock Hudson, strapped to gurney with a gag in his mouth, is being wheeled down the corridor to a room where he will be put to death so that his body can be used to fake someone else's death. The camera is planted directed over Hudson's head, and Hudson is thrashing around and screaming.

And screaming.

And screaming.

And screaming . . .

And I found myself smiling. Pulled out of my life once again by this movie, I was looking at the single most terrifying scene ever filmed, and I was smiling from ear to ear for the first time in many months because right there, right there in front of me, right there in front of me in glorious black and white was the perfect outward expression of everything that I was feeling and *had been* feeling for a long time.

Hudson kept on screaming.

I kept on smiling.

Screaming.

Smiling.

Screaming louder.

Smiling wider.

It was great. I was in tears, but it was great.

As soon as the movie was over, I turned off the television and VCR, went up to my room, popped *Quadrophenia* into my CD player, and listened to "The Rock."

Looking at a picture of my parents—the one I would use on the dedication page of *Graveyard People*—I turned up the volume just as the four themes began to merge into one, placed the photograph on my desk, rubbed my face, and thought: *This is where I came in.*

I have loved the darkness my entire life; from watching re-runs of *Zontar: Thing From Venus* on *Chiller Theater* with my dad to seeing *Christine* and *Cujo* with my mom to all the novels and short stories that have kept me awake nights with the shivers and the jumps, I have loved the darkness and it, in its own way, has loved me in return.

That is why I have dedicated my life to horror fiction, and have never once regretted it.

Well, maybe sometimes, once in a great while, but never for long.

It's the sentiment that counts, not the precision of the statement.

I can't speak for other writers, but I'm aiming for a small piece of immortality: the stories in my head will not allow anything less.

I try every month to read at least one novel or a couple of short stories in a genre that I've not read much before, if at all. High fantasy, sword and sorcery, historical fiction, romance fiction, children's books, mystery, suspense, erotica, even the dreaded western. And the more I read across the board, the more I see that all forms of genre fiction have a great deal in common; the more I see that all forms of genre fiction have a great deal in common, the more convinced I become that in order for genre fiction to prevail, a form of communion must take place—merging numerous forms of fiction into one—so that speculative fiction can take the next necessary step in its aesthetic evolution, but this communion cannot be forced, it has to come about naturally. Yes, I'm talking cross-genre fiction; storytelling unbound. The type of richly imaginative, wildly exciting, joyously unpredictable storytelling where you get everything from a straightforward character study to a hard-boiled mystery and even a ghost or two; not only ghosts, but cowboys, as well, if the writer feels they need to yippee-ki-yi-yea their way into a chapter or two. Time travel and high-tech intrigue, alternate universes and comedies of error; passionate romance and nerve-wracking terror—hell, throw in the kitchen sink and a robot domestic while we're at it. Go for broke—just don't go for the easy out. Read everything you can in as many different genres as possible. Don't feel that you as either writer or reader have to restrict your interest to "only cyberpunk" or "just the gaming-related fiction" or "SF, SF, and only, only, only SF!" And God please don't exclude the opinions, observations, or insights of those readers and authors who toil in fictional fields beyond the boundaries of yours.

This goes so much deeper than simply wanting all forms of speculative fiction to march to a different drummer; it's a fervent prayer that all of us will learn to foster a need and desire beyond all the needs and desires that have come before to catapult ourselves into the burning core of our imaginations and meet the whirling, winged, wondrous things that have been waiting for us to take that next step in our creative evolution. "Look at us," they'll whisper. "See what we are and know that you mustn't ever settle. Don't just be—*become!* And don't just become—*transcend!*" It's a prayer that we'll someday be able to get rid of all the misconceptions that insultingly oversimplify what the work is about because it will be impossible for anyone, no matter how hard they try, to put a label on our fiction.

Storytelling unbound, wherein we can do anything we want, anytime, and in any manner, knowing that there are truly no limits—and God, is that kind of knowledge power. We'll know, then, that a summer sky can be poured into a silver chalice and drunk down like Bacchus' headiest brew, that the touch of a lover's fingertips against the skin or the brushing of lips holds the answer to what love and life were supposed to be, every emotion revealing the sensual, smoldering, staggering beauty of the cosmos.

Storytelling unbound.

To live a thousand lives where every second is drenched in overpowering wonder, then turn yourself loose on an empty sheet of paper to see if you can possibility convey this amazement to others, rejecting rationality enough to have faith in the unnamable *something* that drives you to want more out of your fiction than simply "a good read," that pushes you to push yourself and your work to new heights and maybe, just maybe, capture a piece of the Divine.

And you know where this revolution should start?

Down there in the darkness that I have loved all my life, that darkness in Literature's basement, with that drooling, scab-picking embarrassment of a bastard child called horror that no one wants to admit exists. No one's paying attention to it, not really, and those chains on the wall won't hold forever, so why not start now, while the shadows are there to protect us? By the time the lights come back on and the chains fall away, we'll be armed to the teeth with our stories and ideas and memories of drinking the sky from a silver chalice, and *then* just let 'em try to ignore us or lock us away once again.

Let 'em try.

My favorite poem is "I Saw a Man" by Stephen Crane. God, I get chills every time I read it or hear it read:

> I saw a man pursuing the horizon;
> Round and round they sped.
> I was disturbed at this;
> I accosted the man.
> 'It is futile,' I said,
> 'You can never—'
> 'You lie!" he cried.
> And ran on.

That should be the horror writer's battle cry against those who would tell him or her that their work must conform to specific genre boundaries and never, ever, ever dare venture beyond those boundaries because something that is too different isn't acceptable, even in speculative fiction.

"You lie!" we cry, and then on we go, chasing the horizon, freed from illusionary boundaries implied by popular misconceptions. Don't you want that from our fiction? To capture the horizon, to drink down the sky from a silver chalice, to know that, whenever you need it, a dream will call and raise its head in majesty?

Storytelling unbound.

But know this: You may be forced to live outside their city walls when your fiction "doesn't quite fit anywhere" because they'll be scared of you. "He must be mad," they'll say. "How else do you explain his producing this sort of stuff?" Then they'll go on coughing up safe, derivative fiction, occasionally looking down at the asphalt to make sure their feet are still on the ground while *you*, you'll be kissing the hem of Venus' gown and flying alongside Daedalus and solving crimes with Marlowe and dancing with Gatsby atop the pyramid of the moon at a celestial ball given by the gods of ancient Mexico while vampires, ghosts, and robots gather 'round the base and sing otherworldly chants.

It's really nice outside those city walls, trust me. You don't have to write what they say you should write, you don't have to settle for reading the same old same old thing repackaged and rewritten for the umpteenth time. You can be, you can become, you can transcend! So come on, all ye cyberpunks, ye gamers and dreamers of darkness, ye techno-files, *X-Files*rs, *Babylon* 5ers, and Trekkers true, come on all ye mystery mavens of the hard-boiled and cozy schools, ye romance writers and historical scribes with your sense and sensibilities refined, ye rusty-spurred cowpokes and poets of brilliant brevity, over there, ye comics connoisseurs and artists, with pencil and paintbrush and airbrush raised high, step outside, join us beyond the city gates; you'll see our campfires burning in the night as we gather 'round to spin our tales in the manner, *any* manner, we damn well choose. Join us. Our ranks are growing. You'll find no prejudice here by our fires, no one who'll say "It just doesn't fit." Bring your dreams, your angers, your sadnesses and passions as we begin our communion: all fictions merging into one.

And when you hear them calling to you from behind the city walls to come back, come back, come back here where everything is safe and in its place, remember the sacred words as you reach toward the horizon's hands:

"You lie!" we cry.

Storytelling unbound.

Sneaking back into that theater where I'm sitting, watching Rob Zombie's *House of a Thousand Corpses* ooze its way across the screen, we see that the credits are rolling and I am rising with a glassy look in my eyes. Everyone who saw this with me is wasting no time spewing their venom at Zombie, at the movie, and the state of horror in general . . . but mostly at the movie.

I should have hated this thing.

But I didn't.

Why did I think about art while watching it?

Because it disturbed me on a very primal level, which is what art is supposed to do. Does it bother me that I'm grouping this movie and the concept of art in the same thought—and now in the same sentence?

Hell, yes.

But that's part of the game, isn't it—having to consider the merits of something on its own terms and not those you try grafting onto it through your own sensibilities.

I still can't put my finger on why I liked this movie, but I'll figure it out eventually.

Stay tuned.

Time to make a semi-graceful exit, fellow revolutionaries. Take up those swords. Kick down those boundaries the next time you try to scare the shit out of me.

You know the battle-cry now, so—

—turn out those lights. Do it now.

Ready? I thought so.

Onward . . .

GARY A. BRAUNBECK is the author of the acclaimed Cedar Hill cycle of novels and stories, among them In Silent Graves, Coffin County, the recent Far Dark Fields, and the forthcoming A Cracked and Broken Path from Apex later this year. His work has garnered five Bram Stoker Awards, three Shocklines "Shocker" Awards, an International Horror Guild Award, a Dark Scribe Magazine Black Quill Award, and a World Fantasy Award nomination. To read more about Gary and his work, please visit www.garybraunbeck.com.

ARTIST STEVEN GILBERTS: In 1962 in the bucolic region of southern Indiana, a peculiar child was born and given the name of STEVEN GILBERTS. Being the only Indiana-bred person in a family of Wisconsin origin, this led to the unfortunate child being labeled "hoosier" by his extended family; a group collectively known as "badgers," "cheese heads," and perhaps most frightening of all, Norwegians.

LaVergne, TN USA
06 December 2010
207605LV00003B/2/P

9 780984 553518